INTRODUCTION
TO THE OLD TESTAMENT

INTRODUCTION

TO THE

OLD TESTAMENT

BY

Dr. E. SELLIN

(PROFESSOR IN THE UNIVERSITY OF BERLIN)

TRANSLATED BY

W. MONTGOMERY, M.A., B.D.

WITH AN INTRODUCTION AND A BIBLIOGRAPHY
FOR ENGLISH READERS BY

Professor A. S. PEAKE, D.D.

HODDER AND STOUGHTON
LIMITED   LONDON
1923

Made and Printed in Great Britain.   R. & R. CLARK, LIMITED, *Edinburgh.*

INTRODUCTION

By Professor A. S. PEAKE, D.D.

THE name and work of Dr. Sellin have long been familiar to British students of the Old Testament, but there will be many readers of this book who will be glad to learn something of the author and the significance of his work. He was born May 26, 1867. He studied at the universities of Rostock, Erlangen and Leipsic, then after a brief experience as school teacher he became privat-docent at Erlangen in 1894. He became Professor at Vienna in 1897, went to Rostock in 1908, to Kiel in 1913, and in 1921 became Professor of Theology in Berlin. To his study of the Old Testament he added residence in Palestine, as he conducted important excavations at Taanach and at Jericho while he was Professor in Vienna. His many-sided literary activity has been remarkable; more than ten years ago his antagonist, Professor Cornill, said that in this respect he was surpassed only by König among Old Testament scholars. His books, his pamphlets, and his valuable surveys of publications reveal a very wide familiarity with the German literature. But they are all distinguished by exceptional freshness and independence; on whatever subject he writes the reader feels that he is in contact with a mind of great acuteness, penetration and originality. That his novelties of criticism or interpretation do not always find acceptance is not of special importance. Their value lies in their suggestive and stimulating quality, in the discovery of new problems and unsuspected difficulties. And he is of all men the most ready to revise his opinions, the least fettered by his past. No better example of this need be given than is afforded by his successive identifications of the Servant of Yahweh with Zerubbabel, Jehoiachin and Moses.

While the technical students of the Old Testament valued Professor Sellin's elaborate investigation of special problems or his stimulating and instructive popular lectures, a more general interest was created by the publication of the first edition of his *Introduction to the Old Testament*. But here also the interest of professional students was keenly aroused, for it was now possible to learn the author's views on many controverted questions and to find new problems suggested. The book was erroneously taken by Professor Cornill to be an attack on his own *Introduction*; and he published a severe criticism of it, to which Dr. Sellin replied. These controversial writings—each published under the title *Zur Einleitung in das Alte Testament*— are of great value to students, who can see here perhaps more clearly than anywhere else the differences, alike in principle and in important details, which divide the two scholars and the tendencies which they represent. They indicate with unusual sharpness the lines on which the debate among Old Testament scholars is proceeding. But for a wider public the *Introduction* itself is naturally more serviceable, and it is specially useful to British students at the present time.

In the first place, it is valuable for its references to the most recent German work and its information as to the latest developments of criticism. The best British works on Biblical Introduction have been exemplary for the fullness with which they have registered the German literature and ex-pounded and discussed the views of German scholars. But Old Testament experts in Germany have published a great deal since the ninth edition of Dr. Driver's *Introduction* was issued ten years ago. And it is a great advantage to British students to have Dr. Sellin's record and estimate of this work on its critical side. In this respect indeed the English edition is more useful than the original, inasmuch as some account has been taken of work which has appeared since the third edition of the work was published in 1920. In particular, Dr. Sellin's own studies, especially in connection with his massive commentary on the Minor Prophets and the monographs he has written on Shechem and still more on Moses, in preparation for his manual on the *History of Israel*, have left some traces on the book.

In the second place, it has seemed to me that a translation would render a great service to us at this juncture because of what I feel to be the illegitimate use of Dr. Sellin's name by some defenders of the traditional view of Scripture. The impression they are apt to give is studiously one-sided. They lay emphasis on the points in which the author accepts a position more in harmony with traditional views and ignore the extent to which

b

he is at one with advanced critics.   It is accordingly desirable that readers should be able to ascertain for themselves precisely what the author's views are. They will learn that he denies the Mosaic authorship of the Pentateuch, accepts the view that it has been made up from the sources into which critics have with practical unanimity analysed it J, E, D, P; that the main part of Deuteronomy is not earlier than Hezekiah, and that in its present form it belongs to the reign of Josiah; that the Priestly document was written at the date to which the Grafian scholars assign it (about 500); that the Book of Isaiah is a highly composite work; that Habakkuk belongs, as Duhm suggested, to the time of Alexander the Great; that Zechariah 9-14 was written about 200 B.C.; and that the Book of Daniel, while containing some earlier material, belongs to the Maccabean period.

But more important than either of these reasons is the fact that Professor Sellin's work represents a type of criticism which is unfamiliar to the English reader.   It will be seen from what I have said that in many of the crucial problems of Introduction he has definitely broken with the traditional position. How radically he is prepared to break with it may be illustrated by his monograph on Moses, in which he reaches the conclusion that Moses was martyred, and finds evidence of a persistent tradition to that effect.   At the same time there is a marked con- servative strain which leads him to what, from the standpoint of the dominant critical school, can only seem reactionary conclusions; for example, the acceptance of the Decalogue and the Book of the Covenant as Mosaic.   This combination is naturally unacceptable to the more thorough-going scholars who believe that it is an attempt to unite elements which are mutually contradictory. As Cornill wittily puts it, Dr. Sellin wishes to have his omelette but to refrain from breaking his eggs. I have no wish to discuss the issue between them ; but I think that it is highly desirable that the British student who is limited to English should have before him an authoritative statement of this position. The reaction, it must be remembered, is not against the Grafian criticism as such, for the author fully accepts the Grafian criticism. It is in large measure a reaction against that view of the original character and the development of the religion of Israel which is specially associated with the names of Kuenen, Wellhausen, Stade and Duhm.

In reaching this position he has been much influenced by the consideration that we must take far more account in our future Old Testament work of Israel's environment than earlier scholars recognized. They were too content, he believes, to isolate the religion and the literature and treat the development as largely due to forces operative within Israel itself. In this respect he joins hands with such scholars as Gunkel, Gressmann and Eduard Meyer, though he is far from adopting their general standpoint. In particular, while Wellhausen and his associates were profoundly influenced in their criticism of the prophetic literature by the belief that eschatology was a late development in Israel, Dr. Sellin holds, with Gunkel, Gressmann and Meyer, though on different grounds, that eschatology was one of the primitive factors in the religion.   Similarly the problem as to the origin of Hebrew monotheism is one that is bound to engage more and more attention.   At present it is less important for the student to take sides in these controversies than to have the case for both sides presented to him.

It was with these thoughts in my mind that I suggested to the Publishers the desirability of issuing a translation of Dr. Sellin's *Introduction*. And I am grateful to them for the service they have done to Old Testament scholarship in accepting the suggestion.   The author cordially consented to the invitation, and we are indebted to him for the additions he has made for the English translation to the last edition of the original.   We have also good reason for satisfaction in the consent of Mr. Montgomery to undertake the translation. His earlier translations of Pfleiderer, and especially of Schweitzer, are so widely known and so justly esteemed that our readers will count us fortunate in securing him for this work.

As the work was primarily intended for German students, the bibliographies were naturally limited almost entirely to works in German.   Since we hope that the book in its English form will be used by a large number of our own students, I have thought it desirable to add a bibliography for the English reader.

ARTHUR S. PEAKE.

September 5, 1923.

AUTHOR'S PREFACE TO THE ENGLISH EDITION

IT is with much satisfaction that I have accepted Messrs. Hodder & Stoughton's proposal to issue an English translation of my *Introduction to the Old Testament.*

It should be said, however, in this connection, that to my regret the book suffers from one serious omission : of the literature of the subject in English which has appeared since 1914 I have hardly been able to take account at all.*   On the other hand, it seems probable that a parallel disability applies to English scholars, and I believe that many will find it interesting and useful to be informed by this book of the lines followed by the Science of Old Testament Introduction during the last few years in Germany.   And, at the same time, I hope that the book may be of some small service in preparing the way for a resumption of that co-operation in theological studies which we all must equally desire, not only in the interests of sound learning, which knows no national boundaries, but also of that Kingdom of God which is destined to extend over all the nations of the earth.

THE AUTHOR.

* So far as concerns the Bibliography, this omission has been made good by Professor Peake.   See pp. xxxiii-xxxviii.

PREFACE TO THE FIRST EDITION

THE composition of a succinct handbook like the present demands, it can readily be imagined, great self-denial on the part of the author, and the sacrifices become the greater in proportion as he diverges from the beaten track. For in that case he must often be content to base upon a mere reference a statement which, in view of its novelty, might well claim a thorough discussion; or merely to point out a line of thought without following it up; and, moreover, when he differs from other authorities he cannot give his reasons with the fullness which courtesy towards them would seem to require.

In spite of all this, I did not hesitate a moment when the editor of the Series invited me to undertake this volume; on the contrary, I felt it to be an unquestionable duty to do so. For it seems to me that there is no better way than that offered by such succinct handbooks of introducing our scientific theological work to the many who, more especially at the present time, have the ardent wish and the undeniable claim to make acquaintance with it. And obviously, too, there is no better means of preparing our theological students for the work of the class-room.

But I should like, at the same time, to express the earnest hope that these little handbooks will serve the purpose of stimulating an interest which will lead to the study of the excellent larger works which we already possess. For the student who is previously acquainted with the former will derive an immensely increased benefit from the reading of the latter.

It will be my aim in the following work to combine, as best may be, the didactic standpoint with independent critical investigation. Any one who expects to find a compendium of all the views which have been put forward on the various problems of Old Testament Introduction, will be, in so far, disappointed. A book of that kind is already in existence. It has been my view that even the didactic aim could not be better fulfilled than by putting the reader in direct contact with the Scholar's processes of thought and letting him take his share therein. In this way, instead of confronting him with a multitude of diverse views between which he must make an unsatisfactory choice, I have given him a single reasoned view, while of course keeping constantly in touch with the results of previous research. This too has no doubt been attempted before. I venture to hope, however, that the greater succinctness of the form, as well as the new lines that I have in many cases followed, will be felt to justify the existence of my attempt, alongside of the others which have been made.

The alternation between larger and smaller print is not to be taken as indicating the greater or smaller importance of the subject-matter. It is in fact my constant practice (apart from B1, § 4) to use the smaller print whenever I enter upon a continuous discussion ; the larger, to set forth the conclusions which I conceive to follow, whether from my own arguments or those of others. This principle explains the preponderance of the small print in the first half of the book.

I am far from claiming completeness in the references to the literature of the subject, especially as regards foreign works. At the same time I believe that I have not overlooked anything of real and abiding value. In regard to the express quotation of the opinions of others I had necessarily to confine myself to what was original, character-istic, and permanently deserving of respect. And I call attention at this point to the fact that com-mentaries are not cited with the remainder of the literature at the beginning of the paragraphs but are enumerated, once for all, at the beginning of the book.

Readers will, I think, be grateful to me for having given in the form of an Appendix a short intro-duction to the Apocrypha and Pseudepigrapha. But I have not thought it necessary to enter in detail into the literary problems connected there-with, as might indeed be inferred from the definition which I have given of " Old Testament Introduc-tion " (see § 1). It would give me peculiar satisfac-tion if I could think I had succeeded, in this little book—which has behind it more work than its size might at a hasty glance suggest—in giving to many persons, beyond the ranks of professed students as well as within them, a serviceable instrument, which will help them in the performance of that first duty of every theologian, nay, of every Christian seeker after knowledge : " Search the Scriptures."

In addition, I should like to think that my fellow‑scholars will recognize that in spite of the restricted space at my command I have done something to further the study of Old Testament Introduction, which at the present time presents a larger number of burning questions than at any earlier period.

I am indebted for the Index to my former pupil, Dr. Jirku.

THE AUTHOR.

ROSTOCK,
Whitsuntide, 1910.

PREFACE TO THE SECOND EDITION

THE pleasing fact that the first edition, in spite of its extending to 3000 copies, has been totally exhausted within three years, shows that my little book has filled a gap. I have therefore not hesitated to bring out another edition at once, although I am very conscious of the responsibility of writing a handbook at the present time, when so strong a ferment is in progress in many departments of Introduction.

That Criticism has not stood still in the last three years is obvious. And that I myself have not remained immobile will be evident. In particular, the portions dealing with the Pentateuch and the historical books have been largely recast. I am myself convinced that in this department none of us, not even the most confident, have reason to feel that we have entered in and possessed the land. And for this very reason I wished to give my pupils a vivid impression of the fact that we are here confronted by problems, the solution of which demands from all of us persistent and untiring efforts.

I owe my warmest thanks to all those who by their friendly criticisms " made straight the way " for the first edition and at the same time called my attention to its defects and deficiencies. I hope that they, as well as those who have so kindly written to me privately about it, will observe that they have not written in vain.

But I am under still stronger obligation to express my thanks to the author of a polemical pamphlet "On the Question of Old Testament Introduction," who subjected my first edition to a keen and depreciatory criticism. I have not, as I showed in my reply—published under the same title—seen reason to alter my opinion in any one of the more important points on which he attacked me ; and indeed am now more decided than ever in maintaining the positions which I then took up ; but I am nevertheless indebted to his microscopic criticism for a number of corrections in regard to matters of subsidiary importance. And the growth of interest in the burning questions of Introduction which has resulted from our controversy will no doubt continue to be a source of satisfaction to us both.

THE AUTHOR.

KIEL,
New Year's Day, 1914.

PREFACE TO THE THIRD EDITION

In the second edition the paragraphs relating to the Pentateuch and the historical books were subjected to a specially thorough revision; in the present edition the section on the Minor Prophets, to which my studies in the years just past have been principally devoted, has undergone, in many respects, a far-reaching transformation.

In addition, change, and in some cases expansion, will be noted in the discussion of Deuteronomy, Deutero-Isaiah, and the Book of Job. In matters of detail there have been extensions and improvements in nearly every chapter. It is my earnest hope that the book in its new form will add new friends to the old ones, who share my gratitude to the Publishers for having, in spite of the unfavourable circumstances of the time, made possible the printing of a new edition.

THE AUTHOR

Kiel,
September 1920.

CONTENTS

INTRODUCTION

c

ABBREVIATIONS

HRE	. .	Herzog, Real. Encyklopädie für protestantische Theologie und Kirche.
ThStKr	. .	Theologische Studien und Kritiken.
ZAW	. .	Zeitschrift für die alttestamentliche Wissenschaft.
ZWTh	. .	Zeitschrift für wissenschaftliche Theologie.
NKZ	. .	Neue kirchliche Zeitschrift.
WZKM	. .	Wiener Zeitschrift für die Kunde des Morgenlandes.
ZLTh	. .	Zeitschrift für lutherische Theologie.
ZThK	. .	Zeitschrift für Theologie und Kirche.
BZAW	. .	Beihefte zur Zeitschr. für die alttest. Wissenschaft.
BzA	. .	Beiträge zur Assyriologie.
KAT	. .	Die Keilinschriften und das Alte Testament (The Cuneiform Inscriptions and the O.T.).
SchAT	. .	Die Schriften des Alten Testaments in Auswahl neu übersetzt und für die Gegenwart erklärt von Gressmann, Gunkel, usw. (A selection from the Old Testament writings newly translated and explained for the present age by Gressman, Gunkel, etc.)
HSAT	. .	Die heilige Schrift des A.T. Ed. Kautzsch.
ZEAT	. .	Sellin. Zur Einleitung in das Alte Testament, 1912.
ASt	. .	Alttestamentliche Studien. Dedicated to Rudolf Kittel on his 60th birthday, 1914.
Wellhausenfestschr.		Studies in Semitic Philology and History of Religion. Dedicated to J. Wellhausen on his 70th birthday, 1914.

Baudissinfestschr. .   Essays on Questions of Semitic Religion and
                       Philology, offered to Count von Baudissin
                       by friends and pupils on the 26th Sept.
                       1918.
Buddefestschr.   .   Contributions to O.T. Criticism.   Dedicated
                       to K. Budde on his 70th birthday.

Titles are, as a rule, given only once, generally at
the head of the paragraphs in which they are
referred to, and afterwards cited simply by a " short-
title " or by the above abbreviations.   If they are
not found in the paragraph headings they may be
looked for at the beginning of the chapters, where
the expository literature relating to their subjects
is collected.   The " introductions " and literary
histories which cover the whole domain of introduction are cited by their full title only once, in the
Introduction, § 2, but of course they are to be
considered as referred to in each of the chapters
and paragraphs.

THE MOST IMPORTANT COMMENT-ARIES ON THE OLD TESTAMENT

There exist in Germany at present five great Commentaries on the whole of the Old Testament.

1. The *Biblischer Kommentar* on the Old Testament, edited by Keil and Delitzsch, Leipzig, 1861 ff. (abbreviation B.K.). Delitzsch's commentaries are still to be recommended, Keil's are obsolete in regard to questions of Introduction.

2. The *Kurzgefasstes exegetisches Handbuch zum A.T.*, begun by F. Hitzig and others, Leipzig, 1838 ff. (K.E.H.). Represents a moderate criticism. The portions reissued in the last twenty to twenty-five years can be strongly recommended; in the other portions it is obsolete.

3. Strack and Zöckler's *Kurzgefasster Kommentar zu den heiligen Schriften Alten und Neuen Testaments*, Munich, 1886 ff. (K.K.). Conservative in tendency and critically cautious, but does not everywhere consistently respond to the legitimate demands of a scientific study of the Old Testament.

4. *Handkommentar zum A.T.*, edited by Nowack, Göttingen, 1892 ff. (H.K.). In questions of Introduction it is in many cases too strongly influenced by the critical and religious-historical schematism

of Wellhausen, otherwise in every respect on a high
level of scientific criticism.

5. *Kurzer Handkommentar zum A.T.*, edited
by Marti, Tübingen, 1897 ff. (K.H.K.). Very
valuable contributions to the exegesis of particular
passages; but often based on unsound religious-
historical presuppositions, and in some parts,
especially those due to the Editor and Duhm, not
free from an excessively radical criticism and
arbitrary reconstruction of the development of the
Old Testament Literature.

6. At present in process of appearing is the
Kommentar zum A.T., edited by Sellin, Leipzig,
1913 ff. (K.z.A.T.).

Among commentaries on particular books the
following are especially deserving of mention for
the purposes of serious study.

Genesis . . .	Delitzsch (N.K. 1887).
	Dillmann (K.E.H.[6] 1892).
	Strack (K.K.[2] 1905).
	Gunkel (H.K.[3] 1909–10).
	Holzinger (K.H.K. 1898).
	Procksch (K.z.A.T. 1913).
Exodus . . .	Ryssel (K.E.H.[3] 1897).
	Strack (K.K. 1894).
	Baentsch (H.K. 1903).
	Holzinger (K.H.C. 1900).
Leviticus . . .	Ryssel (K.E.H.[3] 1897).
	Baentsch (H.K. 1903).
	Bertholet (K.H.K. 1901).
Numbers . . .	Dillmann (K.E.H. 1886).
	Baentsch (H.K. 1903).
	Holzinger (K.H.K. 1903).
Deuteronomy . .	Dillmann (K.E.H. 1886).
	Öttli (K.K. 1893).
	Steuernagel (H.K. 1900).
	Bertholet (K.H.K. 1899).
	Koenig (K.z.A.T. 1917)

Joshua . . .	Dillmann (K.E.H. 1886).
	Öttli (K.K. 1893).
	Steuernagel (H.K. 1900).
	Holzinger (K.H.K. 1901).
Judges . . .	Öttli (K.K. 1893).
	Nowack (H.K. 1902).
	Budde (K.H.K. 1897).
Samuel . . .	Löhr (K.E.H.³ 1898).
	Klostermann (K.K. 1887).
	Nowack (H.K. 1992).
	Budde (K.H.K. 1902).
Kings . . .	Klostermann (K.K. 1887).
	Kittel (H.K. 1900).
	Benzinger (K.H.K. 1899).
Isaiah . . .	Delitzsch (B.K.⁴ 1889).
	Bredenkamp (1887).
	Kittel (K.E.H.⁶ 1898).
	Orelli (K.K.³ 1904).
	Duhm (H.K.² 1902).
	Marti (K.H.K. 1910).
Jeremiah . . .	Cornill (1905).
	Orelli (K.K.³ 1905).
	Giesebrecht (H.K.² 1907).
	Duhm (K.H.K. 1901).
	Volz (KzA.T. 1922).
Ezekiel . . .	Smend (K.E.H.² 1880).
	Orelli (K.K.² 1896).
	Krätzschmar (H.K. 1900).
	Bertholet (K.H.K. 1897).
Minor Prophets .	Steiner (K.E.H.⁴ 1886).
	Orelli (K.K.³ 1900).
	Nowack (H.K.² 1904).
	Marti (K.H.K. 1904).
	Wellhausen (Skizzen und Vorarbeiten 5³, 1898).
	Duhm (Anmerkungen zu den Zwölf Propheten, 1911).
	Sellin (K.z.A.T. 1922).
Psalms . . .	Delitzsch (B.K.⁵ 1893).
	Kessler (K.K.² 1899).
	Bäthgen (H.K.³ 1904).
	Duhm (K.H.K. 1899).
	Hupfeld-Nowack³ (1887, 8).
	Kittel² (K.z.A.T. 1922).

BIBLIOGRAPHY FOR ENGLISH READERS

BY

PROFESSOR A. S PEAKE, D.D

Introductions to the Old Testament : Driver, *An Introduction to the Literature of the Old Testament,* [1]1891, [9]1913 ;
Bennett, *A Biblical Introduction : Old Testament,* 1911 ;
Cornill, *Introduction to the Canonical Books of the Old Testament,* 1907 ; J. E. M'Fadyen, *Introduction to the Old Testament,*
1905 ; G. B. Gray, *A Critical Introduction to the Old Testament,* 1913; W. R. Smith, *The Old Testament in the Jewish
Church*[2], 1892 ; Orr, *The Problem of the Old Testament,* 1906.

Kautzsch, *An Outline of the History of the Old Testament,*
1898 ; H. T. Fowler, *A History of the Literature of Ancient
Israel,* 1912 ; Creelman, *Introduction to the Old Testament,
chronologically arranged.*

Dictionaries : Smith, *A Dictionary of the Bible* (3 vols.),
1863, vol. i., revised edition, 1893 ; Hastings, *A Dictionary
of the Bible* (5 vols.), 1898–1904 ; Hastings, *A Dictionary of the
Bible* (an independent work in one volume), 1910 ; Cheyne
and Black, *Encyclopaedia Biblica,* 1899–1903 ; Orr, *The
International Standard Bible Encyclopaedia* ; Piercy, *Murray's
Illustrated Bible Dictionary,* 1908 ; Jacobus, *A Standard
Bible Dictionary,* 1909 ; *The New Schaff-Herzog Encyclopaedia,*
1908–12 ; *The Encyclopaedia Britannica*[11].

Commentaries : The chief series are *The International
Critical Commentary* (ICC) ; *The Cambridge Bible for Schools
and Colleges* (CB) ; *The Century Bible* (CentB) ; *The West-
minster Commentary* (WestC). There are also two one-volume
commentaries—Dummelow, *A Commentary on the Holy Bible,*
1909 ; and *Peake's Commentary* (PC), 1919. In the following list the series are indicated by the symbols in brackets
in the list just given. Other commentaries are added which do

not appear in a series. For the convenience of readers the order of books in the English Bible is in this instance followed.

Genesis : Skinner (ICC) ; Ryle (CB) ; Bennett (CentB) ; Driver (WestC) ; Peake (PC).

Exodus : Driver (CB) ; Bennett (CentB) ; M'Neile (WestC) ; Harford (PC).

Leviticus : Chapman and Streane (CB) ; A. R. S. Kennedy (CentB) ; Lofthouse (PC).

Numbers : Gray (ICC) ; M'Neile (CB) ; A. R. S. Kennedy (CentB) ; Wade (PC).

Deuteronomy : Driver (ICC) ; G. A. Smith (CB) ; H. W. Robinson (CentB) ; T. Witton Davies (PC).

Joshua : G. A. Cooke (CB) ; H. W. Robinson (CentB) ; S. Holmes (PC).

Judges : G. F. Moore (ICC) ; G. A. Cooke (CB) ; Thatcher (CentB) ; J. Strahan (PC) ; Burney, *The Book of Judges*.

Ruth : G. A. Cooke (CB) ; Thatcher (CentB) ; J. Strahan (PC).

Samuel : H. P. Smith (ICC) ; Kirkpatrick (CB) ; A. R. S. Kennedy (CentB) ; Bennett (PC) ; Driver, *Notes on the Hebrew Text of the Books of Samuel*.

Kings : Barnes (CB) ; Skinner (CentB) ; Foakes Jackson (PC) ; Burney, *Notes on the Hebrew Text of the Books of Kings*.

Chronicles : Curtis and Masden (ICC) ; Elmslie (CB) ; Harvey-Jellie (CentB) ; Oesterley (PC).

Ezra and Nehemiah : Batten (ICC) ; Ryle (CB) ; T. Witton Davies (CentB) ; Oesterley (PC).

Esther : Paton (ICC) ; Streane (CB) ; T. Witton Davies (CentB) ; Duff (PC) ; P. Haupt, *The Book of Esther*.

Job : Driver and Gray (ICC) ; A. B. Davidson (CB) ; Peake (CentB) ; Gibson (WestC) ; Franks (PC) ; Buttenwieser, *The Book of Job* ; Ball, *The Book of Job* ; J. Strahan, *The Book of Job* ; J. T. Marshall (in American Commentary on the Old Testament).

Psalms : Briggs (ICC) ; Kirkpatrick (CB) ; W. T. Davison and T. Witton Davies (CentB) ; Addis (PC) ; Cheyne, *The Book of Psalms*.

Proverbs : Toy (ICC) ; Perowne (CB) ; G. C. Martin (CentB) ; S. Hooke (PC).

Ecclesiastes : Barton (ICC) ; Lukyn Williams (CB) ; G. C. Martin (CentB) ; A. J. Grieve (PC). J. T. Marshall (as in *Job*) ; P. Haupt, *The Book of Ecclesiastes*.

Song of Songs: A. Harper (CB); G. C. Martin (CentB); Jordan (PC); P. Haupt, *The Book of Canticles.*

Isaiah: Gray [chaps. 1-27] (ICC); Skinner (CB); Whitehouse (CentB); Wade (WestC); Peake [chaps. 1-39], Wardle [chaps. 40-66] (PC); Cheyne, *The Prophecies of Isaiah*; G. A. Smith in the *Expositor's Bible.*

Jeremiah: Streane (CB); Peake (CentB); Binns (WestC); H. W. Robinson (PC).

Ezekiel: A. B. Davidson (CB); Lofthouse (CentB); Redpath (WestC); M'Fadyen (PC).

Daniel: Driver (CB); Charles (CentB); Andrews (PC); A. A. Bevan, *Commentary on Daniel*; C. H. H. Wright, *Daniel and his Critics*; Prince, *A Critical Commentary on Daniel.*

The Minor Prophets: Horton [*Hosea to Micah*], Driver [*Nahum to Malachi* (CentB); G. A. Smith in *Expositor's Bible*; Pusey, *The Minor Prophets.*

Hosea: W. R. Harper (ICC); Cheyne (CB); Box (PC).

Joel: Bewer (ICC); Driver (CB); Wardle (PC).

Amos: W. R. Harper (ICC); Driver (CB); Edghill (WestC); Canney (PC).

Obadiah: Bewer (ICC); Perowne (CB); H. W. Robinson (PC).

Jonah: Bewer (ICC); Perowne (CB); Peake (PC).

Micah: J. M. P. Smith (ICC); Cheyne (CB); H. W. Robinson (PC); P. Haupt, *The Book of Micah.*

Nahum: J. M. P. Smith (ICC); A. B. Davidson (CB); Gordon (PC); P. Haupt, *The Book of Nahum.*

Habakkuk: W. H. Ward (ICC); A. B. Davidson (CB); Gordon (PC).

Zephaniah: J. M. P. Smith (ICC); A. B. Davidson (CB); Gordon (PC).

Haggai: H. G. Mitchell (ICC); Barnes (CB); Kennett (PC).

Zechariah: H. G. Mitchell (ICC); Barnes (CB); Kennett (PC).

Malachi: J. M. P. Smith (ICC); Barnes (CB); A. J. Grieve (PC).

Introductory Chapter, § 2. Cheyne, *The Founders of Old Testament Criticism*, 1893.

A. § 1. Gordon, *The Poets of the Old Testament*, 1912; G. A. Smith, *The Early Poetry of Israel*, 1912; Cobb, *A Criticism of Systems of Hebrew Metre*, 1905; Gray, *The Forms of Hebrew*

Poetry, 1915 ; G. A. Cooke, *A Text-book of North-Semitic In-scriptions*, 1903.

§§ 2-4. Driver, *Notes on the Hebrew Text and the Topo-graphy of the Books of Samuel*[2], 1913, pp. i-xciv ; Geden, *Out-lines of Introduction to the Hebrew Bible*, 1909 ; Ginsburg, *Introduction to the Massoretico-critical Edition of the Hebrew Bible*, 1897 ; T. H. Weir, *A Short History of the Text of the Old Testament*, 1899 ; Buhl, *Canon and Text of the Old Testament*, 1892 ; Swete, *Introduction to the Old Testament in Greek*, 1900 (2nd edition by R. R. Ottley). Articles on the text and the different versions in the dictionaries of the Bible.

B. I. Kuenen, *The Hexateuch*, 1886 ; Wellhausen, *Prolego-mena to the History of Israel*, 1885 ; *The Hexateuch . . ., arranged in its Constituent Documents*, edited by J. Estlin Carpenter and G. Harford-Battersby, 1900 [the first volume in an expanded form was published as *The Composition of the Hexateuch*, by J. Estlin Carpenter, and an Appendix on Laws and Institutions, by G. Harford, 1902] ; Addis, *The Documents of the Hexateuch*, 1892, 1898 ; Chapman, *An Introduction to the Pentateuch*, 1911 ; Simpson, *Pentateuchal Criticism*, 1914 ; Bacon, *The Genesis of Genesis*, 1892, *The Triple Tradition of the Exodus*, 1894 ; Finn, *The Unity of the Pentateuch*, N.D. ; Skinner, *The Divine Names in Genesis*, 1914.

§ 5 (1) Gordon and G. A. Smith as in A. § 1. (2) S. A. Cook, *The Laws of Moses and the Code of Hammurabi*, 1903 ; Johns, *The Relations between the Laws of Babylonia and the Laws of the Hebrew Peoples*, 1914 ; Kennett, *Deuteronomy and the Decalogue* (1920).

§ 8. M'Neile, *Deuteronomy, Its Place in Revelation*, 1912 Kennett (as above).

II. A. 1. Holmes, *Joshua, the Hebrew and Greek Texts*, 1914.

B. Gordon, *The Prophets of the Old Testament*, 1916 ; T. H. Robinson, *Prophecy and the Prophets in Ancient Israel*, 1923 ; Edghill, *An Enquiry into the Evidential Value of Prophecy*, 1906 ; Bennett, *The Religion of the Post-Exilic Prophets*, 1907 ; Buttenwieser, *The Prophets of Israel*, 1914 ; Peake, *The Roots of Hebrew Prophecy and Jewish Apocalyptic*, 1923.

§ 1. Driver, *Isaiah ; his Life and Times*[2], 1893 ; Cheyne, *Introduction to the Book of Isaiah*, 1894 ; Glazebrook, *Studies in the Book of Isaiah*, 1910 ; Kennett, *The Composition of the Book of Isaiah*, 1910 ; Gordon, *The Faith of Isaiah*, N.D.

§ 2. Cheyne, *Jeremiah, his Life and Times*, 1888 ; J. R.

Gillies, *Jeremiah, The Man and his Message*, 1907 ; W. R. Thomson, *The Burden of the Lord*, 1919 ; Skinner, *Prophecy and Religion : Studies in the Life of Jeremiah*, 1922 ; Driver, *The Book of the Prophet Jeremiah* (translation, introduction, and notes), 1906.

§ 3. Lofthouse, *The Prophet of Reconstruction*, 1920.

§ 4. Farrar, *The Minor Prophets*, 1890 ; Orchard, *Oracles of God*, 1922.

§ 5. Melville Scott, *The Message of Hosea*, 1921.

§ 9. C. H. H. Wright, *Biblical Essays*, 1886.

§ 11. Gray, *Expositor*, Sept. 1898.

§ 12. Budde, *Expositor*, May 1895 ; Stevenson, *Expositor*, 1902 ; Peake, *The Problem of Suffering in the Old Testament*, 1904 ; Stonehouse, *The Book of Habakkuk*, 1911.

§ 15. C. H. H. Wright, *Zechariah and his Prophecies*, 1878.

III. Lowth, *De sacra poesi Hebraeorum*, 1753 ; Gordon, *The Poets of the Old Testament*, 1912. See further under A § 1.

§ 1. Cheyne, *The Origin and Religious Contents of the Psalter*, 1891 ; W. T. Davison, *The Praises of Israel*, 1893 ; Jordan, *Religion in Song*, N.D. ; Peters, *The Psalms as Liturgies*, 1922.

§ 2. Cheyne, *Job and Solomon*, 1887 ; W. T. Davison, *The Wisdom Literature of the Old Testament*, 1894 ; W. A. L. Elmslie, *Studies in Life from Jewish Proverbs*, 1917.

§ 3. Cheyne and W. T. Davison as under § 2 ; J. E. M'Fadyen, *The Problem of Pain : A Study in the Book of Job*, N.D. ; Dillon, *The Sceptics of the Old Testament*, 1895 [reproduces Bickell's theories].

§ 4. Budde, *The New World*, 1894 ; D. R. Scott, *Pessimism and Love*, N.D.

§ 7. Tyler, *Ecclesiastes*,[1] 1874,[2] 1899 ; C. H. H. Wright, *The Book of Koheleth considered in relation to modern criticism and to the doctrines of modern pessimism*, 1883 ; M'Neile, *An Introduction to Ecclesiastes, with Notes and Appendices*, 1904 ; Cheyne and Davison as under § 2 ; D. R. Scott, *Pessimism and Love*, N.D. [on the lines of Siegfried].

§ 9. Pusey, *Daniel the Prophet*, 1865 ; C. H. H. Wright, *Daniel and his Prophecies*, 1906 ; A. C. Welch, *Visions of the End*, 1922 ; R. D. Wilson, in *Biblical and Theological Studies by the Members of the Faculty of the Princeton Theological Seminary*, 1912.

§ 10. C. C. Torrey, *Ezra Studies*, 1910.

Apocrypha and Pseudepigrapha: Charles, *The Apocrypha and Pseudepigrapha of the Old Testament in English*, 1913; Drummond, *The Jewish Messiah*, 1877; Oesterley, *The Books of the Apocrypha: their Origin, Contents and Teaching*, 1914; Andrews, *The Apocryphal Books of the Old and New Testament*, 1908; Porter, *The Messages of the Apocalyptic Writers*, 1905; Burkitt, *Jewish and Christian Apocalypses*, 1914; Charles has published editions of *Enoch*, [1]1893, [2]1912; *The Secrets of Enoch*, 1895; *Apocalypse of Baruch*, 1896; *The Assumption of Moses*, 1897; *The Ascension of Isaiah*, 1900; *Jubilees*, 1902; *Testaments of the Twelve Patriarchs*, 1908. The following may be added: Ryle and James, *The Psalms of Solomon*, 1891; Box, *The Ezra Apocalypse*, 1912; R. Harris, *The Odes and Psalms of Solomon*, 1909, new edition by Harris and Mingana, 1916–20.

C. Buhl, *Canon and Text of the Old Testament*, 1892; Ryle, *The Canon of the Old Testament*, 1892; Wildeboer, *The Origin of the Canon of the Old Testament*, 1895.

INTRODUCTORY CHAPTER

§ 1. *Definition and Divisions of Old Testament Introduction*

Hupfeld, *Über Begriff und Methode der sogenannten biblischen Einleitung*, 1844, and ThStKr, 1861, p. 3 ff.; Köhler, *Über Berechtigung der Kritik des Alten Testaments*, 1895; *Die heilige Schrift als Gottes Wort* (NKZ, 1896, p. 429 ff.); Köberle, *Heilsgeschichtliche und religionsgeschichtliche Betrachtungsweise des Alten Testaments* (NKZ, 1906, p. 200 ff.).

OLD TESTAMENT INTRODUCTION is that branch of theological study which deals with the origin and history of those Old Testament writings which were taken over by the Christian religious community from the Jewish, and, on the testimony of Jesus and the Apostles, were acknowledged as Holy Scripture. It thus differs from the secular study of the history of Jewish literature in the same way as the study of the Old Testament history of the way of salvation differs from the study of the history of the people of Israel, and as the study of Old Testament theology differs from that of Israelitish-Jewish religious history. These latter have their rights as scientific studies alongside of the theological studies, while in regard to most of the particular problems they stand in the closest relations with them. But the aim and purpose of the two kinds of study are different. In the study of the Old Testament under the head of history of literature the aim is the investigation of the origin and history of the literary monuments of Israel and Judah ; in " Introduction " the aim is the investigation of the origin and history of a collection of writings which, for the Church of God upon earth, constitute the archives of revelation and an ethico-religious norm.

Introduction falls naturally into three parts :

(*a*) The History of the Text of the Old Testament Scriptures.

(*b*) The Examination of the circumstances and date of origin of the individual writings.

(*c*) The history of the collection and setting apart of the Books, and formation of the Canon.

The at one time most widely accepted Division into General Introduction (*a* and *c*) and Special Introduction (*b*) is misleading, and brings together under (*a*) material which is wholly disparate. Cf. Koenig, *Einleitung*, p. 8 ff.

§ 2. *History and Literature of Old Testament Introduction*

The history of Old Testament Introduction has passed through the following periods :

1. The Early Church handed down to us only isolated materials for Introduction (referring to language, geographical and historical statements of the Old Testament, etc.), no complete treatment of the subject. (Origen, Eusebius, Epiphanius, Jerome, Augustine, Julius Africanus, etc.)

2. The way was first cleared for Introduction as a scientific study by Humanism and the Reformation, the former of which directed attention to the Hebrew language and the original text, while the latter aroused an entirely new interest in the contents of the Scriptures, and raised the question

of the trustworthiness of the tradition which had come down to the Church through the Synagogue. (The Humanist Reuchlin, the Catholic Sixtus Senensis, the Reformed scholars Rivetus and Capellus, the Lutheran Walther, the Jew Spinoza.)

3. Introduction first acquired an independent position through the Rationalistic criticism which sought to understand each Book in the light of its own period and to discover the time of its origin from the historical circumstances which it implied. (Semler, Herder, Eichhorn—who was the real father of the study, in his *Einleitung in das A.T.*, 1780–82—J. D. Michaelis, G. L. Bauer, De Wette, Bertholdt, Vatke, Ewald, Bleek, etc.)

4. In opposition to this there arose about the middle of last century an attempt to revive the Church-Synagogue tradition (Hengstenberg, Hävernick, Keil and, as a last representative, Green in America).

5. The fathers of the modern scientific study of Introduction, which endeavours in investigating the date of the various writings to make use alike of language, history and the history of religion, are Kuenen in his *Historisch-kritische Einleitung in die Bücher des Alten Testaments* (translated from the Dutch by Weber and Müller, 1887–92) and Wellhausen, *Geschichte Israels*, I., 1878 (since 1883 *Prolegomena zur G.*); *Einleitung in das A.T. von Bleek*, 4th ed., 1878. Their conception of the tasks and methods of Introduction is the same as that of the writers named under 3, but they start out from an essentially new conception of the history of Israel. In the science of Introduction as influenced by the epoch-making work of these

scholars, especially Wellhausen, there are to be observed during the last four decades two streams of tendency.

(*a*) A first, which accepts the main lines of Wellhausen's conception of the history almost unconditionally. (Reuss, *Die Geschichte der heiligen Schriften A.Ts.*, 1881 ; Stade, *Die Geschichte des Volkes Israel*, 1881–88 ; W. Robertson Smith, *Das A.T., seine Entstehung und Überlieferung* (*Old Testament in the Jewish Church*[2], 1892), translated by Rothstein, 1894 ; Cornill, *Einleitung in die kanonischen Bücher des A.T.*[7], 1913 ; *Zur Einleitung in das A.T.*, 1912 ; Steuernagel, *Lehrbuch der Einleitung in das A.T.*, 1912.)

(*b*) A second, which adopts a less sceptical attitude towards the Jewish tradition than Wellhausen, and consequently refuses to accept his critical results, so far as these depend on his reconstruction of the religious history. (Riehm, *Einleitung in das A.T.*, edited by Brandt, 1889 ; Driver, *Introduction to the Literature of the Old Testament*, translated by Rothstein, 1896 ; Strack, *Einleitung in das A.T.*[6], 1906 ; Koenig, *Einleitung in das A.T.*, 1893 ; Baudissin, *Einleitung in die Bücher des A.T.*, 1901.

6. Starting from the foundations laid by Wellhausen there has grown up in the last three decades, alongside of the form of Introduction which treats the individual Old Testament Books in their order, a parallel study—Israelitish Literary History—which treats the various component parts of the Old Testament in their historical order and development. (Wildeboer, *Die Literatur des A.T.*, translated from the Dutch by Risch, 1895 ; Kautzsch,

Abriss der Geschichte des a.t. Schrifttums, 1897 ; Budde, *Geschichte der althebräischen Literatur*, 1906 ; Gunkel, *Die israelitische Literatur* in " Die Kultur der Gegenwart," 1906 ; Meinhold, *Einführung i. d. A.T.*, 1918 ; Bertholet, *Kulturgeschichte Israels*, 1920.)

7. From two directions, but finally converging on one point, the way has lately been prepared for an advance beyond the Wellhausen conception of the Science of Introduction. On the one hand, a more strictly historical attitude towards literature has given its attention primarily to the *history* of the various literary forms in the Old Testament, in contradistinction to the previously prevailing *literary criticism*, which held its task to be fulfilled when it had analysed the Old Testament writings into their various " sources " and affixed a date to these. This method has led to the recognition that the critical standards hitherto applied had been too one-sidedly derived from the specimens of literary art which had come down to us, and were inadequate for dealing with the real life, of which Old Testament literature was just one of the products, alongside of others which have not come down to us. It has therefore pointed out that incomparably more early material is to be found, even in writings which received their final form at the hands of a relatively late redactor, than had long been assumed.

On the other hand, in the main the same result has been arrived at by placing the Old Testament literature in the framework of Early Oriental Literature, and more especially by bringing it into relation with the Babylonian and ancient Egyptian literatures. The scheme into which Wellhausen, looking at it too much in isolation, tried to fit the Old Testament Literature, has thus proved in many respects inadequate.

Up to the present both tendencies embrace many views on particular points which diverge widely from one another and give no consistent and comprehensive presentation of the Old Testament Literature as whole. (The stimulus to these studies was given especially by Gunkel (cf. 6), and in his *Schöpfung und Chaos in Urzeit und Endzeit*, 1896; Hommel, *Die altisraelitische Überlieferung in inschriftlicher Beleuchtung*, 1897 ; Winckler, *Alt-orientalische Forschungen*, 1897 ff. ; also *Arabisch-Semitisch-Orientalisch*, 1901 ; Winckler and Zimmer in Schrader's *Die Keilinschriften und das A.T.*[3], 1902 and 3; Jeremias, *Das A.T. im Lichte des alten Orients*[3], 1916 ; Gressmann, Gunkel and others, *Die Schriften des A.T. in Auswahl*, 1909 ff.; Kittel, *Die alttestamentliche Wissenschaft in ihren wichtigsten Ergebnissen*[4], 1921 ; Sellin, *Zur Einleitung in das A.T.*, 1912.)

Old Testament Introduction is therefore at present in a transition stage. The history of the literature as such will become more consciously differentiated from it as time goes on. But the old method of dealing with the books in their traditional order will always retain a practical advantage as a method of initiation into the subject. And Introduction will retain its justification in principle so long as there exists a Christian Community which regards it as guaranteed by its Lord and His Apostles that it possesses in the Old Testament, as we now have it, an entirely unique literature, the archives of the preparatory Divine revelation. Moreover, this view, even as regards the assertion of the ethico-religious superiority of the Old Testament as compared with all other early Oriental literature, is only confirmed by the science of Comparative Religion. On the other hand, Introduction will always remain in mutual relations with History of Literature.

For to trace the methods by which it has pleased God to cause
this unique literature to arise is purely a matter of scientific
historico-critical investigation. And the latter moves, by zig-
zags it is true—but in a forward direction, and approximates
more and more closely, as time goes on, to historical truth

A. THE HISTORY OF THE TEXT OF THE OLD TESTAMENT SCRIPTURES

§ 1. *Poetry, Narrative, the Art of Writing and Literary Art in Israel*

Kittel, *Die Anfänge der hebräischen Geschichtsschreibung im A.T.*, 1897 ; Gunkel, *Die israelitische Literatur*, 1906 ; *Das Märchen im A.T.*, 1917 ; Lidzbarski, *Handbuch der nordsemitischen Epigraphik*, 1898 ; Benzinger, *Hebräische Archäologie²*, 1908 ; E. Koenig, *Die Poesie des A.T.*, 1908 ; Bertholet, *Kulturgeschichte Israels*, 1920 ; Volz, *Die biblischen Altertümer*, 1914.

THAT in Israel, as among all other nations, the period of literary composition was preceded by a period of singing and tale-telling might be taken for granted. But it is in fact confirmed in the Old Testament tradition. For in the historical Books, which, according to the tradition, are the oldest, there are two other books quoted, unfortunately now lost, which must have been older than the books in which they are cited, and which were obviously collections of songs. These are " The Book of the Wars of Yahweh " quoted in Numbers 21. 14, and the " Book of the Valiant " * which is cited in Jos. 10. 13 and 2 Sam. 1. 18, and perhaps also in 1 K. 8. 53 (LXX).

* German " Buch des Braven," which retains the ambiguity of the original (cf. the Latin use of *virtus*). The singular may, according to various theories, be taken collectively, or as referring to a personified Israel.—Translator.

Read, in the latter passage, instead of הַשִּׁיר as implied by the LXX (ἐν βιβλίῳ τῆς ᾠδῆς), with Wellhausen הַיָּשָׁר. It is probable that this, like יְשֻׁרְאֵל in Micah 2. 7,* and יְשֻׁרוּן, Deut. 32. 15 ; 33. 5, etc., is a title of honour in opposition to the hostile mockery of Jacob as the betrayer. Cf. Hos. 12. 3, 7 ; Gen. 27. 36. When these collections were first instituted—whether under David, the Sweet Singer of Israel, 2 Sam. 23. 1, the leader in the Wars of Yahweh, 1 Sam. 18. 17 ; 25. 28—we do not know. In any case, in one of them songs continued to be inserted under David and Solomon.

But beyond this, the historical books offer abundant evidence that Israel, from the days of Moses downwards, made use of song on every occasion, cheerful or solemn, private and public, secular and religious.

There are allusions to Drinking Songs, Taunt Songs, Love Songs, Gnomic verses, and Elegies. Moreover, all the important events of the history are preserved in Songs — War Songs in Ex. 17. 16 ; Jos. 10. 12 ; Jud. 5. 12 ; Taunt Songs, Nu. 21. 27 ff. ; as Praise of Heroes and Song of Victory, Ex. 15. 21 ; Ju. 5. 1 ff. ; 11. 34 ; 1 Sam. 18. 6 ff. ; and also in the form of elegy in 2 Sam. 1. 17 ff. ; Amos 5. 16. But there was, moreover, from the earliest times a religious poesy. It was not merely that the whole of the historical poetry had also a religious character—was a celebration of " the righteous acts of Yahweh," Jud. 5. 11—but there was also a specifically cultus poetry, Nu. 6. 24 ff. ; 10. 35 ; 1 K. 8. 53 ; hymns for singing in public worship, Amos 5. 23 ; Hos. 9. 1 ; Ex. 32. 18 ; Processional Hymns in Ps. 24. 7-10 ; 2 Sam. 6. 15 ; Isa. 30. 29 ; hymns of supplication, Ps. 20 ; thanksgiving, Jer. 33. 11 ; lamentation and penitence, Hos. 6. 1-3 ; 14. 1-3. Cf. the resemblance between certain phrases in the Old Testament penitential psalms and the Babylonian, which were in existence in the second millennium B.C. (Ps. 6. 3 ; 32. 5a ; 51. 7 ; 130. 1).

To the religious poetry belong also the formulas in which Blessing and Cursing were laid upon persons or things, Gen. 27. 27 ff. ; Jos. 6. 26 ; Deut. 11. 29 ; and oracles and eschatological utterances, which are often given in close association, Gen. 25. 23 ; 49. 1 ff. ; Nu. 23 ; 24, etc.

---

* The author adopts this reading in his Minor Prophets, p. 272f.— Translator.

The most important characteristic of Hebrew poetry, which was long ago recognised by Bishop Lowth (*De sacra poesi Hebraeorum* 1753), is the "parallelism of the members," the combination of usually two, but sometimes three or four verse-lines, answering to one another by way of synonym, antithesis or synthesis, to form a verse. That the poetry had also a metre, or more strictly speaking a *rhythm*, is self-evident. For a good while past the rhythm of the elegy (discovered by Ley and especially Budde, *Das hebräische Klagelied*, ZAW, 1882, 1 ff.) has been held to be demonstrated. This is the *Kinah*, the so-called halting verse, in which the second line is regularly shorter than the first, in the proportion 3 : 2. Cf. Amos 5. 2, etc. It is used later in the taunt song in Micah 2. 4, and even in the didactic poem, Ps. 19. 7 ff.

The metrical theory of Bickell, which assumes a metre in which the syllables were counted, as in Syrian, and of Grimme (a rhythmical law of *morae* *) have found little favour. The most important attempt to work out a metrical theory is that of Sievers, *Studien zur hebräischen Metrik*, 1901 ff. (equal stress-groups,† the basic foot being the irrational anapaest, combined in two-stress, three-stress and four-stress lines), with which Rothstein's *Grundzüge der hebräischen Metrik*, 1909, is largely in agreement. Against these Stärk, in *Ein Hauptproblem der hebräischen Metrik*, ASt., 1913, p. 193 ff., maintains the theory that mixed metres are normal in the lyrical poetry of Israel. Cf. also Koenig, *Hebr. Rhythmik*, 1914.

That Hebrew poetry, in addition to verses, was acquainted with larger units of the nature of strophes is proved by the poems with a recurrent refrain, like Ps. 42 and 43 ; Isa. 9. 8 ff. But how far the existence of these is to be assumed when such clear indications are lacking is at present far from certain. On this point, however, Duhm, Marti and others have recently committed themselves to very arbitrary assertions. D. H. Müller in his *Die Propheten in ihrer ursprünglichen Form*, 1896, *Strophenbau und Responsion*, 1898, has sought to prove the existence of strophes by the evidence of thought answering to thought and word to word, especially in the prophetic orations.

---

* The Latin *mora*, delay, in the sense of lapse of time. The most nearly corresponding English technicality would probably be " time-beat."

† Sievers has himself fortunately provided an authoritative translation for the difficult term " *Sprechtakte*." Sweet, he says, calls them " stress-groups." By a stress-group is meant the run of syllables, containing one stressed syllable, which are naturally pronounced together ; *e.g.* in " Give me that book there " (supposing there to be no *special* emphasis on one of the words) the stress-groups would be giv'e-me-that | bo'ok-there.—Translator.

That during the whole of Israel's history there existed alongside of the singer's art a custom of story-telling in non-metrical language, the handing on of traditions in a simple narrative form, we have not so much direct evidence; but cf. Deut. 32. 7; Jos. 24. 2 ff.; 1 Sam. 12. 7 ff. It is, however, just as clearly implied indirectly.

If we distinguish poetic narrative (myth, saga, legend, tale and fable) from strictly prosaic narrative (history), there can, in the first place, be no doubt that the Myths, when we come upon them for the first time fixed in writing—in the David-Solomon era, as we shall see under B—have for the most part already been in existence in Israel for centuries. The stories, which in general come from the common storehouse of early oriental material (Creation, Flood, etc.), have in their ethico-religious character been metamorphosed into something so completely new that they must have undergone a long process of gradual transformation. Cf. Sellin, *Die biblische Urge-schichte*[2], 1913.

And the same applies to the Sagas which celebrate the earliest religious figures, the Patriarchs, the Religious Founders, and the Heroes of the period of the Conquest of Canaan. Here too, long before they were fixed in writing in the form in which we find them, the separate sagas must have been joined together into saga-cycles, nay, in some portions worked up with the art of the story-writer, for in these portions the Folk-stories are already made subservient to a higher literary idea which binds them together into a unity.

While it was no doubt mainly the priests who preserved and handed on these stories, in so far as they deal with eth-nology, etymology and the cultus, there must have existed alongside of them professional story-tellers, who journeyed from place to place and brought the materials together. The same doubtless applies to the cultivation of History proper; the *maṣkir* who had a post at David's Court was perhaps, in the first place, nothing else than a relater of historical stories, corresponding to the Egyptian "reading priest" (cf. Erman, *Ägypten*, I. p. 115, II. p. 498 ff.), for the *Sopher*, the scribe, appears alongside of him in 2 Sam. 20. 24 f. And when, for the first time, we meet with a historical narrative of consider-able extent to which a date can be assigned—that of the Philistine

oppression and the relations of Saul and David—it is already
on so high a level that the art of narrative must have exercised
itself long before on the materials of the earlier history, especially
the founding of the nation and the conquest of the country.

But from very early times in Israel there was not
merely an art of singing and of tale-telling, but also
of writing. That the question should ever have
been raised whether Moses, living about 1300 B.C.,
could have known how to write, appears to us now
absurd.

As early as the second half of the second millennium B.C.,
as the clay tablets of Tell el-Amarna and Taannek have shown,
writing in Babylonian cuneiform script was practised throughout the whole of Western Asia, and especially in Palestine.
Every petty Canaanitish " King " of a city-state had his scribe,
who conducted his correspondence and kept the necessary
lists. And the Canaanitish cities were, with a few exceptions,
not destroyed by the Israelites, but gradually Hebraized during
a period of some 300 years. In the period of the Judges,
according to Jg. 8. 14, any chance citizen of Succoth can write
out a list of names ; and from the time of David it was taken
for granted that every educated Israelite could read and write,
2 Sam. 11. 14 ; 1 Kings 21. 8.
More particularly, all *laws* were written, Hos. 8. 12 ;
Isa. 10. 1. They were engraved on stone or clay and laid up
in the Holy Place, Deut. 27. 8 (translate in accordance with
Hab. 2. 2, "graving them well "); Jos. 8. 32 ; 1 Sam. 10. 25 ;
Ex. 34. 1 ff ; Jos. 24. 26. Writing indeed is especially practised
in connection with the sacred places and objects, for writing
is, first of all, "the writing of God," Ex. 31, 18 ; 32. 16. There
were, no doubt, Temple records and archives in Ophra, Dan,
Shiloh, Shechem and Gibeon. But writing was used even
in very early times in Israel for letters, contracts of sale and
purchase, lists of tribute and the like. And if as direct evidence
for this the earliest that we have so far is from the time of
King Ahab (in the potsherds of Sebaste), the existence of stone
seals is in itself a proof for the earlier time, Gen. 38. 18. And
the appointment of a scribe as a functionary of David's Court
does not appear to be any more of an innovation than the
appointment of the priest and the commander of the army,
2 Sam. 8. 16 ff.

But writing is not in itself literary composition. And the latter art only came into being, so far as we can see at present, in the age of David and Solomon.

The first specimen of genuine Israelitish historical writing is, as we shall see later, a politico-religious document which is closely associated with the Monarchy. From that time onwards continuous political annals were kept. And finally in the eighth century, in which the Prophets began to address themselves in writing to the whole nation, Israel became a literary people. In the time of Hezekiah the formation of literary collections of many categories begins. In his days there were in Israel elementary schools which taught reading and writing, Isa. 10. 19, 28. 10; and the ordinary man understood writing, 8. 1. Craftsmen began to immortalise themselves on their productions; and a husbandman in Gezer notes down, from sheer pleasure in writing, to what agricultural tasks the various months are appropriate. Naturally there was always alongside of this general knowledge of reading and writing a class of illiterates, who made use of the public letter-writer, Isa. 29. 12 ; Ps. 45. 1.

In what kind of script were Israel's archives first written? It can now hardly be doubted that we must give a two-fold answer to this question. Israel, like Egypt, Babylon and other countries of antiquity, had two forms of script, as Winckler long ago inferred from Isa. 8. 1, an official and a popular script.

The official was the Babylonian cuneiform, which was the prevailing system in Western Asia. In this, no doubt, were generally written, in the early centuries, official documents, laws, treaties and so forth, and it doubtless remained in use down to the Babylonian Captivity. That has lately become practically certain through the discovery at Gezer of two contracts and a letter in cuneiform writing. Even if the Assyrian garrison was one of the parties to the contracts, the seller, a Jew named Natanjahu, would scarcely have signed a contract which he could not read.

But alongside of this there existed — though we do not, it must be admitted, know from how early a date—a popular alphabetic writing. The only piece of evidence that goes to suggest that Israel may have been acquainted with it as early as the Mosaic period is that the Mosaic oracular symbols, the Urim and Thummim, appear to be not unconnected with the first and last letters of this alphabet (א and ת), but it would be perfectly possible that Moses might have taken it over from the Kenites. Cf. 1 Chron. 2. 55. This alphabet made it possible to express everything with exactitude in the national idiom, which was not possible with the cuneiform, and it was therefore considered, although it was widely used in Western Asia, to be the national script. It is the so-called Old-Hebrew writing, which is closely allied to the Phoenician, and survived to later times as the Samaritan form of writing. Its origin has been variously conjectured to be Babylonian, Cypriotic or Cretan. An origin in David's time under Cretan influence has also been mooted (cf. v. Gall in *Hessische Blätter für Volkskunde*, X. pp. 43-46). Lately, however, it has become almost certain, from the evidence of votive inscriptions from the Sinai peninsula, that it is derived from the Egyptian Hieroglyphic (cf. Sethe, *Nachrichten d. Gött. Gesellschaft d. Wissenschaft*, 1917, p. 437 ff.; Bauer, *Zur Entzifferung der neuentdeckten Sinaischrift und zur Entstehung der semitischen Alphabets*, 1918; Eisler, *Die kenitischen Weihinschriften der Hyksoszeit*, 1920; the last named assumes an older Babylonian origin and only an intrusion of a few hieroglyphs into the Semitic alphabet). This early form of the writing is preserved in the inscription of King Mesha of Moab (first half of ninth century), on about 80 inscribed potsherds, receipts for tribute from Ahab's palace in Samaria, in the inscription in the Siloam tunnel (probably end of eighth century), and the small so-called almanac inscription found at Gezer (end of seventh century), and also upon some 60 Israelitish seals (the most famous of which is that of "Shema', servant of Jeroboam," of the eighth century, from Tell el Mutesellim), about 100 jar-handles of the eighth and seventh centuries, some 20 weights, and on the coins of the Maccabaean period.

This script, however, rapidly went out of use in post-Exilic times, so far as regards everyday matters, as well as in commercial and diplomatic intercourse.

The Dispersion (Diaspora) of the Jewish race brought about the introduction and adoption of a cognate script, which was in use in Babylon and Egypt among both Jews and non-Jews, the Aramaic (cf. recently the Elephantine papyri from the fourth century   Some 15 jar-handles of post-Exilic times, found in Jericho, and four or five in Gezer are inscribed with these characters).

From this developed gradually the so-called square-script which the Jews describe as Assyrian. The earliest inscription which has come down to us in this script is the five-letter inscription of Arak el Emir of the second century B.C., and the next earliest is that of the tomb of James in the Kidron valley, of the first. In the time of Christ it must have been in universal use. Cf. Mt. 5. 18. This also was a consonantal script, without special characters for the vowels; neither the Talmud nor Jerome found these in existence. They must therefore have been introduced between the sixth and tenth centuries, evidently on the principle of Syriac writing. (Two systems are distinguished: that in use in our Bibles, which is known as the Tiberian, and the Babylonian, which was a supra-linear system.)

The earliest Israelitish archives (Laws, Contracts, Letters) are, as we have seen above, written on stone or clay tablets, and this practice continued down to the days of Jeremiah. Cf. also Isa. 8. 1; 30. 8; Jer. 32. 10 ff.; Hab. 2. 2; Job 19. 24. But alongside of this—at least from the later times of the Monarchy—papyrus, and doubtless also prepared animal skins, were used for writing (cf. the expression " to bind," Isa. 8. 16, and the plural *sepharim*, which indicates that the letter was something folded together, 2 K. 19. 14; Isa. 39. 1; Jer. 29. 25; 32. 14; 36. 2 ff., 23 ff.). In this writing, ink was used, Ezek. 9. 2. The writings were in the form of rolls, Ezek. 2. 9; Zech. 5. 1, and the two ends of the roll were wound on staves.

If, as we have seen, a good deal of the early history of Israel as given in the Old Testament must have been first preserved by oral tradition, the portions that were first fixed in writing must have been rewritten—in part three times, in part twice, in part once—in wholly new characters. The originals have all completely disappeared.

§ 2. *The Manuscripts of the Old Testament*

Buhl, *Kanon und Text des A.T.*, 1881 ; *Bibeltext des A.T.* in HRE³ 2.

The manuscripts which have come down to us are divided into sacred or synagogal (unpointed, containing the Torah or the Megilloth) and private (almost always pointed, containing the other Books). The former are without exception on rolls of parchment or leather, the latter are in some cases in folded form (parchment, and, later, paper). They may also be classified according to their origin as Spanish, German, etc. They have been collected to the number of many thousands (especially by Kennicott, De Rossi and Firkowitsch—the last named, however, also forged extensively).

But none of these manuscripts, so far as they are dated, go farther back than the tenth century. The earliest yet discovered is considered to be the *Prophetarum posteriorum codex Babylonicus* in St. Petersburg, which dates from the year 916 and has been edited by Strack. The earliest manuscript of the whole Old Testament dates from the year 1010 (in the Firkowitsch collection). The Nash Papyrus, which doubtless belongs to the second century, contains only the text of the Decalogue and the beginning of the Shema'.

The principal reason for the lack of earlier MSS. is doubtless the Talmudic regulation that every worn-out Synagogue-roll must be hidden and destroyed as soon as possible, in order to preserve the sacred books from profanation by unbelievers. (The place in the Synagogue to which they were relegated was called the *Geniza*; *i.e.* place of concealment, or, treasury.)

§ 3. *The Massoretic Text*

Geiger, *Urschrift und Übersetzungen der Bibel*, 1857 ; Strack, article " Massora " in HRE³ 12.

Even a casual examination of the texts as preserved in the MSS. suffices to show that we cannot regard them as in all respects a faithful reflection of the original text. A certain number of meaningless passages, as well as the numerous parallel texts which we have in the Old Testament (especially in the Books of Samuel, Kings and Chronicles) which offer a large number of variants, make it quite obvious that the originals of the sacred writings have been subjected to the same vicissitudes as all others known to man—obliterations, copyists' errors, misunderstandings, displacements, glosses and the like (cf. *e.g.* Ps. 18 with 2 Sam. 22, etc.). Indeed the MSS. themselves force us to the conclusion that the original text has in many cases been deliberately altered, partly from religious motives, partly from political and patriotic motives, and partly for aesthetic reasons (cf. the alteration of the name Jerubbaal, Jg. 6. 32, to Jerubbosheth, 2 Sam. 11. 21, etc.).

But if these facts, together with the consideration that the oldest MSS. are separated by a period of at least a thousand years from the author's MS. of the latest books, might at first sight incline us to a thoroughgoing scepticism in regard to the traditional text, our confidence might well be revived when we read the regulations laid down in the Talmud, by which—since the end of the first century A.D.—the copyists have been legally bound to treat the letter of the original with the greatest

C

care, not to say with a kind of religious awe ; to alter nothing whatsoever, and so forth.

But the facts do not bear out this suggestion. On the basis of the almost complete absence of any real variants in the different MSS. of the Old Testament and their remarkable, not to say curious, agreement in the writing of certain unlucky consonants, De Lagarde (in his *Anmerkungen zur griechischer Übersetzung der Proverbien*, 1863), following out a suggestion of Spinoza, came to the conclusion that all the MSS. which have come down to us go back to a common archetype, which he considered to be derived from Rabbi Akiba in the time of Hadrian. This cannot so far be designated as more than a very probable hypothesis—it is opposed, *e.g.* by Strack, who referred the agreement to later harmonisation—but it is a simple fact that, notwithstanding a number of periphrastic variants, we find, since the second century A.D., traces of only a single recension of the Hebrew text. And already at that period the vocalic pronunciation was fixed by a firmly established tradition, if not as yet by the addition of signs.

This text has been handed down to us most exactly by the so-called Massoretes (מָסוֹרָה = tradition), who from the seventh century onwards endeavoured to fix the text, down to the smallest details, counting the verses, words and letters of each book, etc. They refrained from the slightest interference with the traditional text : where it was untenable they placed the correction (the Kĕrê) in the margin, merely placing the vowels of the reading which they held to be the correct one under the consonants of the text (the Kĕthîbh). Absolute uniformity was of course not attainable ; but the variants almost all refer to the vocalisation.

The two most famous Masters of the Massorah, who were the antipodes of one another, lived at the beginning of the tenth century. These were Rabbi Moses b. David b. Naphtali in Babylon and Rabbi Ahron b. Moses b. Asher in Tiberias, the latter of whom was probably the author of the famous Massoretic work *Dikduke Hat'amim.*

§ 4. *The Translations of the Old Testament*

Articles in HRE[3] by Kautzsch, Nestle, etc.

The most important Old Testament versions, which are also the most important aid to the testing and restoration of the text, are the following :

1. The Samaritan Pentateuch. The Samaritans, the descendants of the inhabitants of the Northern Israelitish Kingdom, destroyed in 722 B.C., with an intermixture of Assyrian colonists, who, according to Neh. 13. 28, in the year 433 permanently separated themselves, in a hostile spirit, from the Jews, took with them in their schism as their sacred books the first five Books of Moses. They retained, in contrast to the Jews, the Old Hebrew writing. Their Pentateuch offers 6000 variants from the Massoretic Text, including many of special interest, *e.g.* the completely different system of numbers in Gen. 5 and 11.

It has been charged by the Jews, without foundation, with many falsifications, while scientific criticism has attributed to it at least one—namely Deut. 27. 4—though the " Ebal " which the Samaritans read here instead of Gerizim may well be the original reading. Cf. verse 12 and 11. 29.

2. The Greek translation made in Alexandria, the so-called Septuagint. The legend of its miracu-

lous origin is preserved in the Letter of Aristeas.
The valid nucleus of this appears to be that under
Ptolemy II., Philadelphus, about 250 B.C., the
translation of the Torah was begun. The other
Books followed gradually at not excessively long
intervals, for according to the prologue to Sirach
(Ecclesiasticus), about 130 B.C., " the Torah, Pro-
verbs and the rest," had been already translated.
It is obvious of course that various translators of
very different degrees of capacity have had a hand
in it. At first warmly welcomed as a valuable
instrument of propaganda, after the destruction of
Jerusalem and the expansion of Christianity the
LXX was held in absolute detestation by the Jews.
For us it is the most valuable aid to textual
criticism, since its text is centuries older than the
MT.

We do not, however, possess even this in its original form.
The oldest MSS. (Alexandrinus, Vaticanus, etc.) are later
than Origen, who inserted a revision of the text in his Hexapla,
as column 5. Thus the original text of the LXX has first to
be reconstituted ; and for this the establishment of the texts
of the three Church recensions of it (those of Origen, Lucian
and Hesychius, which progressively adapted the LXX text
to the MT) forms a preliminary stage.

3. Further aid towards the reconstruction of the
LXX is given by its daughter translations, above
all by the Syriac translation of the LXX column
of the Hexapla by Paul of Tela (beginning of the
seventh century) ; by the *Vetus Latina*, commonly
called the *Itala*, which perhaps goes back to the
second century, and is only preserved in fragments ;
the Ethiopic, at earliest from the fourth century ;
the Coptic translations (four different ones, from
the second or third century) ; the Gothic of Ulfilas,

from the fourth century, only preserved in quite small fragments; and the Armenian of the fifth century.

4. Much less importance attaches to the later Greek versions: that of the Jew Aquila *c.* 100 A.D., slavishly literal, although its author had a good hellenistic education; that of Theodotion, the Marcionite, which is only a revision of the LXX in the direction of closer conformity to the Massoretic Text; and that of the Ebionite Symmachus, written in polished Greek.

5. After the LXX the greatest value for textual criticism attaches to the so-called Targums, Aramaic translations, with an admixture of paraphrase, which were more and more used in the Synagogues as Hebrew became a dead language.

That they existed as early as the time of Jesus and the Apostles has been justly inferred from Mt. 2. 6; Eph. 4. 8; 1 Cor. 10. 1-5, etc. The two most important Targums which have come down to us are that known as the Babylonian (in which the Torah is ascribed to Onkelos, and the prophets to Jonathan) and that known as the Jerusalem Targum (also, erroneously, ascribed to Jonathan). All, doubtless, of Palestinian origin, the former of the second century A.D., the latter of later date.

6. The Syriac version, known as the *Peshitto*, is of Christian origin, doubtless dating from the second century. (Only the Books of Chronicles were done later, on the basis of a Jewish Targum.) Its value for textual criticism is impaired by the fact that the translators have allowed themselves to be influenced by the LXX and the Targums.

7. The Latin version, the Vulgate, made by

Jerome in the years 392–405. After a long struggle it completely ousted the Itala.

Most of these versions are synoptically exhibited in the so-called polyglots. Of these we have the so-called Complutensian (from Spain, 1514–17), the Antwerp (1569–72), the Paris (1629–45) and the London (1653–57).

B. CIRCUMSTANCES OF ORIGIN AND DATE OF THE VARIOUS BOOKS OF THE OLD TESTAMENT

THE Hebrew Old Testament is divided into three parts—the *Torah, i.e.* the Law; the *Nebiim, i.e.* the Prophets; and the *Kethubim, i.e.* the " Scriptures."

I. THE TORAH OR PENTATEUCH

Dillmann, *Über die Komposition des Hexateuchs* in the *Kurzgef. exeget. Handb. z. A.T.*[2], 1886, 13, pp. 593-690 ; Wellhausen, *Die Komposition des Hexateuchs und der historischen Bücher*[2], 1889 ; Bredenkamp, *Gesetz und Propheten*, 1881 ; Steuernagel, *Allgemeine Einleitung in den Hexateuch*, in the *Handkommentar zum A.T.*, 1900, I. 3, pp. 249-86 ; Gunkel, *Genesis*[2], 1910 ; Kittel, *Geschichte des Volkes Israel*[3], I., 1916, pp. 260-360 ; Holzinger, *Einleitung in den Hexateuch*, 1893 ; Klostermann, *Der Pentateuch*, 1893 and 1907 ; Merx, *Die Bücher Moses und Josua*, 1907 ; Eerdmans, *Alttestamentliche Studien*, I. 1908, III. 1910, IV. 1912 ; Erbt, *Handbuch zum A.T.*, 1909, pp. 9-18 ; Dahse, *Textkritische Materialien zur Hexateuchfrage*, I., 1912 ; Gressmann, *Mose und seine Zeit*, 1913, pp. 345-92 ; Smend, *Die Erzählung des Hexateuch auf ihre Quellen untersucht*, 1912 ; Eichrodt, *Die Quellen der Genesis von neuem untersucht*, 1916 ; Eissfeldt, *Hexateuchsynopse*, 1922.

§ 1. *Contents and Title*

At the beginning of the Old Testament there stands a great work, the influence of which upon the world's literature has been unique, unequalled by any other writing. Not only do Christianity and Judaism see in it an essential part of their archives of revelation, possessing a fundamental significance, but Islam also has been deeply influenced by the history which it embodies. It begins with the creation of the universe and purports to set forth the mighty deeds and revelations of God, which form the foundation for the whole history of the Kingdom of God upon earth ; and, to this end, concerns itself more especially with the gradual separation, election, deliverance and constitution of a special People of God, following the course of the history of this people down to the death of its greatest Lawgiver and Prophet, Moses.

This work is designated by the Jews, from its principal contents, the *Torah*—that is, the Law—but in the Greek and Latin versions is named ἡ πεντάτευχος sc. βίβλος, or *Pentateuchus*—that is, the Book consisting of five parts or volumes. While the Hebrew Bibles name the five Books by their opening words, the Greek and Latin versions give them the titles *Genesis* (Origin), *Exodus* (the Going Forth), *Leviticus* (the Laws of the Cultus), *Numeri* (Numbering of the People), *Deuteronomium* (the Repetition of the Law). As regards the age of this five-fold division, all we know is that it is earlier than the LXX.

§ 2. *Tradition and the Statements of the Work itself regarding its Origin*

Whereas, even in the latest books of the Old Testament, the conception we meet with is that it is the Law which is the work of Moses (Ez. 3. 2 ; 7. 6 ; 2 Chron. 34. 14), Philo, the writers of the New Testament, and Josephus, everywhere start from the assumption that the whole Pentateuch goes back to him. The Talmud (*Baba bathra*, 14*b*) states emphatically that only the last eight verses, dealing with the death of Moses, were added by Joshua. And this view remained the prevailing one—challenged only by certain sects (Nazarenes, Bogomils), by a few Jews (Isaak and Aben Esra, and a few Christian theologians, Karlstadt, Masius) —in Church and Synagogue alike down to the seventeenth century.

It is not, however, supported by the statements of the work itself. It bears no superscription or signature indicating Moses as the author. He is for the most part spoken of in the third person, and it is expressly said that only some of the most important historical, and in particular the legislative, portions are from his hand; according to Ex. 17. 14, the sentence of destruction upon Amalek; 24. 4, the so-called Book of the Covenant, probably including the Decalogue (chaps. 20-23); 34. 27, another collection of the commandments given at Sinai (vv. 10-26); Num. 33. 2, the list of the halting-places during the desert wanderings; and Deut. 1. 5; 4. 45; 31. 9, 22, 24, the whole of the Law given in the Land of Moab, with the so-called Song of Moses. This is in itself indirect evidence that the remaining portions of the Pentateuch do not profess to be derived directly from him.

§ 3. *How the Pentateuch arose out of the Combination of several post-Mosaic Sources*

The view which is suggested by the evidence of the book itself, that the greater part of the Pentateuch is *not* derived from Moses, is confirmed in the first place by several passages which cannot possibly have been written by him. To these belong, Gen. 12. 6; 13. 7, "the Canaanites dwelt then in the land," which is only intelligible as coming from a time in which the Canaanites no longer inhabited Palestine ; 14. 14, " he pursued them even unto Dan," that is to say, as far as the town of which the name was only changed from Laish in the later days of the Judges (cf. Jg. 18. 29) ; 34. 7, " he hath wrought folly in Israel " ; 36. 31, " these are the Kings that reigned in the land of Edom before there reigned any King over the Children of Israel " —a statement which could not have originated before the days of Saul ; 40. 15, " the land of the Hebrews "—only possible after Joshua ; Deut. 1. 1, " beyond the Jordan," as a description of the Land of Moab—which is only explicable as from the pen of one who was writing in Palestine ; 2. 12, " as Israel did unto the land of its possession which Yahweh gave them," only possible after the occupation ; 3. 14, " unto this day," referring to a period which is contrasted with the Mosaic era ; 17. 14-20, the law of the Kingship, which, if Mosaic, would be unreconcilable with the conduct of Samuel in 1 Sam. 8. 6 ff. and with the drawing up of a law of the Kingship by him, 1 Sam. 10. 25.

A closer examination of the Pentateuch shows that it cannot in any case have been written by a single author, but rather has been put together, or perhaps it would be better to say, has grown together, out of various sources and strata, derived from various *milieux* and periods.   That is shown in the first place by the phraseology, which changes completely from one section to another.

One set of sections says for *beget* always *yalad*, others *holid* ; some say *to cut a covenant*, others *to set up a covenant* ; some say *man and woman*, the others *male and female* ; some prefer for the pronoun of the first person *anoki*, the others *ani*; some use *saphah* for speech, the others *lashon*; and so forth.

To the same set of phenomena belongs the alternation of different names for the same person or thing. At one time the inhabitants of Palestine are called *Amorites*, at another *Canaanites*; the mountain where the Law was given is sometimes called *Horeb*, sometimes *Sinai*; the third of the Patriarchs, sometimes Jacob, sometimes Israel; the father-in-law of Moses, sometimes *Raguel* and sometimes *Jethro*. And, best known of all, there is the periodically changing designation of God as *Yahweh* and *Elohim*.

It is no doubt true that the LXX, by its deviation from the MT in this point, shows that the Divine names are not preserved with such certainty that we can use them as an infallible clue to the differentiation of the sources, but have to reckon in many instances with the possibility of later editorial alterations (cf. the editorial touches in the Psalter). It is also true that now the one name and now the other may be designedly used in the same source (cf. Gen. 3. 1, 5, etc.). But nevertheless the Pentateuch clearly shows that there is present in it a two-fold tradition regarding the age of the name Yahweh (according to Gen. 4. 26 it has been in use since the days of Enoch, according to Ex. 6. 3 only in use since Moses, and previously unknown), and consequently that the frequently abrupt periodical interchange of the names cannot be due to chance, but has its roots in a difference of source.

The latest attempt, by Dahse, to invalidate this argument by the hypothesis that the alternation of the Divine names in the LXX is determined by the earlier division into lessons, the so-called *Sedarim*, while that in the MT is due to the later *Parasha* division must be regarded as a failure (cf. Sellin, *Gehen wir eine Umwalzung auf dem Gebiete der Pentateuchkritik entgegen?* (Are we on the threshold of a revolution in the domain of Pentateuch criticism?), NKZ, 1913, pp. 119-48; Koenig, *Die moderne Pentateuchkritik und ihre neuste Bekämpfung* (Modern Pentateuch criticism and the latest attack upon it), 1914).

But this brings us to the second category of reasons, the *contradictions in matters of fact* which make unity of authorship impossible. These are to be observed in the narrative as well as in the legislative portions.

No observant reader can fail to notice that the Pentateuch offers two inconsistent accounts of the Creation (Gen. 1. 1—2. 3 and 2. 4-25). According to the former the creation occupies seven days, in the latter one; in the one case the order is plants, animals, man, in the other man, plants, animals; in the one man and woman are created simultaneously, in the other successively; there are two accounts of the Flood, which, though interwoven, are inconsistent (6. 19, of every kind of beast one pair; 7. 2, of the clean beasts 7 pairs, of the unclean 1; in 7. 4 the duration of the flood is 40 days, in 7. 24, 150, and so forth); there are two inconsistent accounts of Joseph's coming into Egypt (37. 22-24, 28a, 29 ff.; 40. 15, by Reuben's advice he is thrown into a pit and stolen by Midianites; 37. 25-27, 28b, by Judah's advice he is sold to Ishmaelites); there are two widely different accounts of the Call of Moses, Ex. 3 and 6; two wholly different statements regarding the position of the Tabernacle (Ex. 33. 7, always outside the camp; Num. 2. 2 ff., in the middle of the camp). But in this discrepancy we are already touching on the discordant legal enactments. Ex. 20. 24 prescribes that in every place which God shall appoint for the praise of His name an altar (definite article to be omitted, with LXX) is to be erected to Him; in Deut. 12. 14, only in the place which He shall choose in one of the tribes are sacrifices to be offered; according to Deut. 18. 7 f. all the Levites have the right to offer sacrifice, according to Ex. 28. 1 ff. only the sons of Aaron; according to Deut. 16. 15 the Feast of Tabernacles is to be a seven-day, according to Lev. 23. 36 an eight-day, festival.

In addition to all this we have to take into account that, besides the directly discordant accounts of one and the same fact, there is a whole series of *parallel narratives* which may easily be recognised as doublets (*e.g.* Gen. 12. 10-20, the denial of Sarah by Abraham in Egypt, and 20. 1-18, again, in the land of the Philistines; in 16. 4-14 and 21. 8-21 two accounts of the expulsion of Hagar ; 21. 22-34 and 26. 26-34 two accounts of the reason for the naming of Beersheba) ; indeed, when closely examined, almost every occurrence from the creation of the world to the death of Moses is related to us twice, and in some cases three times, always with the regularly recurring slight changes of diction. The conclusion to which we are forced, then, is that while all theories as to the number, origin and age of the different sources are only working hypotheses, scientifically justified as such, the one absolutely established scientific fact which emerges is that the Pentateuch grew up in the post-Mosaic period out of the combination of several sources which were written in Palestine. That is the immovable basis on which Protestant Pentateuch criticism unanimously takes its stand at the present day.

§ 4. *The History of Pentateuch Criticism*

While it is true that Spinoza had assumed an evolution of the Pentateuch going far beyond the Mosaic era and coming down into the period of the Exile, the real father of Pentateuch criticism was Astruc, the Court Physician of Louis XIV., who, in his *Conjectures*, 1753, gave expression for the first time to the view that Moses had composed Genesis by combining two primitive documents, an Elohistic and a Jehovistic source. Eichhorn, in Germany, gave to this hypothesis of two primitive documents a more scientific form. A step in advance was made by Ilgen, *Die Urkunden des Jerusalemer Tempelarchivs in ihrer Urgestalt* (The primitive documents of the Jerusalem Temple Archives in their original form), 1799 ; by distinguishing, alongside of the Jehovistic writer not one only but two Elohists. This view was extended in 1802–1805 to the whole Pentateuch by Vater, who, however, saw in the sources not primitive documents but fragments.

This " fragmentary " hypothesis was corrected into an " expansion " hypothesis by Ewald, von Bohlen, Tuch, Delitzsch and Stähelin, who saw in the Elohistic writing the primary document which, some hundred years later, was discovered by the Jehovist and expanded by him.

In contradistinction to this, there soon developed a more modern version of the "primitive document" hypothesis, the most important defenders of which were Ewald (in his later years), Hupfeld, Knobel, Schrader, Nöldeke and Dillmann. They went back to Ilgen's hypothesis of two Elohists, and, in addition, following the lead of De Wette, pointed to Deuteronomy as an independent source, and thus obtained four sources, which originally existed in separate form, and later were united by a Redactor. These were the primary document (First Elohist), the theocratic document (Second Elohist), the prophetic document (Jehovist), and Deuteronomy.

Just as this hypothesis seemed about to acquire an almost exclusive dominance, there arose another which gradually pushed it aside. This was started by Graf, *Die geschichtlichen Bücher des A.T.*, 1866, who declared the source which had been known as the "primitive document" to be not the earliest but the latest, and to have first arisen after the Exile. This hypothesis was brilliantly defended and elaborated, and supported by a consonant theory of the whole religious development of Israel, by Wellhausen and Kuenen. Both arrived at the conclusion that the Jehovist, whom they now began to call the Yahwist, is also older than the source which had formerly been called the Second Elohist, and was thus the oldest source of all. This view encountered, on the one hand, enthusiastic assent, on the other—although the priority of the "primary document" was soon generally abandoned and only its pre-Deuteronomic origin was maintained—it met with vigorous opposition. Thus, at the close of the last century there were three main currents in Pentateuch criticism.

1. The Kuenen-Wellhausen School : Yahwist (J) *c.* 850 B.C., Elohist (E) *c.* 750, Deuteronomy (D) *c.* 623, Second Elohist (P standing for Priestly writing) 500–450 B.C. Principal adherents : Reuss, Duhm, Stade, Smend, Marti, Budde, Cornill, Baentsch, Benzinger, Holzinger, Bertholet, and in the main also Kautzsch and Steuernagel.

2. The Dillmann School : E 900–850, J 800–750, P 800–700, D 650–623. Adherents : especially Kittel and Baudissin.

3. A number of individual scholars who, while not in complete agreement with one another, agreed in claiming for E, J, and D. a higher antiquity—*e.g.* Koenig : E 1200, J 1000,

D 700–650, P 500; Köhler: E 1200, J 1000, P 700, D 700–650. Similarly Orelli, Strack, Lotz, Öttli and others.

In the last two decades there is to be observed in three directions a modification of the picture that has just been drawn. In the first place, a more penetrating analysis of the sources, combined with growing knowledge of the Ancient East, has led to the conclusion that there must be a much larger amount than had previously been assumed of extremely early material, preserved by popular tradition, in even the later sources, in the narrative as well as in the legislative portions, and that therefore the sources must be much more complex than seemed at first to be the case. Cf. Gunkel, Merx, Kittel *Geschichte des Volkes Israel*[3], and Gressmann's *Mose*. In the second place, the question of tendency, religious and political, has been raised. Cf. Winckler, Erbt and others. In the third place, the present book raises the question of a liturgical, cultual derivation of the sources.

A few investigators attack the whole theory of the four sources. Klostermann substitutes for it a gradual crystallisation round the nucleus of the original Mosaic Law of Sinai, which, from being constantly read in public worship, was also expanded and cast into new forms. At two periods, moreover, it received a wealth of new material—under Solomon, when the cultual prescriptions associated with the Tabernacle were interwoven with it, and once under Josiah, when Deuteronomy was incorporated with it. An entirely different solution of the problem is offered by Eerdmans. According to him the primitive stock is a Book of Adam, which is still polytheistic, also called a " Jacob " recension (beginning Gen. 5. 1; cf. 37. 2), originating sometime before 700. With this there was worked up, still in the pre-Deuteronomic period, an " Israel " recension, which was also polytheistic. Both were worked over in a monotheistic sense after the discovery of Deuteronomy, and the book which thus arose was expanded in the post-Exilic period.

Finally, Dahse proposes a simple division — between the early narrative material, a prophetic redaction and a priestly-liturgical redaction of it.

Obviously we are at present in a period of ferment and transition; and accordingly, in what follows, I offer my own view simply as the hypothesis which appears to me to have the firmest foundation.

§ 5. *The Earliest Materials in the Pentateuch*

In §§ 6-9 we shall find ourselves led to the conclusion that, in spite of all the arguments which have been brought against it, the hypothesis that the Pentateuch has grown up out of a combination of four historico-legislative sources or strata, which were not fixed in writing before, at earliest, the beginning of the Monarchy, has the highest degree of probability in its favour. But there has been taken up into these documents some much earlier material, partly from oral tradition, partly from earlier writings which have disappeared. This material has of course in many cases been so thoroughly recast, both in spirit and expression, in the course of its incorporation into the four sources, that it does not visibly stand out from them ; but, on the other hand, in some cases this material was so characteristic, even in its outward form, that this in itself betrays its higher antiquity and affords sufficient proof of its origin prior to the Monarchy ; that is to say, in the period of Moses and the Judges. This applies primarily to the poetic, in the second place to much of the legislative, and in the third place also to some of the narrative portions of the Pentateuch.

(1) *The Poetic Elements in the Pentateuch*

Cf. A, § 1 (p. 8) ; Land, *Disputatio de Carmine Jacobi*, 1858 ; von Gall, *Zusammensetzung und Herkunft der Bileamperikope*, 22-24, 1900 ; Kamphausen, *Das Lied Moses*, 1862 ; Graf, *Der Segen Moses*, 1857 ; Volck, *Der Segen Moses*, 1873, and *Festschrift für Öttingen*, 1898, 196-219 ; Van der Flier, *Deuteronomium* 33, 1895 ; Budde, *Der Segen des Mose*, 1922.

Almost all the poetic elements in the Pentateuch

are much older than the prose sources in which they are preserved to us :

(*a*) The *Song of Lamech* or *Sword Song*, celebrating a blood-revenge, Gen. 4. 23 f., is obviously not really of Israelitish origin at all, but has been taken over from Midianites or Kenites (Jg. 4. 11), perhaps as early as the Mosaic era.

(*b*) The *Noachic Oracles* regarding Shem, Japhet and Canaan, Gen. 9. 25-27. Here there are two alternatives. Either they take us back into the pre-Mosaic period, for the early inhabitants of Canaan, being subjugated partly by Semites who came from the East and conquered the country (Amorites or Khabiri ; cf. 10. 21), partly by Japhetites coming in from the North (Aryans or Hittites, 10. 2 ff. ; Ezek. 16. 3), about the middle of the second millennium B.C. were crowded back into a narrower territory (so, *e.g.*, Gunkel and Böhl, *Kananäer und Hebräer*, 1911, p. 68 f.). Or, on the other hand, they may date from the time when the Canaanites began to be subjugated by the Israelites, and at the same time the Philistines (Japhet = *Keft*, the Egyptian word for Phoenician ?) began to spread from Phoenicia into Palestine, say about the twelfth century B.C.

The period of Solomon, to which the oracles are generally referred (cf. Cornill, p. 52), is excluded not only by the name Shem and the oracle on Japhet, which can find no explanation at that time, but also by the burning hatred against Canaan which betrays itself in the whole collection of oracles.

(*c*) *The Oracles on the Patriarchs :* Abraham, Gen. 12. 2 f. 7 ; 13. 14-17 ; Isaac, 26. 4 ; Jacob, 27. 27-29 ; 28. 13 ff. ; also on Esau, 25. 23 ; 27. 39, 40 ; and Joseph, 48. 22. All these utterances, preserved from disintegration by the poetic form of speech, and in part closely associated with specific sanctuaries, 12. 7 ; 28. 13 f., lived on the lips of the people and were counted a sacred heritage (cf. ZEAT, p. 8).

In the main they take us back to the period of the first expansion of Israel and its occupation of the country.

(d) *The Blessing of Jacob*, Gen. 49, is a collection of sayings about the different tribes—partly laudatory, partly condemnatory, partly prophetic—which are referred to the dying Patriarch, and were no doubt traditionally preserved at one of the sanctuaries. They all presuppose that the tribes are already settled in their Palestinian territories. Cf. vv. 7 f., 13, 14 f., 16, 20, 26. It is certainly in the main the circumstances of the time of the Judges which are implied—note especially the reference to a tribe of Simeon, which entirely disappeared soon after the settlement in Palestine, also the sayings about Reuben, Levi, Zebulon, Issachar, Dan and Benjamin. The last, more especially, would have been simply impossible after the time of David ; and Zebulon in the period of the Monarchy no longer lived by the sea, Jos. 19. 10 ff.

But some of the sayings may have been in course of time expanded or transformed ; though this can be actually proved only in the case of the oracle about Judah, which cannot have assumed its present form earlier than the time of David. Cf. Sellin, *Schiloweissagung*, 1908 ; also ZEAT, p. 6 f. None of them is definitely later than this. There are no grounds for the wide-spread opinion that the reference to Joseph, on account of the word *nazir*, implies the period of the Divided Kingdom, for this word never means " the crowned," but simply describes the Tribe as " the dedicated "—dedicated, that is, to a constant warfare on behalf of Yahweh, like Samson and Samuel (cf. Schwally, *Der heilige Krieg*, 1907). The lines allude to

Ephraim as the leader in battle in the time of Joshua. The reference to Dan, from which Smend argues (*ut sup.* p. 112) that this Tribe had already been subjugated by the people of Damascus and was no longer one of the tribes of Israel, takes us back, on the contrary, to the times of the Judges (cf. Jg. 17 and 18), since this Tribe is in process of organising itself in the north (cf. 18. 1). It is also possible that the Babylonian Zodiac is reflected in the whole collection.

(*e*) *The Song of Triumph at the Red Sea*, Ex. 15. 1-18, preserved by the Yahwist. Verses 1-3, 4-10 show clearly that the song belongs to the same historical era as the events which it celebrates. Soon after Israel had got a firm footing in Palestine the song must have been expanded from the earlier shorter form (v. 21) to the present hymn, which has been rightly described as a Passover hymn. The conceptions of Yahweh as " a man of war," v. 3, and as King, v. 18, and the wars in which He is placed in comparison with other gods, v. 11, are confirmatory indications of high antiquity.

Verses 13 and 17, in which some have seen a reference to the Jerusalem Temple, and hence an argument for post-Deutero-nomic, or at least post-Solomonic, origin, refer in reality to Palestine as the Mount of Paradise (cf. Ezek. 28. 16), that is, to the mountainous country of Palestine in contrast with the wilderness (cf. Deut. 1. 7, 19, 44; Isa. 11. 9; also Hos. 9. 15); even the verb " prepared," v. 17*c*, might quite well refer to this, Ex. 23. 20; Ps. 68. 10, but in point of fact this part of the verse is probably a later gloss. There were, moreover, other sanctuaries, such as Shechem, Shiloh, Gibeon, at which the Song might have been sung long before the existence of the Jerusalem Temple.

(*f*) A whole series of shorter poetic formulae from the time of the wilderness journeyings, chiefly preserved by the Elohist. An imprecation of high antiquity used at the taking up of the ark of the Covenant, or of the Mosaic standard, Ex. 17. 16;

" Hand upon Yahweh's seat (or : upon the Staff of
Yahweh) : war hath Yahweh with Amalek from
generation to generation " (cf. Gressmann, *ut sup.*
157 ff.) ; the address to the ark on breaking camp
and on making halt, Num. 10. 35 f. ; the so-called
Aaronic Blessing, Num. 9. 24-27 ; the so-called
Song of the Well, Num. 21. 17 f. ; the poetic
quotation about the *halting-places*, 21. 14 f.; the
Taunt Song about the overthrow of the Amorite
King, Sihon, 21. 27-29.

These are all only explicable as dating from the time when
Israel came up out of the desert into Canaan.   To seek in
them allusions to events of the time of the Monarchy is merely
to involve oneself in quite unnecessary contradictions with the
Book of Kings, and, in fact, the inconsistent statements about
Sihon are the best evidence that this form of the story belongs
to a hoary antiquity (cf. ZEAT, p. 8 f.; Gressmann, *Mose*,
p. 306 ff.; and Böhl, *ut sup.* p. 59 f., where the attempt to
connect the Sihon Song with the Moabite wars of Omri is
refuted).

(*g*) The Balaam Oracles, Num. 23. 7-10, 18-24 ;
24. 3-9, 16-19.   The first two are preserved by the
Elohist, the last two by the Yahwist, but both
sources found the sayings already in existence.   Cf.
23. 5 and, *e.g.*, the *Yahweh* in 23. 21.   It is certain
that these cannot belong to the time of the Divided
Kingdom, and still less to the post-Exilic era, as is
now assumed in many quarters.   All Israel is ruled
by *one* sceptre, 23. 21 ; 24. 7.   In the prophecies
incorporated by the Yahwist in chapter 24 it is
only possible to see evidence of the time of David—
both the allusion to Agag (v. 7), who still lived
in the popular memory (cf. 1 Sam. 15. 1 ff.), and
that to David himself (v. 17 f.), point clearly to this.
On the other hand, the Elohistic prophecies in

chapter 23 are later modifications in a theocratic direction ; it is the theocracy of the period before Saul which is presupposed. Cf. v. 21*b*, and also vv. 9 and 21*a*.

Here already we meet, as in the later Prophets, with pro-phecies of disaster directed against the other nations as a pendant to the prophecies of salvation for Israel, 24. 20 ff. In the post-Davidic period the references to Amalek and the Kenites would be meaningless. The Asshur mentioned here is not the kingdom of Nineveh, but the Arabian Shur. Cf. Hommel, *ut sup.* 240 ff. ; also Böhl, *ut sup.* p. 70. The whole of these prophecies seem to have been composed in order to be sung at the yearly Feast of the Tabernacle of Yahweh. Cf. Sellin, *Das Zelt Jahwe*, ASt, p. 191.

(*h*) *The Song of Moses*, Deut. 32. The first point to be emphasised here is that this song has not been preserved by the Deuteronomist (cf. § 8), as is now almost universally assumed, but by a (later) Elohist (cf. § 7).

For to the latter and not the former belong Deut. 31. 16-22, 28-30. This has been proved to demonstration by Klostermann (*ut sup.*, 1893, p. 237 ff.) on linguistic grounds, (cf. v. 16 with Gen. 35. 2 ; Jos. 24. 23, etc.) ; verses 24-27 of chapter 31 are an interpolation by the Deuteronomist, in order to place the Law alongside of the Song.

But of course the author of that source himself took over from an earlier one this song, which purports to express the feelings of the dying Moses himself. According to verses 7, 10, 13-17, however, the nation has already a long history behind it since its entry into Canaan. That in itself, quite apart from the language, excludes a Mosaic origin. It may well be that we owe to some pupil of Elijah, in whom was reincarnated the Spirit of Moses, this glorious, tremendously earnest poem, which has helped to mould the thought and style of a Hosea

(cf. 9. 7; 13. 1), an Isaiah, a Micah and a Jeremiah.
Most critics, however, hold the poem to be Exilic
(cf. especially Löhr, " Monatshefte," 1903, pp. 1-31,
and Budde, *Das Lied Mose*, 1920).

According to verses 19 ff. Israel has now fallen away to
" gods that are no gods," and in punishment therefor it shall
be outstripped by " a people that is no people," which, as a
people, cannot set itself in comparison with Israel, v. 21.   This
people shall execute vengeance upon Israel (v. 31) : a single man
of them shall put to flight a thousand Israelites, v. 30, etc.
The assumption that this is an allusion to the Assyrians—not
to speak of the Babylonians—is, in view of the description of
the character of the enemy, hardly possible (Klostermann, p.
302).   Moreover, there is no mention of any carrying away
into captivity.   The supposed *Deuteronomic turns of expression*
will be patent only to those who see in Deuteronomy a book
which fell from heaven in the year 622 B.C. (cf. ZEAT, p. 30 ff.).
We find ourselves here, with most probability, in the reign of
Ahab, when the worship of false gods was eating like a canker
into the national life.   The Aramaeans, with their rudimentary
political organisation, who had formerly been subject to Israel,
are to be the rod of the Divine chastening.   If the Song is
not admitted to belong to E², it will be best to place it in the
Greek period.   The enemy of verse 21 is in that case, on the
analogy of Hab. 1. 6 ff.,* the Macedonians.

(*i*) *The Blessing of Moses*, Deut. 33.   This has
been preserved by the Elohist.   It is a collection
of oracles upon the different tribes, like Gen. 49.
That it is not derived from Moses is evident
especially from verses 7, 12, 22, 23 (cf. also v. 4).
These oracles point without exception to the time
of the Judges, but on the whole to a rather later
date than Gen. 49.   Simeon is here passed over in
silence.

The widely held view that the oracles belong to the early
days of the Divided Kingdom is based upon a series of exegetical
errors and has had a disastrous influence on Pentateuch criti-

---

* See II. 12 *infra* for the explanation of this statement.—Translator.

cism generally. The oracles which have aroused most controversy are (a) that referring to Judah, v. 7. The interpretation which makes Judah's aspiration refer to the removal of
the division between the kingdoms is a pure impossibility,
for even a North-Israelitish poet could not, after the division,
so represent things as to make Judah petition to be reunited
with *his People*. The reference to the division of Judah from
the rest of the nation in the struggles of the conquest (cf.
Gen. 38. 1; Jg. 1. 17; Jg. 5, where Judah is not mentioned)
is by all means to be adopted. (β) The oracle on Levi, vv.
8-11. The prominence given to the *Urim* and *Thummim* in
itself suffices to indicate the period of the Judges rather than
the middle period of the Monarchy, while Levi's struggle for
existence is not less decisive evidence (verse 10*b* is perhaps a later
gloss). (γ) The Oracle on Benjamin, v. 12. The interpretation of the words " he shall dwell between his shoulders " as
a reference to the Temple is untenable (cf. Böklen, ThStKr,
1894, p. 365 f.). That Jerusalem since David's time belonged
to Judah was doubtless known even in the Northern Kingdom,
and, besides, men would not there have acknowledged such
a pre-eminence as belonging to the Jerusalem Temple. We
have to think rather of either Gibeon or Bethel (so, *e.g.*, Knobel,
and recently Dalman in the volume of studies dedicated to
Baudissin on his birthday, 1918, p. 111 f.); or, again, the verse
may refer to the fact that Benjamin is in possession of the
portable sanctuary, the tabernacle (so Sellin, *ut sup*. p. 184 ff.).
In either case there is no reason to bring it down later than
the time of the Judges. (δ) The oracle on Joseph, vv. 13-17.
The false interpretation of *nazir* has already been corrected
under (*d*) above. Here again the campaigns of Ephraim
which began in the days of Joshua form the starting-point of
the Poet of verse 17. As all the remaining oracles can also be
best explained as belonging to the period of the Judges ; as
v. 5 implies the Divine Kingship of the pre-Monarchic period,
and indeed, like verses 28, 29, implies a united Israel ; and as,
finally, the tribal organisation lost its importance after the time
of Solomon (1 K. 4. 7 ff.), while here—as the passing over of
the extinct tribe of Simeon shows—it is no mere artificial poetic
framework, but an institution which existed in full vigour, we
have certainly to see in the Blessing of Moses a product of the
period of the Judges. It also was perhaps originally intended
for the Feast of Tabernacles (cf. Sellin, ASt, p. 191 ; and, on
the whole problem, ZEAT, p. 36 ff. ; and Gressmann, SchAT,
p. 176 ff., who rightly compares Gen. 49 and Deut. 33 with

Jg. 5, and holds the two former passages to be earlier than the latter).

(2) *Legislative Portions*

Meisner, *Der Dekalog*, 1893 ; Matthes, *Der Dekalog*, ZAW, 1904, p. 17 ff.) ; Koenig, *Neueste Verhandlungen über den Dekalog* (NKZ, 1906, p. 565 ff.) ; Rothstein, *Das Bundesbuch und die religionsgeschichtliche Entwickelung Israels*, 1888 ; Baentsch, *Das Bundesbuch*, 1892 ; D. H. Müller, *Die Gesetze Hammurabis*, 1903 ; *Semitica*, II., 1906 ; J. Jeremias, *Moses und Hammurabi*, 1903 ; Oettli, *Das Gesetz Hammurabis und die Thora Israels*, 1903 ; Erbt, *Die Hebräer*, 1906 ; E. Meyer, *Die Israeliten und ihre Nachbarstämme*, 1906, pp. 542-61 ; Klostermann, *Beiträge zur Entstehungsgeschichte des Pentateuchs* (ZLTh, 1877, p. 401 ff.) ; Baentsch, *Das Heiligkeits-Gesetz*, 1893 ; Volz, *Mose*, 1907, p. 84 f. ; Kittel, *Das Alter des Dekalogs*, GVJ², I. pp. 653-56, 1916.

(*a*) Of primary importance here is of course the Decalogue, the Ten Commandments given at Sinai, which are recorded for us twice, in Ex. 20. 1-17 and Deut. 5. 6-18, passages which agree in substance, the former being from the Elohist, the latter from the Deuteronomist, so that the evidence is two-fold. That the Yahwist also was acquainted with them we shall see later under (*c*), and there is, further, the testimony of Hosea 6. 5 ; 8. 12. That the Decalogue, with its succinct and clear-cut form, and embodying, as it does, only the very simplest cultual (1-4) and ethical (5-10) commandments, is well adapted to be the fundamental Law-code of the newly created People of God, admits of no denial. It is therefore not to be wondered at that the hypothesis of its Mosaic origin has begun again lately to gain many adherents, seeing that the Egyptians and the Babylonians undoubtedly, from the very earliest times, summed up the demands of ethics and religion in similar short formulae.

Nevertheless, even now its Mosaic derivation is contested in many quarters, and the Decalogue is brought down into the

Prophetic, or even into the Exilic period. The arguments for this are in the main four : (α) It is asserted that the Fourth Commandment (the Sabbath), and the Tenth, imply that Israel was already settled in Palestine. This argument is not valid, for, on the one hand, it was the purpose of Moses to settle his people in Palestine, and, on the other, even his contemporaries were by no means Bedouins of the desert, but had been accustomed to practise agriculture in Egypt. The Sabbath, as originally a moon festival (cf. Am. 8. 5 ; Isa. 1. 13), points directly to the desert as its place of origin.

(β) That the prohibition of images cannot go back to Moses, since in the time of the Judges and the early days of the Monarchy Yahweh was worshipped without scruple under images, especially that of a bull.

But the evidence always cited in support of this, the Ephod which was used especially by David, is inapplicable, for this Ephod was in no sense a divine image, but a garment which was assumed when waiting to receive an oracle (cf. Sellin, *Das israelitische Efod*, 1906) ; while the setting up of the bull-images in Dan and Bethel (1 K. 12) is quite obviously an innovation due to political motives. The absence of any images which is so indubitably attested as regards the sanctuaries of Shiloh and Jerusalem must, after all, have had some reason. Finally, how comes it that the early stories never make the Patriarchs set up an image of God, while they represent them as setting up, without scruple, the Maẓẓebahs and sacred trees, though this was later a penal offence ? And while the worship of idols certainly occurred in early Israel (cf. Jg. 17 ; 18), proof is completely lacking that this was normal or legitimate ; in fact the aim of this narrative is to pour contempt upon the sanctuaries of Micah and of Dan. While the priests there may have appealed to the authority of Moses for this also (Jg. 18. 30), the authentic Mosaic tradition is doubtless to be sought in the image-less Shiloh (1 Sam. 2. 27 f.).

(γ) It is asserted that in Ex. 34 an older Decalogue is preserved for us by the Yahwist. But this interpretation of the chapter is unsound. Cf. (c) *infr*.

(δ) The *language* is said to be that of the period of the kings and prophets. But that only shows that the Decalogue was no dead letter. See, on the whole question, ZEAT, p. 17 ff. Koenig, *Geschichte der alttest. Rel.*, p. 148 ; Eerdmanns, *ut sup*. III. pp. 131-46 ; Gressmann, *Mose*, p. 471 ff.

It is true, no doubt, that a comparison of Ex. 20 with Deut. 5 suffices to show that the Decalogue is no longer in the actual

original form. In Ex. 20. 5, 6, the reason given for the prohibition of image-worship is obviously based on Deuteronomistic redaction, and the reason given for the Sabbatic law,
20. 11, is perhaps also of later date. But it is highly probable
that by setting aside all explanations and expansions we can
arrive at the primitive form of the Decalogue, in which it was
preserved by the priesthood (cf. also Hos. 4. 2).

(b) The Book of the Covenant, Ex. 20. 23–23. 19.
This consists of "statutes", introduced by the word
" if " and " words," categorical commands. Cf.
24. 3 and 21. 1 ff. on the one hand and 20. 23 ff. ;
22. 19, 27; 23. 1 f., etc., on the other. This also is
preserved by the Elohist. But it has long been
recognised that it is no longer in its original place,
but was only brought into connection later, and
loosely, by means of 20. 22; 24. 3-8, with the Sinai
section. Its original position is a matter of controversy. It has been conjecturally placed in
Joshua 24 (as the Law read before the People by
Joshua in Shechem) or in the place of the present
Deuteronomy (as the Law given in Moab). It
may, however, be concluded, with the highest probability, from the sections which belong to the
Elohist, Deut. 27. 2a, ba, 8, 5-7a (cf. with 11. 29 f. ;
the oldest version speaks of the stone altar at Gilgal
near Shechem, the later of the altar on Mount
Gerizim), that the Book of the Covenant once
stood immediately before this, and was displaced
from its original position by Deut. 12–26. For it
is absolutely impossible that 27. 3, 8 referred originally to Deuteronomy, and it is also quite impossible
that a later writer should have put into the mouth
of Moses a command to place the permanent
record of Deuteronomy at Shechem. It follows
that the Book of the Covenant was, according to

the Elohist, a Law which was given by Moses shortly before the crossing of the Jordan (it may be conjectured, at the installation of Joshua in the leadership, Jos. 31. 14 ff.) and was carved upon stones in the neighbourhood of Shechem, v. 8 (according to a later tradition written upon stones prepared with plaster, vv. 26β - 5). In striking agreement with this we find that, precisely at Shechem there was worshipped in the time of the Judges, according to Jg. 9. 46, a God of the *Covenant*, and that it was precisely there that Joshua, according to Jos. 24. 25 f., performed, with reference to a Law, the ceremony of making a *Covenant*, and precisely there that an altar in accordance with the Book of the Covenant was set up, cf. 8. 30 ff. In view of this unimpeachable evidence of the age of the Book of the Covenant it would need very strong internal reasons to justify us in relegating it to the period of the Monarchy.

But it is hardly too much to say that no such reasons exist. It is true, indeed, that three arguments have been brought forward in many quarters. (*a*) It is urged that the Book of the Covenant everywhere implies a civilised agricultural community, and that this excludes the possibility of Moses' being the legislator. But this argument is based on incorrect and now obsolete ideas. It was Moses' purpose to make his people into a civilised people, and the fundamentals of civilised life were familiar to him, as to his contemporaries generally, from Egypt and Midian. (*β*) The assertion that 22. 20-26 implies an advanced social development is simply incorrect. Verses 25 and 26 are evidence of the most primitive social conditions possible. (*γ*) It is said that 23. 19 implies the existence of the Temple. But a " house of God," for the Elohist more especially, exists wherever God has revealed Himself—in Bethel, in Shechem, and elsewhere—Gen. 28. 17 ; Ex. 20. 24 ; 21. 14 ; 22. 9 f. ; 23. 17, etc. ; and that even as early as the times of the Judges there was a certain centralisation of the cultus, *e.g.* at Shechem

or Shiloh, cannot be denied Jos. 24. 1 ff. ;   Deut. 27. 11 ff. ;
1 Sam. 1-4.

On the other hand, the following elements take us back to
the most primitive stage of the national history.   The settlement in Palestine is still, according to 20. 24 f. ;   21. 13, a thing
of the future ; there is no King, but only tribal leaders (22. 27)
—sheiks—of the character suggested in Num. 7. 10 ff. ; but
also in Gen. 34. 2 (in contrast with, *e.g.*, Deut. 17. 14) the whole
administration of justice is still in the hands of the priests ;
there is no trace of a class of secular judges or officials, 21. 6 ;
22. 8, 10 (cf., on the other hand, Ex. 18. 21, and still more
Deut. 17. 9 ff. ; 19. 17 f.).   Seeing that the whole of the state
and civic life which developed in and after the time of David
and Solomon is still wholly unknown, it is not permissible to
relegate the compilation of this law-book to the period of the
Monarchy.   We have rather to look to the time of the Judges as
the period in which Mosaic principles were combined with
early Canaanitish " common law " into a legal *corpus*.

The discovery of the Code of Hammurabi in
Susa, and of the Hittite Laws, mark a new stage in
the critical study of the Book of the Covenant.   It
has become evident that both in the substance and
the arrangement of the legal enactments (especially
the *Mishpatim*—A.V. "judgments"—of the Book
of the Covenant) there are striking points of contact
between these three.   But this places the Book
of the Covenant in an entirely new light.   The
Israelitish law-giver has not created an entirely
new law out of nothing, but has revised a code
of laws which, since the beginning of the second
millennium B.C., was current throughout the whole
of western Asia, in the spirit of the revelation
given to his people, and in so doing has purified
and deepened it.

In respect of social organisation the Code of
Hammurabi is in advance of it (cf. the regulations
regarding blood-revenge, etc.) ;   but on the ethico-
religious side the Mosaic code stands incomparably

higher (cf. the relation to slaves, debtors, wizards, enemies, etc.).

(c) The so-called Yahwistic Decalogue, Ex. 34. 10-27. The Yahwist as well as the Elohist handed down a series of precepts, on the basis of which God is represented as making a covenant with the People at Sinai. Since Goethe in his *Was stund auf den Tafeln des Bundes?* (What did the Tables of the Law contain?) gave expression for the first time to the idea that we have here the original tradition regarding the contents of the Decalogue, this view has found supporters down to the present day (cf. Wellhausen, etc.). But it is not tenable.

In the first place, it is not possible without violence to get ten commandments out of it (cf. Cornill's attempt in the set of studies presented to Wellhausen on his birthday, 1914, pp. 109-13), for 34. 28 does not belong to the Yahwist at all, but to the Elohist, and, moreover, "the ten words" is an editorial addition to the Elohist. Secondly, such very diverse material is here brought together that it is impossible to think of it as all belonging together from the first (v. 18, Feast of Unleavened Bread; 19, 20, Law of the First-born; 21, Law of the Sabbath; 22, Feast of Weeks and Feast of Ingathering!). Particularly naïve is the assertion that Ex. 20 must be later than 34, because in the latter passage only molten images, whereas in the other images of all kinds, are forbidden, for if molten images are an offence against the Deity, carved images or those in plastic material can certainly be no less so!

It is, on the contrary, easy to see that we have here a confused medley of fragments from the Decalogue which is preserved in orderly form in E and the cultual precepts of the Book of the Covenant. Verse 14=first commandment; 17= second commandment; 18=B. of C. 23. 15, 19 f. =22. 29*b*, 30; 21=third commandment; 22 f.= 23. 16 f.; 25 and 26=23. 18 f. Whether the

Yahwistic tradition was limited from the first to these fragments of the Mosaic code, or whether it was reduced to these by a later redactor, who confined himself to giving a few passages in which J diverged in form from E, is hardly likely ever to be decided. Cf. ZEAT, pp. 23-26 and Gressmann, *Mose*, p. 473 f.

But in spite of the unsatisfactory state of the tradition in this regard, there are three important conclusions which may be drawn from it. (a) The laws are given with greater exactitude in the (later) Elohist than in the (earlier) Yahwist. And this is not to be wondered at, for the former embodies the priestly tradition, the latter is much more of a popular tradition. Cf. §§ 6 and 7. In regard to the Priests, who were charged with the administration of justice, it is said even in the times of the Judges that they had the duty of guarding the word of God and preserving His Covenant, Deut. 33. 9; cf. Hos. 8. 1. (β) J as well as E refers not only the Decalogue but also the B. of C. to Moses. (γ) On the other hand, we see how free an attitude, in the first period of its history, the People took up towards the letter of the Divine Law; even the Decalogue underwent, in view of the actual circumstances in Canaan, formal modification—in the first commandment, " not another God " instead of " other Gods "; in the second, " molten image " instead of " graven image or likeness "; in the fourth, the limitation of the rest to " seed-time and harvest."

(d) The Shechem Decalogue, Deut. 27. 15-26. A still more independent by-form of the Decalogue, the formulation of which probably dates from the time of the Judges, has been in the main taken up without alteration into the present Deuteronomy, but it is derived, like all the fundamental parts of the chapter, from the Elohist. The verses contain a part of the liturgy used in celebrating the festival of the making of the Covenant at Shechem (after the reading of the B. of C.). The fact that Deut. 12—26 is now interpolated between 11. 29 f. and chapter 27, and that 27 has been worked over from the Deuteronomic point of view, has made the connection in many respects obscure. In verse 14 " the Levites " is an interpolation, which does not agree with verses 11-13. But the mere fact that in these verses Levi appears as a Tribe, like the others, proves its early date. In the curses we see reflected the whole religious, family and civic insecurity of the time of the Judges; the second, fifth, seventh, eighth and sixth commandments of the Decalogue have again been recast in relation to the concrete circumstances of the time in Canaan. (Cf. Gressmann, SchAT, II. p. 235 ff.; and, rather differently, prior to him, Erbt, *Hebräer*, p. 33 ff.)

That verses 15-26 are not Deuteronomic is generally admitted; but to hold the passage to be on that ground post-Deuteronomic is to turn history upside down. We find in it turns of expression which occur in none of the other Law codes; on the other hand, many which are found also in P; but P has incorporated much early material.

(e) *The Law of Holiness*, Leviticus 17-26. In the Priestly Writing (cf. § 9) there has been incorporated an extensive code of laws, which, while it has certainly been worked over by the author of that writing, has yet not been so completely transformed as not to proclaim itself, by the contrast which it offers to the remainder of the writing, as a much older code, which had had an earlier independent existence. Klostermann was justified in the title which he introduced for it, *the Law of Holiness*, for the fundamental commandment in it is to be holy as God is holy, 19. 2; 20. 7, etc.

The long discussions as to whether this Law, which has particularly close points of contact with **Ezekiel**, is prior to or subsequent to him have tended more and more to favour the former view ; only, in adopting this it is necessary to hold also that the Law of Holiness may have undergone redaction later on the basis of Ezekiel, say by the author of P, from whom, *e.g.*, chapter 27 is derived.

But that is a solution only of the first stage of the problem. The second question is whether the author of this code (known as H) wrote before or after D (the Deuteronomist). The former is the more probable, because in chapter 17 he makes no distinction, as D does, between the slaughtering of animals for secular and for religious purposes. But, be that as it may, in any case the author of H has himself worked up older materials. Merx in particular has lately pointed out how we can still perceive, just beneath the surface, the evidences of the ritual of the period of the numerous High Places. And even if this ritual continued to be in the main the same throughout the centuries, at any rate the laws against Egyptian and Canaanitish ethical and cultual abominations, 18. 1 ff. ; 20. 2 ff. (the latter a variation of the former with a statement of the penalties), show that this code has its ultimate roots in the period before the Monarchy, reaching back in some cases beyond that to the period of the Desert wanderings. Cf. 17. 7. Chapter 19 is simply another version of the Decalogue and the Book of the Covenant, like Ex. 34, and shows us how these took shape at some time in Gibeon or elsewhere. Even in the laws relating to the priests and sacrifices, chaps. 21 and 22, as also in the legislation for the festivals, chap. 23, it is not difficult to disentangle the early material (cf. " the priests " *without* the addition " the sons of Aaron," etc.). Even the regulations relating to the High Priest, 21. 10-15, may be very early, for every ancient sanctuary had a High Priest. Cf. Shiloh, Nob, Bethel, Jerusalem. The homily in chapter 26 of course comes from the prophetic period (cf. Deut. 32), but to say that it must be Exilic is to make a very insecure assertion. If it had been, would not the blessing, vv. 3-13, have been omitted ? Whether Ezekiel 34. 25 ff. is dependent on Leviticus 26. 3-13, or conversely, cannot be decided with certainty. Cf. ZEAT, pp. 26-29. Eerdmanns has lately made a new and vigorous attempt to disentangle the early material in Lev. 17-26, which he, however, does not hold to be a definite code (*ut sup.* IV. pp. 83-135).

(3) *Narrative Portions of the Pentateuch.*—
Genesis 14

Nöldeke, *Untersuchungen zur Kritik des A.T.*, 1869, pp. 156-72 ; Sellin, *Melchisedek*, NKZ, 1905, p. 929 ff. ; Wilke, *War Abraham eine geschichtliche Person?* 1907 ; Meinhold, *1te Mose 14*, 1911 ; König, NKZ, 1912, p. 425 ff. ; Böhl, *Die Könige von Genesis 14*, ZAW, 1916, p. 65 ff.

The chapter narrates how Abraham made a victorious foray, and recovered spoil from an army of the Kings of the East; and also his meeting with Melchizedek, King of Salem. Both in form and content it stands in contrast with all that is related elsewhere in Genesis, and cannot therefore be referred with certainty to any one of the later "Sources."

Its closest affinities are with E (cf. Gen. 21. 22 ff. ; Jos. 10. 1 ff., 24. 2), and we have to take into account the possibility that it is simply the introduction to this document (therefore Abraham on his first appearance, v. 13, is called "Abraham the Hebrew," v. 12b, where he is mentioned without the appellation, being in this case a gloss). If not, it must have been a later interpolation.

In contrast with what was long the prevailing view, viz. that we have here a later "Midrash" from Babylonian or even Maccabaean times, written with the purpose of glorifying Abraham and Jerusalem, recent studies of oriental antiquity have made probable the early date of the chapter and the view that it possesses a historical basis.

Two of the names of the Kings of the East have already been found in the cuneiform inscriptions (Amraphel = Hammurabi, Arioch = Eri Aku), the third has been shown to be good Elamite (Chedorlaomer = Kudar Lagamar) ; those of the Canaanitish kings have their analogues in the Tell el-Amarna tablets. That Elamite kings exercised lordship over Babylon, and that about 2000 B.C. raids upon the "West Country" were made from Babylon, is now confirmed ; the relation of Abram, the Khabiri chieftain, as client to the Canaanite Princes

E

(v. 13) is illustrated by the Tell el-Amarna tablets; *Urusalim* as the Canaanite name of Jerusalem is confirmed; the belief in God, and the Priest-Kingship of Melchizedek, are rendered highly probable by discoveries in Babylon and Palestine from the middle of the second millennium B.C. The *Chori* (Horites), which used always to be interpreted as a *nomen appellativum*, is now proved by inscriptions to be the name of a people. Is it not probable that the same will prove to be the case with the *Rephaim* and the rest? Moreover, the subject-matter of the chapter is historically realisable—the night attack, for instance—if only it is rightly interpreted and subsequent glosses are cleared away. Of these there are in truth a considerable number. But, apart from these, we have to take into account the fact that, before assuming its present form, it must long have been current orally among the people, and during this period several raids of eastern kings may well have become fused together, and the phrase "four kings against five," as well as the *mythical* number 318 (v. 14) which, differently composed, appears elsewhere in the ancient oriental literature of the fifteenth century B.C. (1 princess and 317 maidens, "the choicest of the enclosed"; see Erman, *Ägypten*, p. 114) may have found their way into the story at a later date.

But, finally, what is the source of the narrative? Everything points to its being a translation of some Canaanite record which was deposited in the archives at Jerusalem some time about the fifteenth century B.C., in cuneiform writing, and fell into the hands of David when he captured "Jebus." In favour of the non-Israelitic origin are : (a) Abram the Hebrew, v. 13 ; (b) the numerous explanations of ancient names which are given; (c) peculiarities of language (especially in verses 14, 15, 17b). If we remove the explanatory glosses, and especially the narrative in verses 17a, 20-24, of the meeting with the King of Sodom, who, according to verse 10 had previously been killed —in which we see an Israelitish addition whereby Abram's subordination to Melchizedek is intended to be counter-balanced—we can still reconstruct, from verses 1-16, 17b, 18, 19, the ancient Canaanitish narrative, which shows us Abram as a valiant Khabiri chieftain, who follows the fortunes of the rulers of Jerusalem, and incidentally provides indubitable proof of his historicity. Israelitish tradition doubtless preserved this narrative because it supported the sacred character of Jerusalem even at this early period. Cf. Gen. 28. 22. Other recent investigators (like Kittel, *ut sup.* I. p. 448 ff. ; Lehmann-Haupt, *Israel*, p. 9) emphasise rather more strongly than we have done the legendary colouring of the chapter, or reduce the historical kernel to a number of particulars (so, *e.g.*, Gunkel, *Genesis*[2], p. 288—the kings' names, the historical setting and the figure of Melchizedek), but the view that a historical kernel really does exist is gaining ground, as compared with the former hypercriticism. As regards the chronological difficulty to which the narrative gives rise by making Abraham a contemporary of Hammurabi (about 2000 B.C.), Böhl has proposed to remove it by identifying the names of the Kings of the East with those which we meet with as Hittite or Mittani chiefs in the tablets of Boghazkoi. In that case the events would have happened in the fourteenth century B.C., a hypothesis which certainly deserves consideration.

Certainly those who are so anxious to deny the existence of any historical basis would do well to await the decipherment of these tablets.

We have treated at some length this one obvious instance, with a view to making clear that even narratives which had already attained a fixed literary form were incorporated into the later sources. It is not by any means the only example.

In the first place, it is obvious that in the numerous lists which occur in the sources there is present older material, in some cases arbitrarily adapted to a fixed plan, in others introduced in an inappropriate connection.

The time has gone by when people supposed that a few post-Exilic priests amused themselves by inventing them. The names recorded have been strikingly proved to be really old by Sabaean and Babylonian discoveries, and the Lists of Taannek have shown how rich in name-lists the Palestinian archives must have been. The list which chiefly deserves mention is that of the Edomite Kings down to the time of David, Gen. 36. 21-39, which is no doubt derived from J; alongside it we may place the list given by P of the Sheiks of the Tribes in the Mosaic period, Num. 1. 4 ff.; 7. 10 ff.; 13. 4 ff., whose names, compounded as they are with Amm, Zur, Shaddai and El, are undeniably appropriate to the first period of Israelitish history (cf. Hommel, *ut sup.* pp. 298-302); also the list of the Israelites' camping-places, Num. 33, which has no doubt been worked over, but is certainly not free invention; and E had another list of the kind which is now out of its place, at Deut. 10. 6 f., but was originally at Num. 21. 11-15. Cf. ZEAT, p. 51 ff.

In this connection it should be mentioned that, the more progress is made with the critical examination of style and metre in the Old Testament—a study which only began in recent years —the clearer it will become what narratives had attained a fixed form, marked by peculiarities of style which later disappeared, before they were taken over by the authors of those " sources " which we are about to distinguish in the following paragraphs, and which of the narratives taken from old material have been recast by the authors of the " sources." Think, for example, of some of the primitive stories (with the earlier polytheism still visible just beneath the surface) : of the stories of Sodom (with the " three men "), of Jacob's wrestling, of the narratives of Joseph and of Balaam, which even when taken up into the later sources have preserved so distinctive a character that lately an attempt has been made to treat them as independent self-contained stories and to deny that they belong to the " sources " at all.

§ 6. *The so-called* Yahwistic Source*

Budde, *Die biblische Urgeschichte,* 1883 ; Luther, *Die Persönlichkeit des Jahwisten,* in E. Meyer's *Die Israeliten,* 1906, pp. 105-73 ; Sachsse, *Die Bedeutung des Namen Israel,* 1910 ; Procksch, *Genesis,* p. 16 ff. ; Kittel, *ut sup.* I. p. 299 ff.

One of the sources of the Pentateuch is called the " Yahwistic," because one of the characteristics by which it is most readily recognised is that it, in contradistinction to the others, even before the point at which Moses appears in the narrative, uses almost constantly, and as if it were a matter of course, the Divine Name Yahweh. It has however, in addition to this, a characteristic language and narrative manner by which the sections belonging to it can easily be distinguished.

The following are some of its characteristics. It calls the mountain where the Law was given " Sinai " (not " Horeb "),

---

* The word *sogenannt,* which can hardly be *translated* otherwise than by " so-called," does not, nevertheless, carry the ironic implication which is usually present in the English word. It does not, that is to say, imply that the author repudiates or criticises the term. One might, of course, turn it by " the Source which is known as the Yahwistic," but the author uses it so constantly that I have preferred to leave it, with this explanation. —Translator.

the third of the Patriarchs " Israel " instead of " Jacob," from Gen. 32. 28 or 35. 18 onwards, and the inhabitants of Palestine Canaanites. Among his characteristic phrases are אֲדָמָה (the ground), יָלַד (beget), אִישׁ וְאִשְׁתּוֹ (man and wife), אָלָה (oath), בְּאֶכָה (as far as), יָדוֹת (parts), יָדַע (to know, of sexual intercourse), שָׂפָה (speech), שִׁפְחָה (a maidservant), and he is fond of the expressions מָצָא חֵן (to find favour), הַפַּעַם (this time), טֶרֶם (before), קָרָא בְשֵׁם (to call upon the name). Characteristic marks of his style are its freshness and vividness, sometimes even a certain bluntness, its *naïveté*, its naturalness, its ingenuousness in the description of everything connected with God and man : appearances of God in simple human form, anthropomorphisms, and, from the earliest times, sacrifice, distinction of clean and unclean, and oracles. Although, in consequence of interweaving and revision, here and there a characteristic mark has been obliterated, and in many verses it is simply impossible to disentangle it, yet on the whole even the non-expert reader can soon learn to distinguish the sections that belong to it from the other sources.

Without entering on a hair-splitting analysis, we may give the sections of the Pentateuch which by almost universal consent are ascribed to J (the sign † signifies " mixed with another source ")— Genesis : 2. 4*b*–4. 26 ; 5. 29 ; 6. 1-8 ; 7 and 8† with P ; 9. 18-27 ; 10. 8-19, 25-30 ; 11. 1-9, 28-30 ; 12 ; 13 ; 15† E ; 16 ; 18. 1-19, 28, 30-38 ; 22. 15-18, 20-24 ; 24-27 ; 28. 13-16 ; 29. 2-14, 31-35 ; 30. 9-16, 24-43 ; 31. 46-50 ; 32–34† E ; 37† E ; 38 ; 39 ; 42. 38–44. 34 ; 46. 28-34 ; 47. 13-31 ; 49. 1-27 ; 50. 1-11. Exodus : 1. 8-12 ; 2. 11-23 ; 3–5† E ; 7–10† E and P ; 11. 4-8 ; 12. 21-27 ; 13. 3-16 ; 14† E and P ; 15. 22-27 ; 16. 25-30 ; 19. 20-25 ; 24. 9-11 ; 32. 9-14 ; 33. 12–34. 28. Numbers : 10. 29-32 ; 13 ; 14 and 16† E and P ; 20–22† E and P ; 24 ; 25. 1-5† E ; 32† E and P. Deuteronomy : 34, a few verses.

The Yahwist thus begins with the Creation of

Man in the Garden of Eden, and describes the origin and growth of sin, and the Divine judgements which again and again overtake it; but these judgements are at the same time a setting apart of men who are to be the object of a new and yet more exalted Divine favour. This process of election reaches its culminating point in Abraham, to whom is promised the possession of the Land of Canaan and who is constituted the starting-point of a new era in the history of mankind. The history of his family is then related down to the time of its coming into Egypt, where it becomes a nation. Then follows the miraculous deliverance of this nation from Egypt under Moses (Aaron does not appear), the journey to Sinai, the giving of the Commandments there, and of the promise that Yahweh will go with them into the Land of Promise, the sojourn in the wilderness and the journeyings, up to the boundaries of the Promised Land, where Moses dies. But it should be added here that the Books of Joshua and Judges form a continuation of this source, recording how, in accordance with the promises given to the Patriarchs, the hill-country was first conquered by the Tribes, while the plains only fell into the hands of Israel later " when Israel had become strong."

The very difficult question of the origin of the source is to be answered in general terms by saying that there is a high probability in favour of its representing the earliest written record of the whole history of the People of Yahweh; and, accordingly, the earliest of the four so-called " sources " of the Pentateuch, and that it came into being in Judah in the period of David and Solomon. It seems to have been composed by a man living at the Royal Court of Judah, who collected the traditions of his people in order to provide documentary evidence of the Divine legitimation of Israel's claim to Palestine and of the status of its Dynasty as a Great Power.

Two preliminary questions which call for an answer are: (*a*) Where was the place of origin of this source? To this we can reply with absolute certainty "in Judah." In the Joseph story Judah plays the part of the first-born, Gen. 37. 26; 43. 3, 8-10; 44. 14-34; the beginnings of the history of this tribe in particular are given in Gen. 38; to it is allotted the richest of the blessings of Jacob, 49. 10-12; upon it primarily is concentrated the interest at the time of the Conquest (Jg. I. 1-21; on this cf. II. A, § 2); and, above all, the Judaean Hebron is regarded as the place which, above all others, has been consecrated by the fact of the Patriarchs dwelling there (Gen. 13. 18; 18. 1; 37. 14).

(*b*) Is this source the oldest, *i.e. older than the Elohist*? This question is very much more difficult to answer than the first; indeed it cannot really be answered with certainty, since opinions differ on the point. Nevertheless it may be said that the probabilities are distinctly in favour of the Yahwistic source being the earlier, in view of the following facts: (*a*) In spite of a number of antique phrases which E has scattered over his narrative, J's whole manner of describing events makes a more natural and vivid impression, and therefore gives a greater sense of originality. Cf. Gen. 30. 28-43 (J) with 30. 1-12 (E); 26. 1-33 (J) with 20. 1-17; 21. 22-31 (E); 30. 14-16 (J) with 30. 17, 18 (E). (*β*) In particular the religious conceptions of E seem to be more advanced than J's. In the latter the Deity appears on earth like a man, comes down from heaven, eats and drinks, is jealous, repents, etc. In the former, He only speaks from heaven, and does not appear in person, 21. 17; 22. 11. In E Yahweh has been known since the days of Enoch, Gen. 4. 26; in J He first reveals Himself by this name in the days of Moses, Ex. 3. 14 f. Again, the fact that E, in contradistinction to J, offers us no history of the beginnings is to be attributed to a more advanced state of religious reflection, for in these narratives there still linger, in spite of the new content of revelation, traces of their originally mythical character. Cf. 6. 1 ff.; 11. 7. (*γ*) Similarly E evinces a keener ethical judgement. Cf. Gen. 27. 11 ff.; 31. 6 ff. and 20. 12 (E) with 12. 10 ff. (J). On the other hand, it must be clearly recognised that this argument is not of irresistible cogency; the different religious plane of the two might after all be explained by their being derived from different sections of the people.

If, however, the answer given to question (*a*) is correct, that in itself suffices to fix the *upper limit* for the date of origin of J. It cannot have been written before the time of David. Its theme is that the Creator of the nations has given His chosen nation Israel the land of Canaan as a permanent and exclusive possession in which it can rejoice, and that this People of Yahweh is the most blessed in the whole world, nay more, a source of blessing for the rest. Since that excludes the period when the Canaanites still dwelt alongside of Israel as lords of the country, and when, moreover, the Tribe of Judah was still cut off from the rest of Israel by the territory of the Jebusites (cf. Jg. 1. 21; 5; 15. 11; Deut. 33. 7; 1 Sam. 15. 2 ff.), and consequently a united Israel did not yet exist, it is clearly evident that this source implies the existence of the Judaean Kingship, Gen. 36. 31; 49. 8 ff.; Num. 24. 18.

But this also gives the *lower limit* for the date. For there is no slightest hint of the division of the kingdoms; indeed, the confident and simple-minded consciousness of the election of the *whole nation*, untroubled by any difficulties and undisturbed by any doubts, which manifests itself throughout the whole work, would hardly be conceivable after that event. Accordingly it must date from the Davidic-Solomonic period. And a whole series of indications are to be observed which point us still more definitely to the second half of David's reign and the first half of Solomon's as the time during which it was composed. (*a*) The constantly recurring allusions to the fact that the Canaanites have not indeed been utterly destroyed, but from being masters have become slaves, Gen. 9. 25; 12. 6; 13. 7; Jg. 1. 21, 28, directly reflect the circumstances of 2 Sam. 5. 6 ff.; 24. 16 ff.; 1 K. 9. 15 ff., 21. It is often assumed that this " forced-labour " only began under Solomon; but was there not already in David's day an officer who was set over the " forced labourers," 2 Sam. 20. 24 ? And it is impossible to suppose that David carried on campaigns in Aram, Edom, and elsewhere without being master in his own country. How much historical material referring to the subjugation of the Canaanites as early as Saul's time (1 Sam. 14. 47 ff.) may have been lost we get a hint from the allusions in 2 Sam. 4. 2*b*, 3 and 21. 2, which give us a glimpse of a picture which surprises us. (*b*) There is no trace whatever of the new constitution set up by Solomon, 1 K. 4. 7 ff.; 9. 23. (*c*) The absolutely confident and unquestioning belief in Yahweh as the God not only of Israel but of the whole world, which we meet with throughout the document, gives no hint of the religious cleavage which after the second half of the reign of Solomon left a scar upon Israel's national consciousness. Cf. 1 K. 11. (*d*) The sense of being the most blessed of all nations, the blind confidence in the Divine election and guidance, shown in Gen. 12. 2 ff. and elsewhere, finds its reflection in 1 Sam. 18. 17; 25. 28; 2 Sam. 5. 12; 8. 14 f.; 14. 13; 21. 3*b*; 1 K. 4. 21-25; 10. 1 ff., etc. (*e*) The conditions implied as regards the cultus, the multiplicity of the holy places and the prominence of the Judaean Hebron (cf. on this point 2 Sam. 5. 3; 15. 7 !), the unquestioning recognition of Shechem and Bethel in Northern Israel alongside of it as places sacred from ancient days, Gen. 12. 6 f., 8, the absolute silence in regard to the Jerusalem Temple (for Ex. 34. 26 is applicable to any of the Tribal sanctuaries, and Jos. 9. 23, 27, where the source is uncertain, might in any case quite well refer to the Yahweh sanctuary at Gibeon (cf. 1 K. 3. 4; 2 Sam. 21. 6, 9)), the mention of the priestly Yahweh-Oracle, Gen. 25. 22, which became famous precisely in the time of David, Jg. 1. 1, and, on the other hand, the absence of revelation through the *Nebiim* ; the assumption, as something self-evident, of an image-less worship of Yahweh in the patriarchal times in contrast to the post-Jeroboam worship of images, etc.—all this points to the period mentioned.

And, on the other hand, no at all tenable argument has been brought forward to prove that this source dates from post-Solomonic times, in spite of the wide prevalence of this view. Gen. 27. 40*b*, an allusion to the breaking away of the Edomites in Joram's day, is a later gloss. This opinion owes its origin to quite general considerations of a literary-historical and religious-historical character, which, however, rest ultimately upon false conceptions—obsolete views regarding the antiquity of the arts of writing and of literary composition in Israel, regarding Israel's acquaintance with the primitive Babylonian myths, and regarding the early Israelitish religious beliefs, which were assumed to be different in kind from the religion of the prophets. But these views are tending to disappear.

A much discussed question is that of the *integrity* of the source. And the doubt raised in these discussions is so far justified that the story of the beginnings, Gen. 2–11, is not an integral unity in the sense that it was all written down continuously by a single individual. But when all is said and done, there is a quite clearly marked religious and literary, one might almost say artistic, individuality which shows itself in the whole writing ; and the work keeps before it a definite purpose, even though it has sometimes difficulty in mastering the diverse materials which it worked up and joined together (cf. Kittel, I. p. 301 f. ; II. p. 244 ff. ; Procksch, *Genesis*, p. 16 ff.).

Quite apart from the language, the close consistency of the ideas resists any attempt to divide the material among the members of a *School*. Luther, it is true, has sought to show the existence of a Rechabite tendency, but there is not the slightest justification for that ; the writing shows throughout an appreciation of all the blessings of civilisation. He is, however, no doubt right in pointing out that in J, and only in J, in contrast with the popular consciousness as manifested elsewhere, the late-born child stands over against the first-born as under a special Divine protection. The conception of God and of the Divine plan in history, and the form of the narrative, also keep their identity throughout the whole source ; everything bears the seal of a single mind. On the other hand, it is quite certain that in the Yahwistic Paradise story we have two recensions (cf. 2. 9 and 3. 3 ; 3. 23 and 3. 22, 24) ; that we have in 4. 16*b* ff. a quite different version of the Cain story from that of 4. 14 f. ; 4. 26 is in direct contradiction with 4. 1 ff. ; and above all there is to be detected in 4. 20-22; 6. 4; 9. 20-27, as Budde has shown, a tradition which knew nothing of the Flood. On the basis of this, Budde wishes to distinguish three strata in the story of the beginnings, while Gunkel goes still further and tries to prove a double thread, not only here but in the Yahwistic stories of the Patriarchs, to which were added later other isolated Yahwistic passages. And, pushing the argument to its limits, Smend, with whom Eichrodt and Eissfeldt are in general agreement, has lately tried to show that there is a continuous J^2 which was intended to supplant J^1. But while it is no doubt true that in much of the material which he assigns to J² a particularly close spiritual relationship is apparent, it is none the less certain that this can never have been an independent continuous document. The threads of literary connection which he tries to join up are often entirely artificial. All these investigations, though they certainly have their use and justification, can scarcely lead to any other result than the resolution of the source into the numerous detached legends of various character and various age which it incorporates, and which certainly at some time or other must have been current in popular tradition in different parts of the country. Much more attractive is the hypothesis that one author, working with a single earlier thread of narrative before him, brought into connection with it stories taken from one source or another, but without having a sufficiently developed historico-critical sense to bring them into harmony, and without venturing to suppress anything that he found before him. (Insertions of this kind are particularly recognisable in the Paradise and Flood narrative, and also in Gen. 12. 10-20; 19. 1 ff., etc. It is no doubt possible that the various traditions had already to some extent become interwoven in the existing popular traditions.) That these so-called strata (J 1-6) are separated from one another by centuries there is no proof whatever. This view had its roots in a false conception of the introduction of the myths in Israel. The material of these myths was certainly current among the Canaanites long before the Israelitish invasion. If we adopt the hypothesis which is the most natural one for that time, that a single man—who was, however, not without assistants—was at work on this writing for some thirty to forty years, everything becomes clear. The whole controversy which now gives rise to so much discussion, whether J was an author or a compiler (cf. Gressmann, *Mose*, p. 372) sets up a false antithesis, where the facts call for a combination of the two. That, in addition, in a writing of the tenth century B.C. there occur isolated instances of later additions and glosses hardly needs to be mentioned.

In II. A, § 1-4, we shall see that probably J does not terminate even in Jg. 1, but is continued throughout the whole of Judges and Samuel down to 1 K. 2. The last words belonging to it which we seem to have are, therefore, "and the Kingdom was established in the hand of Solomon," 1 K. 2. 46; or, if we follow the LXX (in which the above is missing), it ended with the sonorous aspiration, "Blessed be King Solomon, and may the Throne of David be established before the face of Yahweh for ever," 1 K. 2. 45. And if this assumption is correct, no further proof is needed that we have here a writing which was begun, and mainly composed, in the reign of David, and completed in the first half of the reign of Solomon. For a hypothesis regarding the author cf. *infra*, II. A, § 3.

As we clearly recognised under § 3 above, it is not possible in regard to any of the Pentateuch sources to reach more than a hypothetical result. But it must once more be repeated that, even if our hypothesis is correct, we have only obtained a lower limit for the date of the materials of which the document is composed. The individual narratives must previously, centuries earlier, have acquired a more or less fixed form in Judaean oral tradition, and some of them may have been already fixed in writing. (Cf. Gressmann's discussion of the subject in connection with Gen. 2. 14; 10. 9 ff., etc., in the *Archiv für Religionswissenschaft*, 1907, p. 347 ff., and his bold, and in any case suggestive, attempt to reconstruct the primitive sagas of the Mosaic era in his *Mose*, pp. 1-344, and similar attempts by Gunkel for the Patriarchal period in his *Genesis*.)

But out of all these materials there was created a work with a quite definite purpose, a work of such historical breadth and such religious insight and depth, a work through which there so breathes the spirit of a living, saving, sin-punishing, but above all a gracious and all-merciful God, that no nation of antiquity has anything to set alongside of it. The Writing, in spite of its apparently decidedly particularistic tendency, is permeated by a conviction of the unity of mankind and a presage of a mighty and wonderful Kingdom of God upon this earth ; and coming, as it does from these primitive times, with the first freshness of Israel's early days about it, it has proved for mankind a spiritual fountain of youth, from which it can constantly renew its religious vigour.

§ 7. *The so-called Elohistic Source*

Steuernagel, *Der jehovistische Bericht über den Bundesschluss am Sinai*, ThStKr, 1899, p. 317 ff. ; Procksch, *Das nordhebräische Sagenbuch, Die Elohimquelle*, 1906.

The questions regarding the Elohistic source are still more difficult than in the case of the Yahwistic. But we are compelled to accept the view that the existence of such a source can be proved. In particularly close association with the Yahwistic portions are found other sections in regard to which, when they are collected and compared together, it becomes evident that they are so closely connected, and so clearly distinguished from all the other Pentateuch materials, by their characteristic language, religious conceptions and historical tradition, that we are forced to regard them as the products of a definite and well-marked period of the history of Israel.

Among these peculiarities are that it uses exclusively, prior to the Sinai revelation of Ex. 3, as the Divine designation, *Elohim* or *Ha-Elohim* (not *Yahweh*), and even after that event uses this name by preference ; that it calls the original inhabitants of Palestine the *Amorites*, the mount of God *Horeb*, and, from Gen. 32 onwards, prefers to speak of the third Patriarch as Jacob ; and it shows a preference for the expressions הָאִישׁ מֹשֶׁה (" the man Moses "), אָמָה for maidservant (J : שִׁפְחָה), חִזֵּק לֵב " to harden the heart " (J : הִכְבִּיד), הֶעֱלָה מִמִּצְרַיִם " to bring up out of Egypt " (J : הוֹצִיא), קוּץ " to be afraid " (J : גּוּר), etc.

On the basis of these characteristics the following sections are assigned to E : Gen. 15. 1-6 ; 20. 1-22. 14 ; 24 † J ; 28. 11, 12, 17-22 ; 29. 15-18 ;

30. 1-8, 17-23; 31; 32-34 † J; 35; 37 † J; 40–42. 37; 45; 46. 1-5; 48; 50. 15-26. Ex. 1. 15-22; 2. 1-10; 3–5 † J; 7–10 † J and P; 12. 30-38; 13. 17-19; 14. 5-27; 15. 20-22; 17; 18; 19. 2*b*-19 † (in 7-19 small interpolations from J); 20. 1–24. 8, 12-18; 32; 33. 1-11. Num. 10. 33*a*; 11 † J; 12; 13, 14 and 16 † J and P; 20. 14-21; 21; 22 † J; 23; 25. 1-5 † J; 32. 16-40 † J and P. Deut. 10. 6, 7; 11. 29 f.; 27. 5-26 † D; 31. 9-13 † D, 14-23; 32; 33; 34. 3-6, 10.

To E's characteristic religious conceptions belong : the revelation of God through dreams, His manifestation through His angel, His speaking out of heaven ; to his characteristic historical conceptions : that the Patriarchs were polytheists (Jos. 24. 2 ff.) ; it is for this reason that the whole of the primitive history is omitted ; the important rôles played by Aaron and Miriam alongside of Moses, conquest of Canaan within a few years (Jos. 14. 10) by the Tribes operating in concert, owing to miraculous Divine intervention, etc.

This Source begins with the promise of a numerous posterity to Abraham, pictures the patriarchal history in the main in the same way as J, but associates it with other places (and has, additional to J, the sacrifice of Isaac and the burying of Rachel). It dwells with special affection upon the story of Joseph, which it gives in great detail. In Egypt and during the wilderness journeyings Aaron and Miriam are prominent alongside of Moses, and, in the latter part of the journeyings, Joshua also. The making of the Covenant and the words spoken from Horeb are given *in extenso*, and in addition a " Book of the Covenant," which was probably originally given in the land of Moab with a view to its being inscribed, for eternal remembrance, upon a stone near Shechem (cf. § 5, 2*b*).

The nation falls into sin even at Horeb, and as a punishment God does not Himself go with His People but gives them a substitute. It falls to be mentioned here that, as we shall see later, this Source continues beyond the death of Moses into the Book of Joshua, and represents the actual conquest of the country as terminating with a renewal of the Covenant in Shechem.

As regards the origin of the Source, it is beyond all doubt that its provenance is to be sought in Northern Israel, in fact in the territory of Ephraim and Manasseh.

This is clearly proved by the facts that its special heroes are Joseph and the Ephraimite Joshua, that it holds Bethel (Gen. 28. 22 ; 35. 6 ff.), Shechem (33. 18 ff. ; 35. 1 ff.) and Beersheba (Gen. 21, 22 ff. ; cf. Amos 5. 5 ; 8. 14) to be the most sacred sanctuaries of the country, and that it preserves the Blessing of Moses, which was doubtless derived from Ephraim and Manasseh. But it is possible to go even a step further and point to Shechem or Bethel as being, one or the other of them, its place of origin. To the former, according to this Source, appertains in a special sense the name Israel, Gen. 33. 19 f. ; 48. 22 ; here is the grave of Joseph, Jos. 24. 32 ; cf. Gen. 50. 24 f. ; Ex. 13. 19 ; it is the religious centre for the people, Gen. 35. 4, for here the Mosaic Law was commemorated for ever and the Covenant of Horeb renewed, Deut. 27. 5 ff. ; Jos. 24. 1, 26 f. On the other hand, the Gate of Heaven is at Bethel, and God is the God of Bethel, Gen. 28. 17 ; 31. 13.

But if the place of origin is practically certain, it is not possible to fix the time of its origin with exactitude, because this Source belongs to a rather different literary category from that of the Yahwist. It is true that the latter also writes with an eye to a religious idea which binds the whole together (cf. § 6 *sup.*), but in dealing with his materials he gives the popular tradition as he finds it, practically without reflective comment; he tells the story for the pure joy of telling it.   But the Elohist, even in the individual narratives, consciously seeks the ends of religious edification and instruction ; everywhere he gives prominence to the Divine guidance, the Divine miracles, the Divine plan for the education of His People (cf. Gen. 15. 6; 20. 11; 21. 17; 22. 1, 12; 28. 17; 30. 2; 31. 42; 33. 5*b*, 10*b*, 11; 35. 2-4; 41. 15, 52; 45. 7; 50. 20; Ex. 19. 4-6, etc.).   The work seems to have had its birth not in the scholar's study but in the sanctuary, the religious assembly, or the school.   In view of this we have to expect *a priori* that it will have been more frequently redacted, and that means that it cannot be regarded as an integral whole in the sense that J is so.

A concrete example of the way in which the Prophets of the Northern Kingdom made the Elohistic material the foundation of their whole view of, and verdict upon, history, of their instruction as well as their discourses at the Holy Places, is offered to us by the prophet Hosea (cf. especially 12. 3 ff.). And at the same time we see here how at that period they still ventured to deal freely with the form of the narratives, elaborating and reproducing them in an edifying form which already gives some slight suggestion of the later *Midrash*. We must, therefore, take into account the possibility that narratives which had been subjected to this kind of edifying and instructive treatment had already found a place in the early history as preserved by popular tradition.

To come to detail, it is, for example, impossible that the same narrator is responsible both for the narrative of Ex. 4. 32, in its present form, which is pointedly directed against Bethel, and Gen. 28. 11 ff., written in praise of Bethel ; and yet both are Elohistic. Accordingly Kuenen already found traces of a new redaction (E[2]), which was recognisable by its inconsistency with the primary Elohistic document (E[1]). And Steuernagel, and still further Procksch, have gone on to show that one set of narratives continues to use Elohim quite predominantly, even after Ex. 3, while the other thenceforward regularly uses Yahweh, and evidently interpreted Ex. 3. 14

as meaning that at this point the name Yahweh was introduced for the first time by Moses.   To this redactor are to be attributed Gen. 35. 2-4 ; Ex. 3. 15-17 ; 4. 1-16, 27-30 ; 24. 4-8, 12-14, 18*b* ; 31. 18*b* ; 32 ; 33. 3-5*a*, 7-11 ; Num. 11 and 12 ; Deut. 31. 16-22, 28-30 ; 32.   In all these it is to be observed that the purpose of religious instruction is more prominent than in those of E¹.   In places (*e.g.* Ex. 32, and later, Jos. 14-19) it is quite clearly to be seen that we have not to do with an entirely new creation, but that the older material can still be disentangled from it (cf. Ex. 32. 25 ff.).

But even in what remains as the primitive document after making the above division, we find narratives which are on very various religious planes, so that even in it we have to reckon with the possibility of the materials having been shaped and fixed in writing at different periods, without, however, being able to determine exactly the different stages (cf., *e.g.*, the Elohistic Joseph narratives with the Jacob cycle proper).

In view of these considerations, all that can be attempted is to mark within very wide limits the general period of Israel's history from which it is probable that the whole Elohistic stratum of the Pentateuch comes.   The first point to be laid down is that the Elohistic portions are in all probability later than J.

This is shown, in addition to the evidence mentioned in paragraph 6 *sup.*, by the following : (*a*) The overthrow of the Canaanites appears to have been an accomplished fact for a longer period in E than in J ; there is very much less reference to the independence maintained through centuries by Canaanite towns in the plains of Jezreel and Philistia and the mountain country of Judaea (cf. J in Jos. 10. 42, etc.). (*β*) It is not indeed possible to lay any decisive stress upon the fact that in E Abraham, Moses and Miriam are represented as *Nebiim*, "prophets," Gen. 20. 7, 17 ; Ex. 15. 20 ; Num. 11 ; 12, for the inference which is still generally drawn from 1 Sam. 9. 9 that this category of religious persons first occurred in Israel in Samuel's day, is by no means certain (cf. Sellin, *Der altt. Prophetismus*, 1913, p. 9 ff.).   But on the other hand it may fairly be said that it was not until the ninth century B.C. that— —in contrast with 1 Sam. 10. 12, etc.—the *Nabi* became an ideal figure for large sections of the people. (*γ*) In Ex. 18

F

there is a suggestion of the constitution of Solomon, the creation of a body of secular officials, cf. 1 K. 4 ; through which the priests, and the elders of the tribes lost a portion of the duties which had hitherto been assigned to them. (δ) The warning which recurs again and again in this Source, like a refrain, against serving other gods, Gen. 35. 2-4 ; Num. 25. 1-5 ; Jos. 24. 14 ff., at least becomes specially intelligible after Solomon's idolatry had left its mark upon Israel's religious consciousness.

On the other hand there are not, in the material which we can assign to the Elohistic primitive document, any definite *historical* data which would compel us to bring it down lower than the reign of Solomon, that is to say the *narrative* material in it seems to have been completed within the Solomonic period.

It is true that the attempt has been made to find even in this narrative-material traces of a later period, but none of the arguments brought forward in support of this position are really valid. These arguments are : (*a*) It is said that in Gen. 37. 8 the Ephraimite Kingdom " shows through." But here we have to do with a dream, which all his brethren declare to be an arrogant assumption, but which according to the intention of the Source was fulfilled in the position acquired by Joseph in Egypt, and no doubt also in the conquest of the country. That it is quite inadmissible to draw a conclusion of this kind has been shown in § 5 (ii.). (*b*) In Gen. 31. 48 ff., it has been proposed to see a reflection of the Syrian wars of the ninth century. But nothing could be more remote from the ideas of the Source here than a war ; in fact it is absolutely excluded by the Laban story. (*c*) Edom, it is said, no longer, according to Jos. 15. 2, belongs to Judah. But that can be explained even in Solomon's time, cf. 1 K. 11. 4 ff. (*d*) It is said that Jos. 6. 26 presupposes the re-building of Jericho, which did not take place until the days of Ahab, 1 K. 16. 34. But that is to turn the story upside down. Hiel did not sacrifice his children for pleasure, but only in order to release the site from the ancient curse. (*e*) All the remaining arguments do not touch the primary document itself but have reference to a later expansion, Ex. 32, the attack upon the calf worship at Bethel, in which, moreover, the older form of the story, which referred simply to a feast of unbridled license, can still be detected ; to the " Studies in Prophetism " which we find in Num. 11 and 12, and the like. The primary document knows only the holy stone of Bethel, Gen. 28 ; had its material been later than the time of Jeroboam it would certainly have mentioned the calf, as it mentions the tithes offered there, v. 22.

There are however positive arguments which prove that the narrative material of the primary document was complete *before the Division of the Kingdom*.

There is not the slightest allusion in the narratives to the Division. Everywhere it is implied that Israel is an integral unity. A false interpretation of Deut. 33. 7, 16, lies at the root of the whole error. (*b*) The fact that in Jos. 15. 1 ff. Judah stands at the head in the list of the division of the land among the Tribes, points as clearly to the undivided kingdom as the inclusion of Philistia within it (15. 2 ff.) does to the times of David and Solomon, in which alone it is explicable. Cf. also Ex. 23. 31. (*c*) The new Judaean central sanctuary at Jerusalem is perhaps recognized as a place of special Divine revelation, alongside of Bethel, Shechem, and others. We leave out of account here Gen. 14. 20, on account of the uncertainty to which Source it belongs, but we have to reckon with the possibility that Gen. 22 refers to the mountain on which the Jerusalem Temple was built. The interpretation of Wellhausen and Procksch who refer it to Shechem (connection of *Moriah* with *Moreh*, Gen. 12. 6) breaks down in face both of the " three days " of v. 4—a traveller on foot takes at least four days to go from Beersheba to Shechem—and also of the " mountain," for the oracular tree lay not on Mount Gerizim but like Shechem itself on a mere rise in a valley and would not be visible from a distance. Gunkel's reference of it to *Jeruel* is equally impossible, for this is a desert, with no mountain, and the journey to it would only require two days. The statement as to the distance applies well to Jerusalem. No doubt the writer would have in mind not Moriah, but *Ariel*, cf. Isa. 29. 1, with the twofold word-play (*Yahweh*, or *Elohim, jir'eh ayl* and *er'eh el*). The reference to the " Land of the Amorites " could also be best explained on the Jerusalem hypothesis (Jos. 10. 5). But is it likely that after the Division of the kingdoms a legend glorifying the site of the Jerusalem Temple would be put on record in the Northern Kingdom ? If not, it would only be possible to think of Mizpeh (originally *Yahweh yizpeh*, cf.

31. 49 ?). Finally, it may be recalled that it is an Elohistic
narrative which, in Num. 21. 4-9, celebrates the Brazen Serpent,
the means of healing for the snake-bites, which was set up at
Jerusalem, and to later times appeared to be an idol, 2 K. 18. 4.

Following up this hint we observe that in general
the Elohistic material accompanies the Yahwistic
like a shadow.

There is much of course which is found in the latter, but is
missing in the former ; the earliest narratives, the Lot-Sodom
story, the story of Tamar's marriage, etc. But in the whole
of the Elohistic material there is only a single story which
has not, at first sight, a prototype in J—35. 2-4 belongs to E²
—and that is the narrative of the sacrifice of Isaac in Gen. 22.
But is it not probable that the basis of this, like, e.g., that of
Gen. 15, was a Yahwistic narrative ?[1] Consider the whole
extraordinarily lively and vivid description, and note v. 14.
Gunkel had previously recognized that the original narrative
knew nothing of the testing of Abraham's obedience which is
the *motif* of the present Elohistic story.   And it is quite possible
that " Ariel, the town where David encamped " might have
been glorified even in the first half of the reign of Solomon
by a legend of patriarchal times which recognized it as a holy
place.

How are we to explain, then, the extraordinary
parallelism between the sources, alongside of all the
independence in detail which we find in Exodus
and Numbers ?

A particularly determined attempt has lately been made
by Procksch to show that E has preserved, alongside of the
Yahwistic, a second line of tradition regarding the whole of
the early history reaching back into the days of the patriarchs,
which stands over against the Yahwistic tradition as a wholly
independent one, but by the constant similarity of its subject-
matter points back to a common primitive tradition.   But is
it possible to conceive of the maintenance of such an absolute
parallelism in the subject-matter in the case of an independent
development of the tradition in two tribes which were no doubt
allied by blood, but were politically entirely separate, even if

[1] A conjecture which was first suggested to me by my pupil Lic. Bruno.

we consider this development as proceeding during a century and a half only? Would there not necessarily have arisen an incomparably greater number of new *motifs*, and have we not indeed in the early oracular verses about the tribes the unmistakable proof that that is what actually did happen in Israel?

It certainly seems to me that in this point the view is to be preferred which was put forward by E. Meyer and afterwards emphasized by Smend, that the Elohist stands essentially entirely upon the shoulders of the Yahwist, that it is in fact a later revised edition of the Yahwist. That the Yahwistic tradition is an elaboration of the Elohistic will certainly never be proved, but there is a good deal of evidence for the converse (cf. *sup*. p. 55 f.). But Smend, it must be confessed, in solving the enigma has himself introduced a twofold error. In the first place, as we have already shown, the place of origin of this new edition was most certainly quite a different one from that of the Yahwist, and was not therefore Jerusalem, as Smend thinks, but Shechem or Bethel. This explains the much stronger North Israelitish colouring, and also many new, independent, and often earlier traits, drawn from the Ephraimite traditions, in the details of the narrative (very specially is this the case in the Joseph stories), also the interweaving of ancient laws, poems, and so forth which had been preserved by the Northern tradition. Secondly, E had no intention of writing a polemic against J or of violently displacing it but only of adapting it to the times by omission or modification of anything which had become ethically or religiously unacceptable, and by emphasizing more strongly the didactic and edifying elements in the history.

In order therefore to discover the time and manner in which the Elohistic document arose, the most important theory is to determine what precisely are the ideas by which it is dominated. It is, in contradistinction to J, as Schrader long ago denominated it, a theocratic document. The thought which is most prominent in it is this: God alone, by His wonder-working power, laid the foundations of Israel's existence, He alone has ever miraculously guided and educated His People, He

is their sole Lord and King, Gen. 37. 8 ; Ex. 19. 6 ;
Num. 23. 21 ; Deut. 33. 5, etc.

Accordingly the points of difference from J as regards the
dominating ideas are (apart from those already enumerated
in § 6) especially the following : (*a*) The origin of Israel is a
much greater miracle even than it is in J. The Patriarchs
were not gradually, from the Creation onwards, chosen out of
humanity, but delivered from the midst of heathendom, Jos.
24. 2 ff. ; the deliverance from Egypt (Ex. 3-5 ; 7-10 ; 14 ; 15,
etc.), and the conquest of Canaan happen in a much more
miraculous way. (*b*) God " is not a man," and all His revelations are supernatural (dreams, visions, angels—and for that
reason the story of Sodom is rejected, cf. Hos. 11. 9). He
therefore bears no personal name, like other gods. He is
God, " He-who-is," since the days of the Fathers, unchanging,
eternal (this is the interpretation which E gives in Ex. 3. 14
to the name of Yahweh, which it never uses before Ex. 3, and
afterwards as little as it possibly can). (*c*) His will must be
held to and followed with the most meticulous care, and everything connected with heathenism must be scrupulously avoided
(Gen. 35. 2 ; Num. 23. 9, 21). (*d*) The centre of gravity of
Israel's history lay from the first in the tribe of Joseph, and
Shechem was the real central sanctuary of Israel. (*e*) As a
consequence of points (*a*) to (*c*) this source could not refer the
human kingship to the Divine initiative, but is obliged to explain
it otherwise, cf. the brusque rejection of the idea in Gen. 37. 8,
and on the other side the idea of the Divine Kingship, Ex.
19. 6. (On the attribution of this passage to E, see Koenig,
Einl. p. 205 ; *Geschichte des Reiches Gottes*, p. 65.)

What then was the period at which these ideas
emerged in the Northern Kingdom ; or rather,
when did they come to stand in the foreground of
the religious life ? To this we can only give the
quite general answer : The development must have
begun when Ahijah the prophet of Shiloh began to
prophesy against the idolatry of Solomon, and, in
connection with this, against Solomon's Kingship,
and later against the Ephraimite Jeroboam. It
probably reached its culminating point in the

struggle of Elijah and his disciples against the Baal-worshipping dynasty of Omri. Thus, the earliest of the literary Prophets of the eighth century are able to assume these ideas to be already in the possession of their hearers, though the latter as a rule treat them, it must be confessed, with scant respect.

Precisely those two sanctuaries round which, for the Elohist, everything centres, Bethel and Shechem, had in their near neighbourhood in the days of Elijah and Elisha settlements of " Schools of the prophets " 2 K. 2. 1-3 ; 4. 38 ; see also 1 Sam. 7. 16 (perhaps indeed the same applies to Beer-sheba, cf. 1 K. 19. 3 ; 1 Sam. 8. 2 ; as to the site of the Gilgal ᶜnear Shechem, cf. Deut. 11. 30 ; 27. 2 ; Hos. 6. 9, and see my *Gilgal*, p. 3). And, on the contrary, it was later precisely against these two places that the wrath of the earliest literary prophets was poured forth, cf. Am. 4. 4 ; 5. 5 ; Hos. 4. 15 ; 6. 9 f. ; 9. 15 ; 10. 5 ff. ; 12. 12.

If then we can say in general terms that the ninth century is the most probable time and the prophetic movement of that date—which is not to be judged entirely by the legends about Elijah and Elisha (cf. my *Alttest. Prophetismus*, p. 23 ff.)— is the impelling motive in the new North-Israelite edition of the Yahwist which produced the present Elohist, there still remains the further and final question : is there a *terminus ad quem* for the present form of the Source ?

There is of course an obvious lower limit in the destruction of the Northern Kingdom by the Assyrians in 722 B.C. After that year, Gen. 35. 1-4 and Ex. 32, would have completely lost their point. But even for the latest Elohistic redaction we

must go back a few decades before this.   The prophet Hosea
lives and has his being in the whole work.   For him also the
Calf of Bethel is one of the chief sins of Israel, he, too, emphasizes
the thought that " God is not a man," for him, too, Yahweh
is the sole helper, in contrast with the Kingship, and is the God
of Israel first from the deliverance from Egypt, for him, too,
Israel is delivered and watched over by prophets, he is an
advocate of the Law and the Covenant (*Torah* and *Berith*)
of Yahweh, Hos. 4. 6 ; 6. 5, 7 ; 8. 1, 12, etc., etc.   But all the
same Hosea seems to have arisen out of a spiritual movement
which was created by the Elohist, including the so-called Second
Elohist (E²), not himself to have prepared the way for it.   It
is true that in matters of detail he is prepared to remould freely
the Elohistic history (*v. sup*.).   But the form in which we now
have that history must be derived from predecessors of the
prophet.   If the last redaction had taken place in dependence
upon him it would have made short work of those patriarchal
narratives which give special honour to the local sanctuaries
of Bethel, Shechem (Gilgal), and Beersheba, against which
Hosea's wrath, like that of Amos, is specially directed, and
not only of the story of the beginnings and the Lot-Sodom cycle.
The idea which is central with Hosea of the love of God and
love to God, Hos. 3. 1 ; 6. 6, etc., is absent even in E², whereas
it could not fail to be present if the revision had taken place
in dependence upon the prophet (cf. Deut.).   And the conception of prophetism in Num. 11 and 12 has its home rather
among the pupils of an Elijah than among those of an Amos
or a Hosea.   We have, therefore, to place the latest Elohistic
redaction shortly after 800 B.C.   As to where it took place,
we can for the present come to no conclusion ; but in II. §§
1 ; 2 ; and 3 *infra*, we shall see that the continuation of it
beyond Joshua takes us probably to the Benjamite Mizpah,
which, however, stood under Judaean spiritual influences, and
must have had, to judge from Jer. 40. 8 ff., a greater importance
than is usually supposed.

The Elohistic writing became incomparably
more important than the Yahwistic for the religious
development of Israel.   Procksch has shown how
vastly more all the prophets, including the later
prophets of the Southern Kingdom, were influenced
by it than by the other.   And Deuteronomy and the

Priestly-writing simply proceeded further along the path which had been trodden by the Elohist—the emphasizing of the theocracy. And that is not to be wondered at, for the Elohist represents the conception of the early history which was vitally present to the mind of the people after the division of the kingdom, and made its influence felt both in the schools of the prophets and in their discourses in the assemblies for public worship. But the Elohistic development of the ancient history was in fact that which was inspired by the deeper impulse. For we may well ask ourselves whether the deeply earnest interpretation which religion and history received in Elohistic circles was not a more correct representation of the intentions of the Founder of that religion, than that which was given to it in court circles in the brilliant period of David and Solomon. The future, it may fairly be said, belonged to them, because they had a sound grip upon the past. The immediately Mosaic material which we possess, distinctly demonstrable as such, we owe, as we have seen in § 5, to the Elohist.

§ 8. *Deuteronomy*

Stärk, *Das Deut.: Sein Inhalt und seine literärische Form*, 1894 ; Steuernagel, *Der Rahmen des Deut.*, 1894 ; *Die Entstehung des deut. Gesetzes*, 1896 ; Naumann, *Das Deuteronomium*, 1897 ; Herrmann, *Ägyptische Analogien zum Funde des Deut.*, ZAW, 1908, p. 299 ff. ; Sternberg, *Die Ethik des Deut.*, 1908 ; Puukko, *Das Deuteronomium*, 1910 ; Oestreicher, " Die Stellung des Gesetzes in der israelitischen Religionsgeschichte," in *Das Reich Christi*, 1911, p. 89 ff. ; Hempel, *Die Schichten des Deuteronomiums*, 1914 ; König, *Das Deuteronomium*, 1917 ; Kegel, *Die Kultusreformation des Josia*, 1919.

According to 2 K. 22. 3—23. 24 there was found in the Temple in the reign of Josiah, in the year 622 B.C., a book which was wholly unknown, called

in v. 8 " the Book of the Law " and in 23. 2 and 21
" the Book of the Covenant." It was sent by the
High Priest Hilkiah, by the hand of Shaphan the
Scribe, to the king, and on the basis of this book
Josiah, strongly supported by the prophetess Hul-
dah, undertook a religious reform. That this book
was our Deuteronomy, in whole or in part, and not
the whole Pentateuch or some other book now lost,
is now almost universally recognized.

It is proved by the following considerations : (*a*) The book
was, according to 22. 8, 10, twice read through—one reading
following shortly after the other—in one day, by Shaphan the
Scribe, once in the Temple, and once when he took it to the
king. (*b*) With the exception of Ex. 20-23 Deuteronomy is
the only book to which the designation " Book of the Covenant "
could be applied, cf. Deut. 5. 2 ; 29. 1 ; 29. 21 ; 30. 10. (*c*)
Above all, the account of the actual reforms undertaken by
Josiah shows that they were based on Deuteronomy and on
nothing else—the centralization of the cultus, 2 K. 23. 8 ff.
goes back to Deut. 12. 13 ; 16. 21 ; the abolition of star-
worship, 2 K. 23. 11 f., to Deut. 17. 3 ; the suppression of the
" Sodomites," 23. 7, to Deut. 23. 17 ; the rooting-out of the
necromancers, 23. 24, to Deut. 18. 10 ff. ; the prohibition of
the sacrificing of children, 23. 10, to Deut. 18. 10 ; the celebration of the Passover in the Temple, 23. 21, to Deut. 16. 1-8.

This book discovered in 622 cannot have been
an ancient Mosaic, or even a Solomonic writing.
But it is equally impossible that it should have
been a book written immediately before, under
Josiah or even Manasseh ; the only thing in fact
that it can have been is the Temple Law upon
which Hezekiah's reform was based.

The first two alternatives are in fact at once excluded by
the fact that the writing could immediately be read freely
and easily, *i.e.* that the language of Deuteronomy is that of the
seventh century, and still more by the fact that had it been an
early book we should have to suppose that the whole of Israelitish
history from the time of Moses (or of Solomon, if that is the

hypothesis) and the religious practice of the pious, of a David, of the earlier prophets, and so forth, had been a studied contravention of this Law (cf. the places, times, and persons at which, and by whom sacred rites are represented in the early history as being performed).

The view, however, which in spite of energetic opposition still prevails (Wellhausen, Marti, and others), that the book was composed *by a contemporary of Josiah*, probably with, though perhaps without the knowledge of Hilkiah, that it represents a compromise between the priests and the prophets, that the discovery in the Temple was only a pretence intended to incline the king to the reforming movement—this view makes shipwreck on the following difficulties. (*a*) It is certainly opposed to the intention of the narrator. And he is a very good witness, for he was obviously not some later so-called Deuteronomist, but, in view of 2 K. 22. 20, some one who drew up the report before the unhappy end of King Josiah—in all probability Shaphan the Scribe or his son Ahikam, for it is only to one or other of these that 22. 7, 12, can naturally be referred. (*b*) Some of the laws are absolutely incapable of explanation as due to a compromise between priests and prophets, and still less as a forgery of the priests ; in particular the regulation in Deut. 18. 7, which was so prejudicial to the interests of the Jerusalem priests that according to 2 K. 23. 9, they simply did not permit its introduction ; also 18. 15 ff., which might easily become a danger to the priests' claim to impart the Law. (*c*) A number of other provisions are unintelligible as owing their origin to a reformation promoted by priests and prophets (cf. Deut. 20 ; 22. 8, 10 ; 25. 4, etc.). (*d*) And on this hypothesis it would be equally impossible to understand why the reforming party had waited until the eighteenth year of Josiah, seeing that from the beginning of his reign he began to seek after the Lord (cf. 2 Chr. 34. 3 ; and with that 2 K. 22. 11 ff.) ; or why, again, Josiah did not simply destroy a book which so strongly condemned himself, his house, and his people (cf. Jer. 36. 23 ff.), unless the circumstances under which it was discovered provided an absolute guarantee that it was really an ancient sacred book.

But equally untenable is the view that we have here to do with a writing compiled by some pious pupil of the prophets, before 623, out of two sources of Manasseh's time (which in their turn were based upon an earlier Hezekian law-code), and then hidden by him in the Temple in the hope of better times—the constitution of an ideal state, a kind of *Respublica*

Platonis, cf. Isa. 30. 8 (so, among others, Steuernagel). Against this there are three arguments : (*a*) Hilkiah's phrase, " *The* Book of the Law," 2 K. 22. 8, shows clearly that he had known before of the existence of the book, it was only its contents which were unknown to him. (*b*) The form of all the Deuteronomic commandments (12-26) is so categorical that it is impossible to suppose it to be anything else than an actual Law-code. (*c*) The content of many of the laws also excludes the possibility that they were mere pious aspirations, and, on the contrary, shows clearly that the intention was from the first that they should constitute a law-code regulating the whole of the national life.

The right solution of the problem has been facilitated by the fact that it has lately been shown by a considerable body of evidence that in ancient Egypt it was customary to build into some part or other of a temple, the " Rule " of the Temple (cf. Herrmann, *ut sup.*). And at least the custom of laying up books of laws in holy places is evidenced within the Old Testament itself, 1 Sam. 10. 25 ; Deut. 31. 26. In view of this evidence it is natural to suppose that at the final consecration of the Temple, which was carried out in the spirit of the Mosaic legislation, such a book of laws, statutes, and rules would be deposited or built in, in the holy place. No doubt the Jerusalem priesthood would keep a copy, but during the long period of reaction in Manasseh's reign this might easily get destroyed. When we find it definitely laid upon the king as a duty in Deut. 17. 16, to have a copy made for himself in a book, that is in itself evidence that no further copies existed. Now, a reformation in the spirit of Mosaism, combined with a purifying of the Temple, is described in the Book of Kings as taking place in the days of Hezekiah, 2 K. 18. 4, 22 ; 21. 3. The conclusion forces itself upon us that the book found by Hilkiah had been the rule and standard of the Hezekian reformation. It was then—after 722—that the moment arrived when Jerusalem took for all Israel the place of the numerous local sanctuaries, and began to occupy the position which Shechem had formerly held in the age of Joshua. The view that Hezekiah's reformation did not extend to the high places can now scarcely be maintained (cf. Kittel, *Geschichte des Volkes Israel*, ii. 548 ff.). And the opinion that the prohibition of star-worship would not as yet have been appropriate is based on an acquaintance with the ancient East which is not exactly up to date. Had not a modification of the cultus been carried out by Ahaz under the influence of the King of Assyria? 2 K. 16. 10 f., 18; 23. 12; cf. ZEAT

p. 44 ff.   Even if one hesitates to place the origin of Deuteronomy in such close connection with the reforms of Hezekiah, in face of the fact that in the account of the reforms there is no mention of such a Law—and in view of the brevity of the report this *argumentum e silentio* can hardly be considered decisive—it must at least be placed in its near neighbourhood, and in spiritual connection with it (so Koenig, p. 51), or regarded as its immediate consequence (so Hempel, pp. 259, 268).

In any case the Law of Hezekiah cannot have been the whole of the present Deuteronomy, but only the nucleus of it.   What exactly this nucleus consists of is a matter of pure hypothesis.   But the assumption which has most probability in its favour is that it more or less coincides with the " Singular-Source " which Steuernagel showed to exist in chaps. 12-26, but which is not strictly confined to the limits suggested by him ; probably with this was combined a short historical résumé and a hortatory introduction, and a conclusion consisting of blessings and curses.   (Cf. the Code of Hammurabi.)   If this is correct, we may seek the original law-code in the following passages, 4. 44 ; 4. 46-49 ; 6. 4-15 ; 12. 13-27 ; 13. 1-18 ; 14. 22-29 ; 15. 1–26. 15 (with the exception of a few interpolations, *e.g.* 20. 1-9 ; 28. 1-25).   This nucleus was enlarged in the days of Josiah by the addition, when it was publicly read, of detailed exhortations to follow its precepts (chaps. 5-11) and by the addition of other laws (in 12-26 ; generally recognizable by the introduction " Ye shall," etc.), these laws being however in part of earlier date.   This *corpus*, 4. 44—26. 15 ; 28, was then in the first place in pre-Exilic times interwoven into the Elohistic writing, 10. 6 f. ; 11. 29 ff. ; 27. 1 ff., and provided with a detailed historical introduction 1. 1—4. 4.

During the Babylonian exile further additions were made, 4. 5-43 ; 28. 26 ff. ; 29 (see further in § 10. 2).

That the historical framework, chapters 1-4, 29-34, is to be distinguished from the nucleus, 5-26, or, it may be, 28, and that in the latter the exhortations, 5-11, are to be distinguished from the laws and statutes, 12-26, was recognized long ago by Kuenen, Wellhausen, and others. But, going beyond this, Stärk, and especially Steuernagel, hold that even the nucleus, 5-26, is not a unity, but is of composite origin. In the first place the latter thought that he could prove by the alternations of the address—" Thou " and " Ye "—that there were here two collections of laws, each of which had a hortatory introduction. In places this argument is absolutely convincing, cf. 12. 13, 14, 16-21, 26, 27 with 12. 8-12, where, apart from some such hypothesis, there would be the most unaccountable repetition. On the other hand the Plural-Source which he constructs can never have existed independently, it has no consistent plan, moreover, it has not always, though it has usually, the plural address. We must, therefore, give up the attempt to distinguish the sources by means of this touchstone. Steuernagel himself has now done so in his *Einleitung*. In this he designates as the " Primitive Deuteronomy " (p. 179), 12. 13-28 ; 14. 22-29 ; 15. 19-23 ; 16. 1-17, 21, 22 ; 17. 1, 2-7 ; 18. 9-12 ; 19. 1-13, 14 ; 21. 1-9, 15-21, 22-23 ; 22. 5, 9-29 ; 22. 30-23. 14, 17, 18, 21-23 ; 24. 1-5 ; 25. 5-10, 13-16 ; 26. 1-15. But it is questionable whether the two principles by which he now effects the separation, the connection of the laws in regard to their subject-matter, or a right arrangement of them, and the question whether or no regard was had to them in the reforms of Josiah, suffice to determine the primary Law-code. Indeed Steuernagel himself takes into account the possibility that the author of this had before him other laws, already formulated, and adopted some of them, and he himself in arguing with Puukko described the second test as misleading. Puukko has made the attempt, on the basis of 2 K. 22 f., to reconstruct the law-code as orginally found by Josiah. But as in the above passage mention is made only of the particular practices which had to be done away with on the ground of this law, the reconstruction is not sufficiently comprehensive. A new method of analysis has been initiated by Hempel, who examines first all those laws which betray the influence of the centralization of the cultus, works out their literary characteristics, their earlier stages, and their place of origin, and then tests the remaining portions by asking how far these can in their present form be derived from the same hand. In this way he arrives at the result that the book found in Josiah's time was not an original work, but that its author revised the old Jerusalem Temple-rule in the interest of the centralization of the cultus, expanded it by adding some social regulations, and provided it with an introduction based upon E. Later on, the same author worked up with it another source directed against the abominations of Manasseh. I doubt the correctness of the latter assumption, and while the main result may well be sound, in regard to many particulars the method does not take us beyond tentative hypotheses (cf. the Josiah book as extracted by him, *ut sup.* p. 261).

In the hortatory portions, 5. 23—11. 32, in which we meet with ever-recurring references to " the commandments, the statutes, and the judgments," without these immediately following, Klostermann has rightly taught us to see allocutions which were delivered at the reading of the Law (*i.e.* 12-26— but not of a lost wilderness-law as Klostermann supposes). This was no doubt a very old custom, cf. 1 Sam. 7. 16. It comes to very much the same thing in practice whether, with Klostermann, we see in it two redactions, 6. 4—8. 20, and 9—11, or like Steuernagel, distinguish between a " Plural-Source," 5. 1-4, 20-28 ; 9. 9-11, 28 ; and a " Singular-Source," 6. 4—9. 7 (+ 10, 12, 14-15, 21 ; 11. 10-12, 14-15).

Of course a considerable number of the " commandments and statutes " in the nucleus-portion, chaps. 12-26, were not a new creation even in Hezekiah's day, but go right back, like those of chapter 5, to the times of Moses and the Judges. This nucleus had been incorporated into the Temple-rule of Solomon's day ; and that of Hezekiah's day was based upon it. The only new thing was the law of the centralization of the cultus, with all its implications. But of course this too must have had a history behind it.

A glance at the subject-matter of the laws suffices to show that what we have here is in large part very ancient popular law, cf. esp. chaps. 22-25. But even in the laws which regulate the administration of justice (in 17. 8-13 if you strike out everywhere "the priest," there remains only "the judge," that is, the king), in the law of the Kingship (17. 14 ff. where v. 16 points to the pre-Assyrian period), in the laws of war (20. 2—4. 8), etc., it is not difficult to separate the new additions from the old foundation. The social laws (*e.g.* 15. 1-18) envisage the peasant farmer of pre-prophetic days, and not the large estate-holders and merchants of the age of the prophets.

On the other hand the new material is especially to be observed in 12. 13-27 ; 13. 1 ff. ; 14. 22-29 ; 16. 1-17 ; 18. 1-8 ; 26. 1, 2, 5-15. Only we must never forget that in Judah the idea of centralization must have been in the air, ever since Solomon built the magnificent Temple over the ancient sacred shrine, the Ark (cf. 1 K. 8. 65 ; Amos 1. 2 ; Isa. 8. 18 ; 18. 7 ; 30. 29 ; 31. 4), and similarly what has been called "Deuteronomic phraseology" had also a long history behind it (cf. the free treatment of the Elohistic writing in Hos. 1. 2*b* ; 2. 5, 13 ; 6. 10 ; 10. 5, 8 ; 11. 2 ; 13. 2, etc.) ; and that we are apt to construct a misleading picture from the prophetic writings, since these were not concerned with a practical reform of the cultus, whereas that was certainly already a dominant interest with other earnest men in the eighth century (cf. Hos. 13. 13). How far Hezekiah's Temple Law goes back to that of Joash (cf. 2 K. 11. 10 ff. ; 12. 1 ff.), and this in turn to that of Solomon, is not likely ever to be exactly determined. (Hempel is probably approximately right in finding the old *corpus* is his QI.) The putting of new laws as well as old into the mouth of Moses is simply a stylistic feature of the Israelitish legislation, for this was all thought of as being merely a reproduction in a form appropriate to the times of the fundamental Law given by Moses.

In making his people bind themselves by an oath to obedience to Deuteronomy, Josiah caused the nation to take a long step forward on the path pointed out by the Elohist, a step on the road which led logically to Judaism. But it was, humanly speaking, the only way to deliver the people from Canaanitish and Babylonian heathenism. And, regarded from a more comprehensive point of view, the introduction of this law may be regarded as at once the noblest and highest, and also, doubtless, the most tragic attempt which has ever been made to bring men the Gospel by the road of the Law. Deuteronomy is penetrated through and through with prophetic ideas; God's love and love to God are its Alpha and Omega, 6. 5; 7. 8, etc. But the vessel in which it was offered was to curdle the noble beverage which it contained. It was a necessity of the time, but to that time only did it belong.

§ 9. *The so-called Priestly Writing*

Giesebrecht, *Der Sprachgebrauch des hexateuchischen Elohisten*, ZAW, 1881, p. 177 ff.; Wurster, *Zur Charakteristik und Geschichte des Priesterkodex und des Heiligkeitsgesetzes*, ZAW, 1884, p. 112 ff.; Baudissin, *Die Geschichte des alttest. Priestertums*, 1889; Kräutlein, *Die sprachlichen Verschiedenheiten in den Hexateuchquellen*, 1908.

The portions of the Pentateuch which belong to the Priestly Writing stand out with peculiar distinctness from the remaining material, so that even the non-expert can recognize them without difficulty.

Among its characteristics are: a strikingly formal style, a special interest in genealogies and numbers, in cultual laws and customs and the rights of the priests, a strong emphasis upon the ideal of cultual purity and holiness; a quite characteristic language, *e.g.* הוֹלִיד (to beget), הֵקִים בְּרִית (to conclude a covenant), אֲחֻזָּה (possession), רְכֻשׁ (substance, belongings), בָּרָא (create), etc. In the historical portions it seeks to avoid all anthropomorphisms. In accordance with its view that Yahweh revealed himself first to Moses (Ex. 6. 2, 3), it never uses this name previously, and similarly it is absolutely silent in the Mosaic period concerning sacrifices, oracles, priesthood, distinction of clean and unclean, etc.

To this source are assigned with great unanimity the following sections: Gen. 1. 1—2. 4*a*; 5. 1-28, 30-32; 6. 9-22; 7 and 8 † J; 9. 1-17, 28, 29; 10. 1-7, 20-23, 31 f.; 11. 10-32; 13. 6, 11-13; 17;

G

23 ; 25. 7-17 ; 27. 46-28. 9 ; 34 † J and E ; 35.
9-13, 15, 22-29 ; 36 ; 46. 6-27 ; 48. 3-6 ; 49. 28-
33 ; 50. 12, 13 ; Ex. 1. 1-5, 7, 13, 14 ; 2. 23-25 ;
6. 2-7, 13 ; 8, 9 and 11 with J and E ; 12. 1-20,
40-51 ; 14 and 16 † J and E ; 25-31 ; 34. 29—40.
38 ; Leviticus entirely. Num. 1-10 ; 13. 1-17 ;
14 † J and E ; 15 ; 16 † ; 17-20. 13 ; 25. 6-31 ;
32 † J and E ; 33-36. Deut. 32. 48-52 ; 34. 1*a*, 7-9.

The Priestly Writing, like the Yahwistic, begins
with a creation-story and, like it, closes, so far as
the Pentateuch is concerned, with the death of
Moses, and, similarly again, finds a continuation
in the Book of Joshua. In the whole outline of
the history it is throughout similar to the Yahwist,
but in the handling of details it goes very decidedly
its own way. For it the whole history is obviously
only an introduction to the Law, and an illustration
of it ; its aim is simply to give the history of the
cultus.

The investigation of its origin is rendered
difficult by the fact that, while it certainly now
bears the impress of a single mind, *it was not
originally a literary unity*, but has been formed by
the combination of the most diverse materials
which in parts have only been superficially connected together.

That is shown in the first place by the large number of
doublets within this document, Ex. 27-29 ; Lev. only one
altar ; Ex. 30. 1-10 ; 35-40 a gold altar of incense beside it ;
Num. 4. 3 f. duties of the Levites, with 30, J ; 8. 23-26, with
25 J ; Ex. 29. 1 ff. only Aaron anointed ; 28. 41 ff. all the
priests. Lev. 17-26, as has already been remarked, § 5 *sup.*,
stands out with particular distinctness as an originally quite
independent stratum. Eerdmans has lately shown that differences of this kind are present not merely in the laws but also
in the narrative portion. It is contrary to P's real fundamental

principles that a cultural institution such as circumcision should go back to Abraham, Gen. 17, and the Sabbath right to the Creation ; that it should be said of the Patriarchs that they had " walked with God," 5. 22, 24 ; 6. 9 ; that the kingship should be considered as specially promised by God, 17. 6, 16 ; 35. 11 ; that a long story should be devoted to an ancestral tomb, Gen. 23. 1 ff. ; that the Ishmaelites should be included in the Covenant 17. 23. (Eerdmans is, however, wrong in thinking that the man who wrote Ex. 6. 2 must previously always have said " El Shaddai " for God, and therefore, while he might have written 17. 1-14 ; 28. 3 ; 35. 11 ; 43. 14 ; 48. 3, could not have written the *Elohim* sections. For this passage (Ex. 6. 2) only says that God had previously always *named Himself* in this way.) The composition of the writing is therefore much more complex than used to be supposed.

In spite of that, the spiritual and literary characteristics of the writing are such, when compared with the rest of the Pentateuch, that we are bound to make the attempt to consider it as a unity and to ask, at what date can it have been published in its present form ? And the answer to that question cannot but be " in the days of Ezra and Nehemiah." It was not until then that the priestly document, worked up in Babylon about 500 B.C., was introduced as a Law and moreover, not until after it had been combined with JED to form the present Pentateuch, between 458 and 444 by Ezra in Jerusalem.

According to Ez. 7. 1 ff., Ezra, who was himself a " priest and a ready scribe in the law of the God of heaven," went in the year 458 B.C. from Babylon to Jerusalem in order to make an inquiry concerning Judah and Israel " according to the law of God that was in his hand." And in the year 444, this law, which was unknown to the people, was, according to Neh. 8-10, solemnly read before the people and introduced as a national law, the people swearing allegiance to it. That this law contained primarily statutes for the priesthood is quite undeniable. Neh. 8. 15 looks back to Lev. 23. 40 ; 8. 18 to Lev. 23. 36 (differing from Deut. 16. 13-15) ; 10. 36-40 to Num. 18. 12-32.

Neh. 10. 34 is a summary of the whole sacrificial ritual of P. On the other hand, the widely prevalent opinion that this law consisted exclusively of P is untenable, for the prohibition of intermarriage with the inhabitants of the land, 10. 31, is found only in Ex. 34. 12, 15 f. and Deut. 7. 2 ff., and similarly the commandment not to demand the payment of debts in the Sabbatic year, 10. 32, goes back to Deut. 15. 2.

But in any case the Priestly Writing was not, previous to this, recognized as law. That is proved by the following arguments : (a) The prophets " Second Isaiah," Haggai, Zechariah, and Malachi refer exclusively to Deuteronomy. (b) Ezekiel certainly implies the existence of Lev. 17-26 and many other laws connected with the priesthood, but by no means of our Priestly Writing as a complete whole; for he knows nothing of the High Priest, and the degradation of the Levites, who in Deuteronomy are still priests, to be Temple servants, only takes place in Ezekiel's time (Ezek. 44. 9-16), whereas in P it is taken for granted as a thing already in exist-ence—only the " sons of Aaron " are there thought of as priests. (c) The account of the introduction of Deuteronomy in 2 K. 22 ; 23, would be nonsense if P had been an existing law ; how could Josiah have been perturbed at the finding of this book if a much stricter law had already been known ? (d) Moreover, Deuteronomy appears to be in almost every respect an older law as compared with the Priestly Writing in its present form (in Deuteronomy the demand is only being made that there should be but one sanctuary ; here it is taken for granted). And, clearly as it goes back in its provisions to Ex. 20-23 ; 34 and to the basis of the Law of Holiness, there is no reference whatever to P. (e) Finally, it is to be observed that on the one hand the pre-Exilic prophets, especially Jer. 7. 22, and, on the other, certain provisions in P itself (e.g. that con-cerning the rights of the High Priest, Num. 34. 17 ff. ; 35. 25, 28 ; in view of which there was no room for a king) absolutely exclude the idea that P can have been recognized in Jerusalem before the Exile as a Divine Law.

If the oath of allegiance to the law which was introduced by Ezra extended not merely to the Priestly Writing but to the older laws as well, the long interval between Ezra's arrival in 458 and the taking of the Covenant in 444 becomes intelligible. Ezra must soon have realized that in spite of the Royal authority which he had behind him an introduction of P in the place of the older law was impossible. He was accordingly obliged to combine the former with the latter, i.e. our Pentateuch is *the work of Ezra and his helpers.* None of the objections brought against this are valid. In particular, the difficulty raised about the shortness of the time for a reading aloud of the whole Pentateuch disappears in view of the wording of Neh. 8. 3, 8, 18 where it is merely said that Ezra read *from* the book, the Law of God, and it is distinctly suggested that there was a need for harmonizing, for interpretation. The heads of the community would certainly never have allowed their ancient law to be reft from them in favour of a mere innovation. This too explains how it is that there belonged to the original Priestly Writing an account of the division of the land which is still preserved in the Book of Joshua. Would it have been possible to excise this so soon, if the People had really taken an oath of allegiance to the whole Book ? And finally, it has justly been pointed out by Dahse in a recent work (*ut sup.*, p. 144 ff.) that in many verses and small sections of Genesis which have hitherto been assigned to P, we have to see simply a liturgical treatment by means of which the whole work was adapted by Ezra for reading at public worship, a theory which receives a remarkable confirmation if we read with the LXX in Neh. 8. 8 " and Ezra taught, and divided it into sections." (Dahse's attempt to divide up the whole of the Priestly Writing in this way breaks down in face of the long law-codes and lists, not to speak of many of the narrative portions.)

If P was brought from Babylon by Ezra in 458 B.C., it must have been written in Babylon before that, but later than 537, the year of the return of the first great company of exiles—say in round figures, about 500 B.C. In view of the veneration with which Ezra regards it, the probability is that it was not written by himself. The language of P is also in entire conformity with this date for the origin of the work, cf. Koenig, *Einleitung*, pp. 229 to 231. The solution of the much canvassed problem, so far as it has proceeded up to the present, has been mainly due to Reuss, Graf, Wellhausen, and Kuenen.

But now comes up a further problem. Whence, and from what period, did the *materials* of this writing originally come ? Only a quite small amount of preparatory work has been done on this problem. But the hypothesis has grown in probability from year to year that the whole representation of the history given by P is an Exi revision of a pre-Exilic historical book of priestly origin.

From Wellhausen onwards various scholars have sought to distinguish *three strata* in P : older priestly records, " Ph " ; a priestly writing containing both narrative and legislation, " Pg " ; and later additions, " Ps." *　But this division, though it appears to be sound—only that Pg needs to be worked out more definitely and freed from later additions (cf. Eichrodt, *ut sup.*, p. 51)—does not touch the heart of the difficulty.　Almost all the narrative material of P in Genesis is worked over—in part superficially, in part thoroughly—but a considerable portion of it is fundamentally as old as or older than that of J or E. The creation story still allows us to recognize its original basis in the Babylonian Creation Myth ; the underlying polytheism is still visible in 1. 26 and 9. 6 ; the " walking with God," 5. 24 ; 6. 9, 10 and the mythological number 365 (of the years of Enoch) and of the days of the duration of the Flood, 6-8, the Covenant rainbow, 9. 12 ff. ; the high antiquity of circumcision and the fact that it was common to the Ishmaelites also, 17 ; the " going up " of God, 17. 22 ; 35. 13 ; His appearing, 48. 3 ; Ex. 6. 3 ; the ancestral tomb, Gen. 23 ; 25. 9 ; 49. 29-32 ; 50. 12, 13 ; in particular the purchase of the burying-place from the Hethites, 23 (cf. on this Winckler, *Vorderasien im zweiten Jahrtausend*, 1913, p. 45 ff.), also the recording of the Divine Name *El Shaddai*—all this points to early pre-prophetic traditions.　And as the study of Oriental antiquity is showing us more and more clearly how early chronological construction and speculation are among the priesthood, and as the names in the genealogies so far as we can check them prove always to be appropriate to the earliest stage of the history of Israel, we are forced to the conclusion that we have to assume here a number of preliminary stages (are we to find the exordium of one of these in 5. 1 ?) and that the priestly historical record, out of which the historical narrative of P has developed, had attained to fixity at least as early as the period of the monarchy, for it is only on this hypothesis that Gen. 17. 6, 16 ; 35. 11 can be explained.　Cf. ZEAT, p. 54, and Eerdmans, *ut sup.*, I. and III. And Gressmann has lately shown that in Exodus and Numbers also, P often represents a tradition which is earlier than J and E (cf. his *Mose*, p. 241 *et al.*).

---

* " h " stands for *H*oliness legislation, " g " *G*roundwork, " s " *S*upplements.—Translator.

But, in addition to the narrative, the whole of the specialized cultural legislation is no creation out of nothing, but, in far the greater part, a *collection* and *codification* of laws and usages which were in force long before the Exile, some of them in Jerusalem, some of them in other national sanctuaries, but a collection made from new and self-consistent points of view.

So far it is only in regard to the Law of Holiness that a convincing argument has been worked out to show that P, in contrast with, if not in direct opposition to D, which was paramount in Jerusalem, is based upon other pre-Exilic codes of law (cf. 1 § 5*e*), but we may conjecture with a high degree of probability that the same thing has happened in other passages also. An attempt to prove this has been undertaken by Merx. He has endeavoured to show that as it is first in Lev. 1-7 that the designation " the sons of Aaron " is set alongside of " the Priests," so also " in the Court of the Tabernacle " is set alongside of " in the holy place," so that here too the ancient laws of the high-places are visible beneath the surface—cf. also 14 and 15 where, similarly, it is taken for granted that the priests are distributed throughout the land. But we must not stop there. Not only does the basis of Lev. 16 go back to the earliest phase of the religion of Israel (cf. 21 ff.) but the same is true of the core of the Nazirite law, Num. 6, and, indeed, of all the dietary laws and laws of purification, Lev. 11-15 (cf. Kittel, *Geschichte des Volkes Israel*, i. p. 50 f.; Bertholet, *Leviticus*, and recently Eerdmans *ut sup.*, III. and IV.). Nay, even in respect of the priestly garments, the Ephod, which is limited to the High Priest, was formerly the right of every higher or oracle priest; there is no material difference between the Ephod of Gideon of Ophrah and that of Aaron. It is only that its significance and the authorization to wear it, and perhaps some details of the ornamentation, have been changed (cf. Sellin, *Das israelitische Efod*). And the case is not otherwise as regards the legislation for sacrifices and feasts; everywhere we can see the old material showing through the later envelope (cf. *e.g.* in the case of the Feast of Tabernacles, Lev. 23. 34, 42, etc.).

Indeed, even in the point in which many have seen P's most original creation—the orientation of the whole law to the Tabernacle, and the description of it—we should probably see a return to a sound historical tradition which was only pushed aside for a time by the Temple of Jerusalem and the Deuteronomic code, and to which men's memories eagerly reverted when the Temple was polluted, and forsaken by God. This tradition was no doubt kept alive even during the Monarchy, in Gibeon-Mizpeh.

That the " ark of Yahweh " went back to the Mosaic era is now very generally recognized; it has only to be pointed out further that, if we might suppose that it remained for a rather extended period at Shechem, even P's designation of it as the " Ark of the Covenant " might well rest on an old tradition. But in the Tabernacle Wellhausen and others see only a reflection of the Temple, projected back—if the phrase may be allowed—into the wilderness-days. But those who make this assumption cannot really have thought out for themselves all that is implied in supposing that the Exilic priesthood based the whole system of Divine worship in the reorganized community upon a sanctuary which not merely was no longer in existence, but up to that time had never existed at all—not even in tradition! But that it did exist in tradition, far back into the pre-Exilic period, is put beyond all doubt by the evidence of 2 Sam. 7. 6 and the Elohist in Ex. 33. 1-11 (cf. also 18. 7, 13 f.); from the latter passage it follows immediately that this " Tent of Meeting " was held to be an independent oracle-tent (vv. 7-11) and to have been exceedingly richly ornamented with gold and other precious materials (33. 6). This verse is generally referred to the making of the *ark*, but wrongly, for in the first place this is against the context (v. 5), and in the second place the ark was not of gold but of wood (Deut. 10. 1). In P also, in Ex. 34. 29-35, the purpose of the Tabernacle is still preserved—it was intended to be a copy of the heavenly tabernacle (cf. the " Mount of Meeting " in Isa. 14. 13, also 33. 20). And we have perhaps further evidence for the historicity of this Tabernacle in Deut. 33. 12, cf. Sellin, ASt *Das Zelt Jahwes*, p. 168 ff., and Hartmann, *Zelt und Lade*, ZAW, 1917–18, p. 209-44.

It is true that David had set up a tent as the abiding-place of the ark, 2 Sam. 6. 17—incidentally a proof that, in spite of

Shiloh, the Tent-sanctuary was the normal form in ancient Israel—but it is never called the "Tent of Meeting." Where then could that tradition have its seat, and the ancient Tabernacle of Yahweh its abiding-place? That in David's time it had a special connection with *Gibeon* may be seen from 2 Sam. 21. 6 (read "on the Mount of Yahweh," cf. v. 11; 2. 12 ff. where we find that the question who should reign on the west of Jordan was decided at Gibeon) and above all 1 K. 3. 4 ff. Here, setting aside for the moment the question of the ark, is in any case the chief sanctuary of the whole country (v. $4a\beta$ is a Deuteronomistic gloss; cf. also Jos. 9. 23, 27?). How is that to be explained, seeing that the place was still Canaanitish? The only possible key is provided by 2 Chron. 1. 3, which critics have dismissed too easily. It is said that it is an afterthought intended to explain Solomon's offering of sacrifices at the High place by suggesting that the Tent of Meeting was here. But the same statement, quite independent of this narrative, occurs in the quite unsuspicious passage 1 Chron. 21. 29 f., and in the second place it is impossible to suppose that the chronicler invented the idea of a rival sanctuary to Jerusalem. After all he might simply have transferred to Jerusalem the scene of the festival on the occasion of Solomon's accession, cf. ZEAT, p. 55 ff. And the seal is set to this by 1 K. 1. 33, 38, 45, where it is clear that *Gib'on* originally stood in place of *Gihon* (cf. the prepositions in vv. 33 and 45, and especially v. 39); a Tabernacle of Yahweh at the brook Gihon would be an absurdity, and to translate by the pluperfect (*i.e. had* taken a horn of oil out of the Tabernacle) is a mere evasion of the difficulty. Adonijah's sacrificial feast would certainly last a full day—cf. 1 Sam. 25. 2-36; Ex. 32. 5 f., so that there would be plenty of time for the journey to Gibeon and back. For the "going down," cf. 1 K. 22. 2; Isa. 7. 1, and had the coronation taken place at the Spring of Gihon the actual shouts acclaiming Solomon king (v. 39*b*) would necessarily have been heard at the well of Rogel (v. 9), which lay only some 700 metres to the south of it.

In any case *it may be regarded as historically certain that the Oracle Tent really had its seat at Gibeon.* While, of course, during the desert journeyings the Tabernacle gave shelter to the ark, later on they became separated. The ark found its home in a ceiled house in Shiloh and, after long wanderings, in Jerusalem. As to the fate of the Tabernacle, after Solomon's day, we have no certain information, as the reference in 1 K. 8. 4 seems to be a gloss. But the tradition regarding it seems to have been preserved especially in the place associated with the later Elohistic tradition, in *Mizpah* near Gibeon, for to the Source which was probably composed here belong both Ex. 33. 1-11 and 2 Sam. 7. 6. (This place is now generally supposed to be at *Tell en Nasbe*, not on the *Nebi Samwil*, but the identification is still uncertain.) And in P, in which the " sons of Zadok " have had to give place to the much earlier and more comprehensive category of " the sons of Aaron," the Shiloh-Jerusalem stream of ark tradition and the Gibeonite stream of Tabernacle tradition have again flowed into one bed. The view of Wellhausen, which always assumed a single line of development, therefore needs drastic revision in this respect. The old opposition between it and the Dillmann view is to be resolved into a higher unity (cf. Kittel, *Geschichte*, ii. p. 525). Throughout, the author of P collected during the Babylonian Exile only old material, but impressed upon it the stamp of the new ideas ; above all, the theory of the absolute Aaronic Hierarchy, and the *motif* which connects the whole, the thought that everything from first to last must subserve the purpose of making Israel a holy nation, separate from all other peoples.

In this way we come to understand how Ezra, in spite of the recentness of the literary work which he brought with him, could believe and teach with all the energy of his nature that these were the ancient and holy statutes of the fathers of the race ; and how for him and those who thought with him the day of its introduction ranked as a great Day of Repentance, on which a whole people, after long wanderings, returned to the sources from which it originally drew all its life and strength.

§ 10. *The Origin of the Pentateuch in its present Form*

If the investigations pursued in §§ 6-9 have given approximately correct results, the combination into one whole of the Sources which we have examined as individual documents must have taken place by four clearly marked stages.

1. In the first place, the Yahwist and Elohist must obviously have been combined into a single work, JE. The union here must have been remarkably close, differing in this from the processes to be noticed under 3 and 4. Moreover— and this is not at present sufficiently taken into account—the process may well have been at the same time a creative one. Much that is now often ascribed to a J³ or E³ may have been the work of this redactor, which indeed can often be recognized by such obvious marks as "*Yahweh* thy *Elohim*," etc.

The most suitable date for this redaction would be the reign of Hezekiah; for just after the destruction of the Northern Kingdom in 722, when Judah could once more feel itself to be the spiritual leader of a united Israel and was making a special effort to concentrate all its religious powers, such a work would have had a natural motive. Moreover, this period was from a literary point of view an exceedingly fruitful one. That there was no need when making such a redaction to destroy the separate sources from which it was made is of course self-evident; we can indeed point to their existence hundreds of years later, cf. 2 *infr.*, and Judges, chap. 1.

2. Once Deuteronomy had been recognized, in the days of Josiah, as a Mosaic Law the desire must soon have been felt to go beyond the historical introduction which it possessed from the first and connect it up with the narratives of the earliest times. That was done in the first place, no doubt shortly before the Exile, by linking it with the Elohistic source which had the closer spiritual affinity with the Deuteronomist by assigning to the latter the place formerly occupied by the Book of the Covenant.

That what happened first was simply a *working-together of D with E* can be proved both on the ground of the close

interweaving of the two in Deut. 10. 6 f. ; 11. 29 f. ; 27. 2-26 ;
31. 9-30, and especially in the Book of Joshua, where, as
Procksch, *ut sup.*, 240 ff., has shown, all the Elohistic parts
have a strong Deuteronomistic colouring, while on the other
hand they are clearly distinguished from the later independent
Deuteronomistic passages like 1. 3 ff. ; 10. 28 ff. ; 11. 10 ff. ;
12. 1 ff. ; 23. 1 ff.   It is true the question cannot as yet be
answered with certainty whether the intention was to produce,
on the basis of Deuteronomy, only a book of the conquest of
the land—and therefore to use only those parts of the Elohist
which were important as giving the historic foundation of the
law and those that dealt with the occupation of the country—
or whether the whole Elohistic writing was worked up with
Deuteronomy.   In favour of the first alternative is Deut. 1—4. 4
which makes the impression of being the introduction to an independent book, a book, however, which, in view of 3. 18—20. 23
—cf. also 31. 7, 8—also proposed to narrate the story of the
Conquest.   In any case, however, it was in connection with
this redaction that the Book of the Covenant was removed
from the position which it first occupied in the last chapter
of the life of Moses, as the law which was to be given at
Shechem, and attached to the Horeb story, in order to make
room for Deuteronomy at the former point.   What easily
suggested the displacement was that E² at Ex. 24. 7 in the
Horeb scene spoke of a *Book* of the Covenant, whereas E¹ in
Ex. 24. 11 only spoke of the conclusion of a Covenant with a
sacrificial meal, and like J knew of Tables of the Law, 31. 18.
What E² means by the Book of the Covenant is, as appears
from 24. 4, the Ten Commandments, cf. 20. 1-17, which now
had to be placed before the ascent of Moses to God in the
Mount, Ex. 20. 18-21.

3. This redaction was followed by the working
up together of JE with ED during the Babylonian
Exile, during which a large part of the ancient
literature was subjected to revision and Deuteronomy was made the norm of all history, and in
which a great Deuteronomistic historical work,
beginning with Gen. 2. 46 and reaching down into
the Exile, came into being.   Of this we shall have
more to say at a later point (cf. II. A § 4 Appendix).

In Genesis this redactor abstained almost entirely from any interpolation. Only in Gen. 18. 17-19; 26. 5 has it been proposed to find a trace of his work. His interest begins only with the time of Moses. Ex. 12. 24-27; 13. 3-16; 19. 21-25 are new Deuteronomistic creations, and indeed in Ex. 4-24 his finger can be traced in many passages, cf. *e.g.* 20. 4*b*, 5; though it is easy to confuse these traces with JE. And, as has been mentioned under 2, there is no doubt about his substantial interpolations in the narrative of the Book of Joshua.

4. The last redaction has already been mentioned under § 9. It took the Priestly Writing as its basis and fitted JED into it. To begin with, the amalgamation was only carried down as far as the death of Moses, for it was as the *Torah* of Moses that the whole codex was put in circulation. And the principle of the redaction in the Book of Joshua is, as we shall see later, quite different. We may conjecture with a high degree of probability that the redaction down to the death of Moses was carried out under the direction of Ezra in the fourteen years which he spent in Jerusalem before the introduction of the Law. The Samaritans, about 430, took with them in their schism the Pentateuch in practically the form in which we now have it. No doubt even after this alterations were made in particular *pericopes*, as is shown especially by the divergent type of reading in the LXX, in which *e.g.* Ex. 37. 25-28 are missing and 35-40 seem only to have been inserted later by another hand, and in any case are in a completely different order from that of the MT.

In the foregoing paragraphs, 1-4, we have been considering the whole process of development as purely *literary*, and that is what up to the present has almost always been done. And of course to a certain extent it was so—the redactor and the diaskeuast were at work from early times in Israel. But now, in concluding the discussion, we must at least call attention to the fact that the problem of the origin of the Pentateuch can never be wholly solved on these lines. In the prevailing view it remains an enigma how it happened that, while in each case it must have been the aim of the later Source to supplant the earlier, in every case it failed to do so ; and similarly, that while in every case it must have been the intention of a redactor who combined two Sources to bring about the disappearance of the individual Sources, nevertheless the attempt was never successful even down to the final redaction which is associated with Ezra. And lastly, the question arises where, in the eighth and seventh centuries, we are to seek the public which read those repeated redactions. Did people really already read edifying literature—for that is what the Pentateuch, from the Elohistic stratum onwards, in large measure is—in their own homes ? These enigmas disappear if we adopt, in addition to the literary explanation, a rhetorico - liturgical explanation, and assume in addition to private readers the body of worshippers who heard it read in public. If we do that we can well imagine that the later source would be quite content to concede the right of the earlier to literary existence, and in the first place hear itself brought in by way of lecture and discourse, as a presentation, better adapted to the times, of the ancient history and the ancient conceptions of the Divine will. So far as its literary form went, therefore, it was simply set alongside of the other, sometimes, when possible, on the same roll ; but at divine service and in the hour of edification, it claimed the preference, until it in turn experienced the same fate at the hands of a younger rival. And only from the time of Ezra onwards did the whole of the historical and legislative literature which had been preserved in the " Book of the Torah " (Ex. 17. 14 ; 24. 4, 7 ; Deut. 29. 19 ; 31. 24) come to be regarded as of equal value for use in public worship.

The majority of scholars have not so much as perceived that there was a problem here at all, not to speak of making any attempt to solve it. It is only quite lately that a beginning has been seriously made in this direction, though earlier a few isolated scholars, like Klostermann, made an attempt to turn investigation into this channel, suggesting, to put it briefly, the hypothesis of a gradual crystallization of the Pentateuch. We saw in § 9 that the view of Dahse, according to which the introduction of P is to be conceived as a liturgical act, is to some extent confirmed by Neh. 8. 8, as well as by the character of P itself. And as we saw in § 8, D consists in part (chaps. 5-11) of purely hortatory matter, and the same applies to other Deuteronomic passages (*e.g.* Ex. 12. 24-27 ; 13. 3-16, etc.), which all make the impression of having at one time been read aloud in a direct allocution to the people. And the key is furnished by Deut. 31. 9 ff., in the regulation, which certainly dates from before the Exile, that the whole Law was to be read aloud at the Feast of Tabernacles.

But the custom was much older and of much more general application. In 1 Sam. 7. 16 ; 12. 7 ff., in a source which goes back to the eighth century, we have a reference to the free reproduction of the ancient law and the ancient history at the popular assemblies for worship. This tradition in fact represents Samuel as an itinerant orator appearing in turn at the ancient sanctuaries of Bethel, Gilgal-Shechem, and Mizpah. In the Elohistic discourse of Joshua at the popular assembly at Shechem this custom is simply taken for granted, Jos. 24. 1 ff. ; and 2 K. 4. 23 suggests that as early as the ninth century prophets observed it at Sabbaths and New Moons ; indeed " remembrance " was the principal feature of the worship of those days, cf. Deut. 5. 15 ; Isa. 1. 13 ; Micah 6. 5 f. Again, in § 7 we inferred from the character of the Elohistic narratives that these, in part at least, must have had their roots in edifying discourses delivered at the sanctuaries or in the schools. (The idea of the ancient history being narrated in public discourses in the post-Davidic period has been followed out still further by Jirku, *Die älteste Geschichte Israels im Rahmen lehrhafter Darstellungen*, 1917. Cf. *Theologie der Gegenwart*, 1917, pp. 199-203.)

If this view of ours is correct, the Pentateuch has grown gradually out of the Yahwistic source by way of constant new editions, which of course also added independently traditions new and old to the original materials. And this took place not merely through literary work carried out in private—this in many cases was a later stage—but in the open course of the religious life and public worship of Israel, during a history of some 600 years.

The Pentateuch forms the foundation for the whole edifice of Judaism. And for the Christian Church also it will always continue to be, on the one hand, the record of the Divine plan for the education of His people in the pre-Mosaic history and of the election and constitution of a people of God upon earth ; and on the other hand a collection of the legislation which was the outcome of the Mosaic religious institutions during a period of nearly a thousand years, and a record—conditioned of course by its historical development—of the holy Will of God towards man, and of the Law which " came in between " as a " schoolmaster to lead us to Christ " in order that thereafter " grace and truth " might the more gloriously abound, Rom. 5. 20 ; Gal. 3. 24, Joh. 1. 17.

II. The Prophets

Under the influence of the idea that the historical as well as the prophetic books were written by prophets (according to Baba Bathra, 14*b*, by Joshua, Samuel, and Jeremiah) the men who formed the collection of the Books of the Hebrew Old Testament placed these historical books, as " the Earlier Prophets," immediately before the prophetic writings proper, which they denominated " the Later Prophets."

A. The Earlier Prophets, or Historical Books

§ 1. *The Book of Joshua*

Hollenberg, *Die deuteronomischen Bestandteile des B.J.*, ThStKr, 1874, p. 462 ff. ; Budde, *Richter und Jos.*, ZAW, 1887, p. 96 ff. ; Albers, *Die Quellenberichte in Jos.*, 1891 ; Sellin, *Gilgal*, 1917.

The Book of Joshua tells the story of the Conquest of Canaan by Israel under the leadership of Joshua, and may be divided into the account of the actual conquest, 1-12, and that of the division of the territory, 13-21 ; with a conclusion, 22-24. It begins with the command to cross the Jordan, and ends with the death of Joshua after the completion of the Conquest, and after the law has once more been impressed upon the people, and the Covenant renewed, on the day of the national assembly at Shechem. The book nowhere professes to be written by Joshua, for 24. 26 refers only to 24. 2 ff. On the contrary, 9. 27 ; 15. 63 ; 19. 47 (cf. Jg. 18), and 24. 29 ff. show clearly that the author, or authors, lived long after the time of Joshua.

It is soon seen that this book, like the others we have examined, is not homogeneous, but has been produced by the working-together of several sources ; here, as in the others, there are a number of contradictions and doublets (cf. 8. 9 with 8. 12 ; 11. 21 f. with 15. 13 ff. ; 15. 63 with 18. 28 ; 23. 8 with 24. 14, and so forth). And a closer examina-

H

tion has shown that precisely the same sources are found here as in the Pentateuch ; and indeed the latter lead us to expect a continuation of this kind (cf. Ex. 13. 19 ; Num. 32. 16 ; Deut. 27. 4 ff., E ; Num. 14. 24, 30 ; 27. 4, P ; Deut. 1. 36 ff. ; 3. 18 ; 31. 7 f., D).

From the pen of the Deuteronomist come obviously 1. 3-9 ; 10. 28-43 ; 11. 10 ff. ; 12. 1-24 ; 23. 1-16, and his hand as redactor can be traced in 8. 33-35. To the Priestly Writing belongs, apart from short glosses, one strand in the history of the Conquest, which is found in 3 ; 4 ; 6 ; 7, and 9. 14, 15*b*, 17-21 ; while in the account of the division of the land, which occupies the "larger half" of the book, 13-21, it forms the general basis. The considerable portion which still remains over raises a very curious problem. That in the main we have here Elohistic material is certain, but none of the attempts to analyse the sources more minutely has led to generally accepted results.

One thing which is clear is that two different conceptions of the Conquest stand over against each other : the Yahwistic, according to which the division of the land took place before the invasion, the various tribes acted by groups or individually, and it was not at first found possible to drive out the Canaanites from the cities in the plains ; cf. 13. 13 ; 15. 13-19, 63 ; 16. 10 ; 17. 11-13, 16-18 ; 19. 47 (Joshua is known to it, though he has not the same prominence as in the other, 17. 16-18, cf. Jg. 1. 22*b* original text ; 2. 23) ; and the Elohistic, according to which Joshua, who plays the part almost of a second Moses, at the head of the Tribes, overthrows with the aid of Divine miracles, in the course of seven years (14. 10, cf. Deut. 2. 14), the twelve Kings of the Amorites (24. 12), and thus, in the main (14. 12, cf. Jg. 3. 1), has in that period taken possession of the whole country. It is thus evident that the interweaving of the two sources by JE, after the fashion of the Pentateuch, cannot have been a very easy matter. That in spite of this it has been attempted is certain (cf. 11. 18-20), but the redaction quite predominantly followed E. Indeed it is questionable whether in 2—11 any traces of J are to be found. Lately Gressmann has claimed to find here the J strand constantly alongside of the E strand (SAT II. p. 127 ff.), while Smend has further tried to prove the presence of a continuous strand of J[2].

But what is more important and more certain—for these hypotheses are rendered very questionable by Jg. 1—is that in these chapters we can still distinguish the *two Elohistic* strata from one another. The break in the Elohistic narrative which we now find before 8. 30 points to the fact that this verse must at one time have come immediately after 5. 30. From this follows that the account of the taking of Jericho and Ai, 6. 1—8. 29, and in connection therewith also chapter 2, as well as one of the strands of narrative in 3 and 4, must have been interpolated into the older Elohistic account. And this later stratum reveals itself by its language and spirit as belonging to E[2]; it makes the Gilgal near Shechem into the Jordanic Gilgal. As, further, it can be shown that 24. 1, 23-27 was once most closely connected with 8. 30 ff., the older Elohistic narrative may be recognised, with considerable probability, in the following passages: 1. 1 f., 10 f.; 3. 1, 5, 14, 16; 4. 4, 5, 7*b*, 19, 20; 5. 2, 3, 8, 10*a*, 11, 12*a*; 5. 13-15; 8. 30, 31; 24. 1, 23, 24, 25; 8. 32; 24. 26*b*, 27; 8. 33, 34; 24. 32; 9. 3-6, 11-13, 15, 16, 22-27; 10. 1-13, 15; 11. 1-9, 20; 14. 6-14; 17. 14, 15; 18. 2-10; 19. 49-50; 24. 29, 30 (cf. *Gilgal*, pp. 28-60). On the other hand, we find E[2] in chapter 2, in one of the strands of 3 and 4 (probably 3. 9-13, 15; the last two words of 3. 16; 3. 17-4. 2; 4. 8, 10-14; the last three words of 4. 19); in 6. 1—8. 29, so far as this passage is not derived from D and P, 10. 16-39 (?); 24. 2-22, 28. It is, however, often difficult to detach this stratum cleanly, because it is in many places very closely combined with D (cf. Procksch, *ut sup*. 243). We are forced to fall back upon the explanation already mentioned in § 10, that there the Exilic Deuteronomistic redactor of the history of Israel had before him not only the earlier amalgamation of J and E, but also a later, produced from E and D, and that he naturally as a rule preferred the latter. The almost entirely Elohistic chapter 24, which records the (now the *second*) Farewell Discourse of Joshua, the (now the *second*) making of the Covenant in Shechem, and Joshua's death, was discarded, or, it may be, put in brackets (cf. also Jg. 2. 6, where Joshua is still living) by this redactor in favour of a Farewell Discourse composed by himself, chap. 23, and

the narrative of the reading of the Law at Shechem (8. 33-35).
In the post-Exilic period, however, the chapter was again
inserted by the latest redactor (like Jg. 17-21; 2 Sam. 9-24,
cf. §§ 2 and 3) as being considered well adapted for reading
at public worship.

The essential point is that this redactor, as we saw in the
purely Yahwistic sections of the list of the divisions of the
land which have been cited above, had before him, in addition to all the previous redactions, the sources J and E still in
separate form; for he took certain excerpts straight from these.
Fortunately, however, the material which he had before him
has been preserved to a considerable extent in Jg. 1. Cf. § 2.

In regard to the redaction of the Book of Joshua
which put it as a whole into the form in which we
now have it, all that can be said is that it must
have taken place soon after that of the Pentateuch.
Had the Hexateuch as a whole been produced by
this redaction, the Samaritans would necessarily
have taken over the Book of Joshua as well as the
Pentateuch. Moreover, in the Pentateuch P is
constantly the basis; in the Book of Joshua only in
13-21, not elsewhere. Finally, there are certain
linguistic peculiarities which are common to the
Pentateuch as a whole but not to Joshua (הִיא f.
used of both sexes; הָאֵל f. הָאֵלֶּה; יְרִחוֹ f. יְרֵחוֹ). The
final redaction must therefore be placed between
430 and 400 B.C.

§ 2. *The Book of Judges*

Stade, *Zur Entstehungsgeschichte des vordeut. Richterbuches*,
ZAW, 1881, p. 399 ff.; Budde, *Die Bücher Richter und Samuel*,
1890; Frankenberg, *Die Komposition des deut. Richterb.*, 1895;
Kittel, *Geschichte des Volkes Israel*, II., 1909, pp. 3-24; Thilo, *Die
Chronologie des A.T.*, 1917.

The Book of Judges in its present form falls into
three parts. An Introduction, 1.1—2.5, narrates

how (after the death of Joshua, Jos. 24) the tribes of Israel (Benjamin, Issachar and the trans-Jordanic Tribes are not mentioned) took possession, singly or in groups, of the districts which had been allotted to them by the oracle, though without being able to expel the Canaanites from their towns, at least in the plains.   The Book of Judges proper— after a foreword (2. 6—3. 6) which casts a glance over the whole period of the Judges and connects with the day of the national assembly at Shechem —relates in detail the deeds of five heroes, Ehud, Barak, Gideon, Jephthah and Samson, and more summarily those of seven others, Othniel (3. 7-11), Shamgar (3. 31), Tola and Jair (10. 1-5), Ibzan, Elon and Abdon (12. 8-15),—in all, therefore, of twelve *Judges*.   Closely connected with the Barak story is Jg. 5, Deborah's song of triumph over the defeat of the Canaanites near Taanach, one of the earliest and most valuable monuments of Israelitish poetry, while with the story of Gideon goes that of Abimelech's usurpation of the tribal headship and his destruction of Shechem, in chapter 9.   Finally, the supplementary chapters 17-21 describe two important episodes from the time of the Judges— 17-18 the founding of a sanctuary in the newly conquered territory of Dan by the appropriation of the sacred objects from an Ephraimite private sanctuary in the house of a man named Micah, and 19-21 the shameful deed at Gibeah, the vengeance exacted for it from the Benjamites, and the means by which the remnant of these were provided with wives by the carrying off of the women of Shiloh.

The main portion, 2. 6–16. 31, is seen to be a book recounting the stories of six Judges (Othniel,

Ehud, Barak, Deborah, Gideon, Jephthah, Samson), edited by a *Deuteronomistic* writer in the time of the Exile.

When this main portion is analysed, it is possible to detach from the narrative matter proper a kind of external envelope, which must be due to a later redactor. This is distinguished both by its language and its dominant ideas from the stories themselves. It is to be recognised especially by the designation of the various tribal heroes as *Judges* over the whole people, *i.e.* righters of wrong, deliverers of the people—a designation of which the narratives know nothing (with the exception of 4. 4, where we have the feminine in the sense of one who delivers judgement); by a chronological scheme into which the narratives are fitted (3. 11, 30; 4. 3, etc.), and, finally, by the constant representation of the national calamities as a punishment for the repeated worshipping of other gods, especially Baals and Astartes. It is characterised, in short, by a consistently carried out religious pragmatism, the theme of which is set forth in 2. 6-21, cf. 3. 7, 12, 15; 4. 1 ff.; 6. 1 ff.; 8. 33 ff.; 13. 1. This redaction from a later religious point of view is couched in the language, and applies the standards, of Deuteronomy. We may therefore describe 2. 6-16. 31 as a Deuteronomistic Book of Judges, which in the main would seem to have received its form during the Babylonian Exile.

Arguing from the chronological scheme, Wellhausen and others have pointed out, and doubtless justly, that this book did not as yet contain the Abimelech story, chap. 9—for this lacks the customary connecting formula, the place of which is taken by 8. 33-35—and the so-called minor Judges 3. 31; 10. 1-5; 12. 8-15. For these destroy the scheme of 1 K. 6. 1, which is otherwise remarkably consistent—the 480 years (12 generations) which the Deuteronomist reckoned as intervening between the flight from Egypt and the building of the Solomonic Temple. What has happened here is evidently interpolation, at a later date, but making use of stories of Heroes of the time of the Judges, with a view to making up the number of the Judges to twelve.

But this Deuteronomistic Book of Judges is based upon two *collections* of much older *Hero-stories* which have been worked up together; and

in these we have probably to recognise the Pentateuch Sources J and E.

The *Hero-stories* as recorded by the Deuteronomist are not
generally literary unities but lie before us in a dual version.
In the Ehud story the audience is twice narrated, 3. 19 and 20,
and similarly Ehud's escape, v. 26 *a* and *b* ; in chapter 4 a story
of Jabin (King of Hazor, v. 17*b*) and a Sisera story have been
worked up together, the latter, however, much preponderating,
while it, again, diverges in some details from the Song of
Deborah, which doubtless dates from nearer the events (cf. 4. 21
with 5. 25 f.).   The different traditions are particularly clear
in the case of the Gideon story, where 6. 2-6, 11-24, 34 ; 8. 4-21
belong to the one, and 6. 7-11, 25-32, 36-40 ; 7. 1–8. 3 ; 8. 22-27
to the other.   In the Abimelech story, too, critics have held
it possible to distinguish the double strand (9. 7-20, 23-25,
42-45, 56 f., and 26-33, 34-40, 46-49).   In the Jephthah story,
again, the double tradition is undeniable.   In the one we have
a chief who is first banished and then returns, who frees his
land from the Ammonites and later smites Ephraim, 10. 7, 17,
18 ; 11. 1-11, 29, 33*b* ; 12. 1-6 ; in the other, he lives in Mizpah,
and smites the Amalekites, and before the battle has made his
disastrous vow, 11. 12-28, 30-33*a*, 34-40.   The Samson story
is generally held to be a unity.   It is worth considering, however, whether we have not in chapter 13 traces of two lines
of tradition, which are harmonised in vv. 8 and 9 (cf. vv. 5*a*, 12,
which do not agree with the context), and whether, further,
14. 1–15. 20 is not to be considered a doublet of 16. 4-31.   In
the one case it would be the spirit of Yahweh which always
descends upon Samson, in the other the influence of his
Nazirite vow ; in the one we have an unnamed Philistine woman,
in the other Delilah.   Cf. the use of the same concluding
words in 15. 20 and 16. 31.   (In this case 16. 1-3 would be an
independent parallel to 16. 23-30.)

In view of the above phenomena it was a natural step to
refer back the dual tradition to the two Hexateuch sources
J and E.   That has been done especially by Budde and Cornill.
Kittel prefers the symbols H and H¹, but in large sections of
these, H^J and H^E, he admits a close relationship with J and E.
For neither source, however, is the matter quite simple.   While
E in Joshua 24 closes with the sonorous ring of a peroration,
J in Judges 1 absolutely compels us to expect a further
narrative of struggles with the Canaanites.   But obviously
in the case of a document in regard to which we have already,

in I. § 7, seen reason to assume a later revision, there is no great difficulty in assuming a later supplement. And in fact the preface to the Deuteronomistic Book of Judges (2. 6—3. 6) is based, unless all indications deceive, on some verses of J and E which show that the stories of the Heroes which are to follow had already been brought partly under the Yahwistic point of view of learning the arts of war from the Canaanites (2. 23; 3. 2), partly under the Elohistic point of view of the religious " proving " of Israel (2. 22; 3. 1). And, above all, the narratives themselves bear in many places the characteristic marks of one or other of these sources. That applies especially to 6. 2-6, 11-24; 10. 17—11. 11; 13. 2-24 (Yahwistic), and 6. 7-10, 25-32, 36-40; 8. 22-27a; 9. 7-20, 50 f.; 10. 10-16; 11. 12-28 (entirely theocratic—pragmatic—Elohistic, cf. the mention of *prophets* in 4. 4; 6. 8). The argument brought against the identification by Kittel and others, that the narratives are obviously in many cases much older than the J and E documents, is sound, so far as the facts are concerned, but not as regards the inference; for exactly the same is true as regards J and E in the Pentateuch.

That the Introduction, 1. 1–2. 5, is in the main from the Yahwistic Source is now admitted with practical unanimity.

The reason for thinking so is that Judah stands throughout in the foreground; moreover, several passages from this chapter are found almost word for word in Jos. 15-17, clearly distinguishable there from the Elohistic parts. The redactor of JE had been unable to use the remainder because of the discrepancy of the Sources; the redactor of our present Book of Judges, however, placed it after the death of Joshua, and was obliged therefore to suppress this at 1. 22, where it certainly once stood (cf. the variant in the LXX; 2. 23 and Jos. 17. 14 f.). The torso 2. 1a, 5, which has been worked over by the Deuteronomist, is almost universally held to be Yahwistic; it is, however, probably Elohistic, since, if in v. 1 *Bethel* is to be read with LXX, it is absolutely incompatible with the Yahwistic section 1. 22-26, and in E in the Book of Joshua the taking of Bethel is missing (cf. Gen. 35. 1, 5-8; also Ex. 23. 20 ff.; 33. 2). And it also presupposes the idea of the people going forward unitedly; that is the Elohistic idea. It stood therefore originally between Joshua 8 and 9 (cf. my *Gilgal*, pp. 40-42).

The supplements to the Book, 17-21, are woven together from two Sources (perhaps in this case also J and E) ; they were again attached after the Exile to the Deuteronomistic Book or, to put it otherwise, they were again permitted to be read at public worship.

In 17 and 18, the narrative of the transference of the idol worship from Micah's house to Dan, the double thread is very obvious.   For, while both represent the private sanctuary as resulting from a theft (for the restitution of the money is twice related, vv. 3 and 4), one Source makes the curse which attached to it turn into a blessing (vv. 2b, 3a, 13), whereas the other simply makes it work itself out.   The one places a graven image and a molten image in the sanctuary (vv. 3b, 4b, etc.), the other an Ephod and Teraphim (v. 5 ff.) ; the one represents it as served by a young Levite (vv. 9, 12 f.), the other by a wandering Judaean (vv. 7a, 8) ; according to the one the Danites steal the Ephod (18. 16 f.), according to the other they persuade the priest to go with them (18. 20 ; cf. also 18. 30 and 31). The attribution of these to J and E respectively is less certain than in the rest of the Pentateuch, but affords the best available hypothesis.   The Deuteronomist omitted the narrative—which is of great importance from the religious-historical point of view, and is intended essentially, in both versions, to pour contempt upon the Danite sanctuary—because it did not really belong to the Story of the Judges ; the final redactor of the whole Book has fortunately reinserted it.

The same applies to 19-21.   Here, too, we are constantly meeting with doublets (cf. 19. 11 and 12), and, above all, the religious centre is at one time Bethel (cf. 20. 18, 23, 26 ; 21. 2), at another Mizpeh (20. 1 ; 21. 1, 5, 8).   The latter Source, as we shall see in § 3, is very probably the Elohistic.   But here, not only have the two Sources been worked up together, and that when the monarchy was still flourishing (cf. 17. 6 ; 18. 1 ; 19. 1 ; 21. 25), but after the destruction of the Northern Kingdom in 734 or 722 B.C. (cf. 18. 30) ; which would fit well enough for the redactor of JE under Hezekiah, but in chapters 20 and 21 there is to be observed in addition to this a midrashic expansion by the hand of the post-Exilic redactor, which in the first narrative is only to be traced in 18. 31 ; cf. 20. 2 f., 10, 15, 17, 21, 25, 27, etc.   Nöldeke has rightly conjectured that

the story of the shameful deed of Gibeah, to which Hos. 9. 9;
10. 9, also makes allusion, has its roots ultimately in the hatred
for the House of Saul, which was of Gibean origin, caused by
the massacre of Nob, 1 Sam. 22. 18, or of Gibeon, 2 Sam. 21. 1
(cf. the way Bethlehem is brought in in 19. 1 ff. with 1 Sam.
22. 8, 13, and Jabesh Gilead in 21. 6-14 with 1 Sam. 31. 11-13;
2 Sam. 2. 5-7). But in spite of that Nöldeke was doubtless right
in assuming a historical kernel (cf. esp. 21. 15-23).

The general outline of the origin of the Book of
Judges is therefore the following. (1) J and E
describe, each from its own special point of view
and making use of earlier Hero-stories, how God,
on the one hand, strengthened Israel by its wars
with other nations, and, on the other hand, tested it
by these and gave it miraculous aid in time of
need. (2) JE worked up the two together, probably
dropping Jg. 1. 1–2. 5. (3) The Deuteronomist
worked up a Book of Judges consisting of 2. 6–
15. 20, or 16. 31, on the basis of JE, but had no use
for chapters 9 and 17-21, as not dealing with the
Judges. (4) A redactor in the post-Exilic period
prepared our present Book of Judges, taking
chapter 1 from the Yahwistic narrative which still
existed in separate form, placing it after the death
of Joshua, and using it as an Introduction (the
kernel of 2. 1-5 came, along with Jos. 24. 23-27, 32,
from Jos. 8, at the end of the activities of Joshua,
cf. § 1), re-inserted the Abimelech story, chap. 9,
brought up the number of the Judges, by using
old materials, to twelve, appended chapters 17-21,
which must have been still current, and expanded
them in midrashic style.

In accordance with the explanations given in I. § 10, we
have to reckon as before with the possibility that the origin
of the Book of Judges is in part to be explained by the custom
of reading aloud at public worship and in schools. That is

to say, E would represent the form in which the Hero-stories of J were given at public worship at the sanctuaries of Shechem or Bethel, or perhaps Mizpeh, in the eighth or ninth centuries B.C., while D would represent the form adapted to edification, in which the whole of this material for public reading (with the exception of a few extracts which were bracketed off) was worked up and expanded in the sixth or seventh centuries at Jerusalem, or, it may be, in Babylon.

§ 3. *The Books of Samuel*

Budde, *Die Bücher Richter und Samuel*; Cornill, ZAW, 1890, p. 96 ff.; Baentsch, *David und seine Zeitalter*, 1907; Kittel, *Geschichte des Volkes Israel*, II. pp. 24-45; Koenig, *Geschichte des Reiches Gottes*, 1908, p. 198 ff.; Luther, *Die Novelle von Juda und Tamar, ut sup.* pp. 175-206; Caspari, *Literarische Art und historischen Wert von 2 Sam. 15-20*, ThStKr, 1909, p. 317 ff.; Steuernagel, *Die Weissagung über die Eliden (1 Sam. 2. 27-36)*, ASt, 1913, pp. 204-21.

That these books are not derived from Samuel is self-evident, for Samuel dies in 1 Sam. 25. The principal personage in them is David, and the LXX is therefore more correct in designating them the First and Second Book of Kings.

They begin with a fragment from the story of Samuel's childhood, 1 Sam. 1-3, then take up the thread of the history at the point where it was broken off in Jg. 16, during the wars with the Philistines, narrate the subjugation of Israel by them and the loss of the Ark, 4-6, the preparing of the way for the liberation by Samuel, 7, the completion of it by the chosen King, Saul, his reign down to his rejection, 8-15, the relations of Saul and David, 16-31; then they describe how after Saul's death a Judaean tribal kingdom arose under David in Hebron, 2 Sam. 1. 1–5. 5, and finally, in great detail, the reign of David over all Israel, 5. 6–20. 26. At the close follow supplements

containing lists, poems and narratives belonging to
the period, 21-24.

From 1 Sam. 7—2 Sam. 1 there runs, as has been
shown especially by Wellhausen, Cornill, Budde and
Kittel, a double thread, which is easily distinguishable, especially by the dual attitude towards Saul's
kingship. This justifies us in assuming, to begin
with, a working-together within these chapters of
two Sources, one of which we can follow with
certainty to the end of the book, while we find
throughout occasional traces of the other.

That the main part of the Books of Samuel is not from a
single Source is obvious from the following undeniable doublets.
There are two accounts of the origin of the saying " Is Saul
among the prophets ? " (1 Sam. 10. 10-12 ; 19. 18-24) ; two
accounts of the coming of David to the Court of Saul (16. 14-23
and 17. 12-58, where, however, the LXX offers a considerably
shorter recension and one more in accordance with what
precedes) ; two accounts of Saul's rejection (13. 8-15 and 15
10-26) ; two, of David's flight from Saul (20. 4-10, 12-17, 24-34,
and 20. 1-3, 11, 18-23, 35-42) ; two, of David's sojourn among
the Philistines (21. 10-15 and 27. 1 ff.) ; two, of the treachery of
the Ziphites, 23. 19-28 and 26. 1 ff. ; two, of the sparing of Saul's
life by David (24 and 26) ; two, of the death of Goliath (1 Sam.
17. 1 ff. and 2 Sam. 21. 19—in the latter he is slain by a man
named Elhanan) ; two accounts of Saul's death (1 Sam. 31. 4
and 2 Sam. 1. 10) ; two, of Absalom's children (2 S. 14. 27 f.
and 18. 18), and so forth.

But the best starting-point for a critical analysis is afforded
by the two accounts of the choice of a king. It is now universally
admitted that two Sources are here involved. According to
one, which we may name provisionally K (1 Sam. 9. 1—10. 16 ;
11. 1-11, 15), the Ephraimite *Seer*, Samuel himself, under the
Divine guidance, gives the impulse towards the choosing of
Saul, which is to become the occasion of the deliverance of
Israel from the Philistines ; the choice is confirmed by the
brilliant campaign of Saul against the Ammonites, and is
consummated in *Gilgal* (of course the Gilgal near Shechem, cf.
Jg. 9. 6 ; 1 K. 12. 1). According to the other version, which
we may call K¹ (1 Sam. 8 ; 10. 17-25*a* ; 12), the Philistines

have already been defeated; Samuel, the *Judge* of all Israel, is forced by the people against his will to give them a king, and the choosing of a king is made to appear an act of apostasy from God, who merely, in anger, permits the institution of the kingship, and in *Mizpeh*, through the casting of lots, directs the choice to Saul. 10. 25*b*-27 and 11. 12-14 are harmonistic attempts to combine the two accounts (10. 27, however, stood originally after 11. 15 and belonged to the Source K; cf. 2 Sam. 20. 1). Having distinguished the Sources here, we can then follow them out both in the backward and forward direction.

The Source K[1], which only gives a conditional recognition to the kingdom and rejects the kingship of Saul, may be delimited with some degree of confidence as follows: 1 Sam. 1-3; a strand of the narrative in 4-6; 7. 2-17; 8; 10. 17-25*a*; 12; 15; 17. 1–18. 5; 18. 6-30 †; 19; 20 †; 21 †; 23. 1-13 †, 14-18; 26; 28. 3-25; 2 Sam. 1. 6-10, 14 ff. The other, the Source K, which hails the kingdom as a blessing from God, consists of: one strand of the narrative in 1 Sam. 1-3 and 4-6; the whole of 9. 1–10. 16; 11. 1-11, 15; 13. 2-6, 15-23; 14. 1-46, 52; 16. 14-23; 18 †; 20 †; 22; 24; 25; 27-31 (with the exception of 28. 3-25); 2 Sam. 1. 17–6. 23; 9-20. And, in the supplementary portions, 21. 1-14, 15-22; 23. 8-39; 24 † and 1 K. 1 and 2. But neither Source is a unity in the sense that it can have been written down at first in the form in which we now have it. On the contrary, they have both taken up into themselves ancient materials from different Sources and of very various kinds.

1 Sam. 8 in K[1] presupposes 7. 5, 6 ff., 15-17, and these passages again presuppose one stratum of 4-6. That there is a doubling here is at once obvious from the alternation of the "ark of Yahweh," 4. 6; 5. 3, 4; 6. 1–7. 1, with the "ark of Elohim" in 4. 11; 4. 13–5. 2; 5. 10. The division cannot, it must be confessed, be clearly made everywhere; Steuernagel

indeed has lately entirely denied it. Again, this Source, in which Samuel appears as the Judge of the whole people, pre-supposes as an introduction to it chapters 1-3, where we are told how this came to be (but Steuernagel has made it probable that in these chapters also there is a strand of K in 2. 12-17, 22-25, 30-33). But in general the difference of opinion among scholars refers to particulars, not to the whole. That we think we can find traces of K^1 extending beyond 2 Sam. 1, to 7 ; 12 ; 24 and 1 K. 3, and why we think so, we shall see later.

A question which arises *in limine* is : What are we to think as to the character of the Sources thus distinguished—were they in any sense at all *literary units* ? Since three different men, Samuel, Saul and David, divide the interest, and since 2 Sam. 9-20 introduce us into the most intimate circumstances of the Davidic Court, the most obvious hypothesis was to assume three, or perhaps four, biographies (so, *e.g.*, Kittel, *Geschichte der Hebräer*, II.). But this hypothesis has not proved to be tenable. In both the recensions indicated above, the story of David interlocks so directly with that of Saul (cf., in K, 14. 52, which is closely connected with 16. 14 ff. ; and in K^1, 17. 2 ff.), and similarly the story of Saul dovetails into that of Samuel (cf., in K, 9. 14 ff., where Samuel appears as one who has long been known ; in K^1, 8. 1 ff.) in such a way, that we have rather to assume continuous histories (so too, now, Kittel himself).

But at the same time we must not assume that these histories were written, to begin with, as straightforward, continuous narratives. Both authors worked upon older material which came to them from various quarters. Let us look first at K^1. 1 Sam. 4—6 does not mention Samuel at all, and is therefore originally unconnected with 7. 2 ff., as also with chapters 1-3 ; it is therefore no doubt taken from a history which was once specially concerned with the ark (as was also, perhaps, 2 Sam. 6), while the other passages just mentioned belong to a biography of Samuel on a considerable scale, in which was no doubt explained, what we do not now learn, viz., how Samuel came from Shiloh to Mizpeh, or Ramah, and the descendants of Eli to Nob. Earlier material can be detected also in the narrative of the rejection of Saul, 1 Sam. 15, and Saul's visit to the witch of Endor, 28. 3-25. In both cases Samuel is not the administrator of justice to the tribes and their intercessor with God, as elsewhere in the Source, but a prophet, with definite messages for the King, and a zealot in the cause of Yahweh. In both cases there is doubtless a historical kernel.

(Budde proposes to assign the latter passage to K; but not only the unsuitable position of it, after 28. 3 instead of after 30. 31, but also the mention of dreams in 28. 16, 17 f., and of prophets in 28. 6, and above all—a point overlooked by Budde—the antagonism, common to this story and K[1], to the sin of divination (cf. 15. 23 with 28. 3 ff.), are decidedly in favour of regarding it as an interpolation from K[1]. But Budde is doubtless right in the conjecture that this chapter, like 15, was removed by D, and later restored again.) But, finally, all this varied material is bound together by the theocratic point of view common to them all, viz. that God by His living instruments the prophets is the immediate Leader of His People, and that it is His will to remain so. For this reason I am inclined to see the same Source in all those passages, even subsequently to the death of Saul, in which this conception meets us; namely, 2 Sam. 7. 1-28 (with the exception of v. 13), the promise through the prophet Nathan; 12. 1-15, his rebuke of David; 24. 11b-15a, the coming of the prophet Gad; similarly 1 K. 3. 4-13. (The friendly attitude of the first and last of these passages towards David's kingship is no reason for thinking of another author than K[1]; a king who allows his footsteps to be guided by prophets, as David does here, is exactly the ideal of K[1]. Cf. 1 Sam. 12. 14, also 10. 24, and, on the other hand, 2 Sam. 7. 15.) Budde has shown in detail how strongly in all these passages, in some cases the context and in others the language, support the claim of K[1]. (For 1 Kings 3. 4 ff. this is evidenced by the dream at a sanctuary. Cf. 2 Sam. 3. 2 ff.; Gen. 28. 11 ff. E, also the whole of the diction and the representing of Gibeon near Mizpeh as a most important place for the offering of sacrifices.)

The Source K makes a decidedly more definite impression than K[1]. But here, too, the assumption that the work is all of one piece, conceived once for all as a whole, would be entirely wrong. Quite apart from the fact that the introductory passages which belong to it in chapters 4-6 are of a different origin from what follows, even from 9 onwards, what we have is no *original unity*. When Saul in 13. 3 ff. is found to have a grown-up son, the original authority which thus pictures him cannot be the same as that of 9. 1—10. 16, where he is represented as a young man living in the house of his father, and so forth. In recent times Gressmann, Luther and Caspari have endeavoured to resolve this large complex into its primary elements in the form of legends, romances, folk-tales, anecdotes and even jests; and the last-named writer has carried the process into the section 2 Sam. 13-20, hitherto regarded as an absolute unity, proposing to distinguish two independently composed stories, 13 ; 14 and 15-20 (in the latter case certainly, it seems to me, without real ground ; for the starting-point, 14. 25-27, is an interpolation). In addition to whatever material of this kind the author had before him, he certainly had at his disposal lists such as that of Saul's children in 1 Sam. 14. 49-51, of the Court officials in 2 Sam. 8. 16-18, and of David's mighty men in 2 Sam. 23. 24-39 ; and annals, etc. (cf. 2 Sam. 21. 15 ff.). But nevertheless all this is now combined under the influence of a single purpose and spirit into a continuous historical work based on the fundamental conception that by means of the kingship Israel has been delivered out of the hand of her enemies, that David in spite of all his sins and weaknesses was the chosen and favourite of Yahweh, and that through him and his House Israel was brought to its Divinely destined place in history. Cf. 1 Sam. 9. 16 ; 11. 15 ; 16. 18 ; 18. 7, 28 ; 20. 15, 31 ; 24. 21 ; 2 Sam. 3. 9 f., 18 ; 5. 2, 12 ; 6. 21 ; 21. 17 ; 2 K. 2. 45. But in practically every respect, language and point of view, objectivity of description and vividness of presentation, the relationship between all the different sections assigned to this Source is so close, and the marks of junction have been so nearly obliterated, that we are obliged to think of a single hand as having ultimately combined them.

The Source K^1 is certainly *earlier* than Deuteronomy and *later* than K. Conjecturally we may assign it to a date about 800 B.C., and its local origin may be sought in the Judah-Benjamin *milieu* of Gibeon and Mizpeh.

While Wellhausen and Stade proposed to assign all the passages belonging to K^1 to the Deuteronomic or post-Deuteronomic period, we owe to Cornill, Budde and Kittel the result, now accepted with practical unanimity, that the Source is to be regarded as pre-Deuteronomic. Jer. 15. 1 alludes to 1 Sam. 7 and 12 ; the real hero of the Book, Samuel, is an Ephraimite, not a Levite ; the cultual usages of 7. 5 ff., 17, are quite un-Deuteronomic ; 8. 10 ff. is prior to Deut. 17, not *vice versa* ; 2 Sam. 7 is essentially a polemic against the Jerusalem Temple ; language and ideas are different from those of Deuteronomy, and, on the other hand, have the closest affinities with those of the Elohist and Hosea.

That, on the other hand, the Source is later than K is equally generally recognized ; it departs much more freely than the latter from the historical events, and is frankly history with a purpose. On the ground of the literary affinities just mentioned, it is usual to place it in the second half of the eighth century—in any case later than Hosea. But in view of the small extent of the literature which is available for comparison, the fact that many of the phrases and ideas of K[1] are found elsewhere first in Hosea, by no means proves that they were not previously in existence. The polemic against the kingship which the Source represents is much earlier (cf. Ahijah of Shiloh, and Elijah). Moreover, the Samuel of this Source shows no traces of the preacher of penitence and judgement such as Amos and Hosea were. Both in the positive and the negative demands of the Samuel of the Source the characteristic *motifs* of these prophets are conspicuously absent (love, etc., rejection of the worship of idols). The Samuel of 1 Sam. 15 and 28 has his prototype above all in Elijah, and the Samuel of 7, 8 and 12 is much more like the Elisha who journeys from place to place, regulates politico - religious affairs, anoints kings, 2 K. 9. 12, and makes intercession, 2 K. 4. 33 ; 6. 15, so that we may well seek among the pupils of the latter—such as they actually were, and not as legend represented them—the origin of the Source from which, it must be remembered, Hosea directly quotes, assuming that Hos. 13. 10*b* is genuine. (Cf. 1 S. 8. 6 ; and 1 S. 15. 22 f. is obviously earlier than Hos. 6. 6.) For its provenance we are almost obliged by 7. 5 ff., 16 ; 10. 17, 25 ; 1 K. 3. 3 to look to the prophetic circle associated with Gibeon and Mizpeh. It was there that, according to 2 Sam. 21. 1 ff. (cf. also 1 Sam. 22. 6 ff.) hatred against Saul was, so to speak, traditional, cf. Jg. 20. 1 ; 21. 1, which belong to the same Source, and—a further surprising confirmation—it is just the place, as being the seat of the oracular Tabernacle of 2 Chron. 1. 3, from which we should expect such a polemic against the Temple as 2 Sam. 7.

In regard to the Source K greater unanimity prevails. There can hardly be any doubt that it was written by an eye-witness of the events of David's reign, *during the reign of Solomon*.

The quite isolated indications which seem to point to a slightly later date, 1 Sam. 30. 25 ; 2 Sam. 18. 18 ; 20. 3, carry

I

no weight in view of the overpowering impression made by
the whole that the narrator was familiar with the minutest
particulars of the events of David's life and reported them
with a most remarkable objectivity. Cf. the pronouncement
of Ed. Meyer: " The stories of David show incontestably by
their contents that they are derived from the period of the
events themselves, and that their narrator must have been
extremely well informed regarding the ongoings of the Court
and the relations and manœuvres of the various characters ;
they cannot have been reduced to writing later than the time
of Solomon " (p. 485 f.). As regards the beginnings of the
growth of legend which we find here and there in it we may
recall, as Meyer suggests (p. 486), that only some forty to fifty
years separated the work of Herodotus from the battles of
Salamis and Plataea. And in the East imagination works
still more rapidly. An attempt has been made to determine
conjecturally who the individual actually was to whom we owe
2 Sam. 9-20 and perhaps also the whole Source K. Klostermann has proposed Ahimaaz the son of Zadok, the messenger
and swift runner of 2 Sam. 15. 36 ; 17. 17 ff. ; 18. 19 ff. A
more plausible hypothesis has been suggested by Duhm and,
following him, by Budde, that the author was the Abiathar,
formerly priest of Nob, who had opportunities of knowing all
that went on, who accompanied David during his outlaw period
and was the medium of all Divine communications to him, who
later on wielded a powerful influence as High Priest, and who,
in the evening of his life, was banished by Solomon to Anathoth.
To this hypothesis it is hardly possible to refuse acceptance.

It may be taken as highly probable that K forms
the continuation and conclusion of the Yahwistic,
K¹ of the Elohistic, writing ; that is to say, the
latter is derived from the same circles as the E²
which we saw reason to assume in I. § 7 *sup*.

This identification has been supported by Cornill and Budde
among others, while Kittel, though admitting close affinities,
is still inclined to separate K and K¹ from K^J and E^E. But
it is scarcely possible to resist permanently the demonstrative
force of the extremely fully worked-out argument of Budde.
Not only do all the fundamental religious ideas of K agree
exactly with those of J, not only does Jg. 13. 5 (J) itself expressly
refer to 1 Sam. 9. 16 (K), but even the language is identical

(cf. יְדוֹת in the sense of parts, shares, Gen. 43. 34; 47. 24; 2 Sam. 19. 43; "to make to stink," Gen. 34. 30; Ex. 5. 21; 1 Sam. 13. 4; 27. 12; 2 Sam. 10. 6, etc.; cf. Budde's *Kommentar zu Richter und Samuel*, and the monograph of Klähn, *Die sprachliche Verwandschaft der Quelle K mit der Quelle J*, 1914).

But if the identification is correct, it follows inevitably that the whole Yahwistic writing was completed in Solomon's reign; and this is the conclusion to which all the other available evidence points. Unfortunately Budde, who has so energetically championed the connection of J and K, has not drawn this conclusion, but only makes a school of writers begin its activity at this time. This school, working backwards from the time of the monarchy in four stages, drew four successive circles, each with a wider radius than the last till finally they worked back to primitive times. But that would have been to begin the building from the top downwards. Where, on this assumption, did that stage of the Source begin which described before the monarchy only the age of the heroes? Here Budde can be countered with his own weapons, for the same arguments which prove that the source J was continued beyond the Book of Joshua prove also that the author or authors began their great work with the creation and carried it down to the days of the reigning dynasty, in which was fulfilled what had been promised to the Fathers. Cf. 2 K. 2. 45 f. See also ZEAT, pp. 61-63.

The position is rather different as regards K[1]. It is true the connection with E, both in the theocratic ideas and in the language, is almost more obvious, and was indeed recognized earlier, first by Cornill (cf., *e.g.*, Gen. 35. 4; Deut. 31. 16; Jos. 24. 20, with 1 Sam. 7. 3). And 1 Sam. 1 ff. is the fulfilment of the programme sketched out in Jg. 10. 6 ff. But, in the first place, the relationship is here of a different kind: it is one of dependence and imitation, not an original continuity as with J and K. And, in the second place, we have already seen in § 2 that E really came to a conclusion in Jos. 24, and that consequently the Elohistic parts of the Book of Judges rest on a later redactional extension of this Source, of which we find traces in the Pentateuch also. The discussion above has led us to the conclusion that the date of origin of K[1] is practically the same which we have already seen reason to assign to E[2], that is to say, about 800 B.C. And in conclusion we may point out a quite unsought confirmation of the connection between the two. We ascribed the polemic against the Temple in the interests of the Tabernacle in 2 Sam. 7 to prophetic circles in Mizpeh in the neighbourhood of Gibeon, the former seat of the Tabernacle ; now, it is precisely in E² that we find, in Ex. 33, the first clear Pentateuch tradition regarding the Tabernacle of revelation ; cf. also the " Book " of 1 Sam. 10. 25 with Ex. 24. 7 ; Jos. 24. 26.

The process by which the book as a whole arose can only be briefly discussed. Here, as in the Pentateuch (cf. I. § 10 *sup*.), we have to reckon with alternative possibilities. The first alternative is that it was *a purely literary process*. In that case, of course, the two originally separate Sources were in the first place worked up together ; cf. 1 Sam. 10. 25*b*, 26 ; 11. 12-14, etc.—very closely and skilfully in 1 Sam. 4–6 and 18. 6-30—probably under Hezekiah. After that came the Deuteronomistic revision. This was much slighter than in the Book of Judges ; it is practically confined to the following passages : 1 Sam. 2. 36 ; 4. 18*b* ; 6. 15 ; 7. 3 f., 13 f. ; 12. 10, 12 ; 2 Sam. 5. 4 f. ; 7. 13. Very important for the history of the book is Budde's discovery that 1 Sam. 14. 47-51 and 2 Sam. 8 are from D, both being short summaries of the reigns of Saul and David respectively, in which older materials are drawn on, the purpose of these summaries being to round off the history of the reigns and provide a substitute for 1 Sam. 15 in the one case, and 2 Sam. 9-20 ; 21-24 in the other.

The first of these passages is easily recognized as Deuteronomistic by the chronological scheme and the reference to " Baalim and Ashtaroth." In 1 Sam. 2. 36 the ancient prophecy dealing with the rejection of the House of Eli (Abiathar) in favour of that of Zadok is expanded by a verse referring to the event of 622 B.C. In 2 Sam. 7 many have seen a purely Deuteronomistic creation ; but wrongly, for this really looks in quite the opposite direction, exalting David because he has *not* built a temple. Only the single verse, 13, which skilfully destroys the whole point of the chapter, is Deuteronomistic. Budde's hypothesis regarding 1 Sam. 14. 47 ff. and 2 Sam. 8 is not yet universally accepted, but it is clearly right. 1 Sam. 14. 47 is in direct contradiction with 14. 52, and 14. 48 is simply a substitute for chapter 15 ; this chapter from K[1] was obviously only reinserted later, for it drives a wedge between 14. 52 and 16. 14 ff., which directly belong together, and the reason for the earlier elimination is not far to seek—it is that in 15. 32 ff. it looks as if Samuel offered a human sacrifice. Similarly 2 Sam. 8 is a Deuteronomistic substitute for 10 ; 12. 26 ff., etc. One thing that shows clearly that 2 Sam. 9-20 was once omitted is the identity of 8. 16-18 with 20. 23-26. The grounds for this omission were no doubt of various kinds. For the suppression of the narrative of the impalement of the sons of Saul in Gibeon, 21. 1-14, with the account which originally immediately followed it, of the numbering of the people, of the plague, and of the purchase of the site of the Temple, 24. 1 ff., which must once have stood before 9. 1 ff., the motive is doubtless to be found in the horror with which human sacrifice had come to be regarded and the disinclination to recall the Canaanitish antecedents of the Holy Place. For the omission of the lists and stories of the heroes, 21. 15-22 ; 23. 8-39, which probably at one time immediately followed 5. 17-25, the reason probably was—as also in the case of the whole Davidic family history in 9-10—simply that they did not make any further contribution to the *Sacred History*, the Deuteronomist following the same lines here as in the Book of Kings, where he excluded everything that appeared to him of merely *secular* interest, without thereby intending to pronounce any condemnation upon it.

Then, in the post-Exilic period a redactor must first have re-attached 2 Sam. 21-24, and then re-inserted 9-20. In the meantime, however, the Deuteronomistic book had been expanded by the addition of certain midrashic narratives, 1 Sam. 13. 7-15 ; 16. 1-13 ; 19. 18-24 ; 27. 11-16. It was probably this same redactor who inserted three poems, the certainly pre-Exilic song of Hannah, 1 Sam. 2. 1-10, and two Davidic poems, 2 Sam.

22. 1-51 and 23. 1-7, the genuineness of which we have no reason to doubt.

That it was first 2 Sam. 21-24 that was reinserted, and only afterwards 9-20, follows from the identity already mentioned of 8. 16-18 and 20. 23-26. The repetition of this list was intended to secure that 21 ff. should follow immediately after the list, as it had previously done. The date of the short midrashes above mentioned, which have no connection with either of the Sources, and at the same time are not Deuteronomistic, is impossible to determine. The narrative in 1 Sam. 13. 7-15, which is not consistent with itself, must, however, have been composed at a time when chapter 15 was omitted, probably from earlier materials, which in this passage told in K also of a breach between Saul and Samuel. That the Song of Hannah is pre-Exilic follows with certainty from 2. 10. The genuineness of the so-called " last words of David " in 23. 1-7 is guaranteed by the obscure, antique style, which is exactly that of the oracles of Balaam. They apply to the actual kingship the old expectation of a saviour. The author of K¹, about 800 B.C., undoubtedly bases himself in 2 Sam. 7 upon these " last words." Cf. Procksch, *Die letzten Worte Davids*, ASt, 1913, p. 112-25. In regard to chapter 22 (=Ps. 18), cf. III. § 1 *infra*).

But alongside of a purely literary development of this kind we have to set the possibility of a development of the ancient history taking place *in connection with the reading of it at public worship.* K¹ would in this case represent a later form in which the history was read during a definite period (about 800) in the meetings for worship, without, however, interfering with the literary existence of K. On the contrary, when the reader came to a part of K which had not been superseded by the new material, he read it as it stood. D, on this hypothesis, would represent a further stage on the same road, and would show us how in the Deutero-nomistic period further portions of K (*e.g.* 2 Sam. 9-20) were excluded from public reading, and new compositions used instead. The whole of the materials would stand side by side upon the rolls, but would have affixed to them distinctive marks to indicate their suitability or otherwise for public reading, and a redactor of the post-Exilic period, to whom all the material would then appear of equal value, would work it up into a united whole.

Here, then, as in the Pentateuch (and the Book of Judges), the problem so far remains unsolved.

In regard to the value which is to be attached to the Books of Samuel as a historical work, we may quote in the first place a remark of the historian, Ed. Meyer, who is speaking of its principal source : " It is a surprising thing that a historical litera- ture of this kind was possible in Israel at that date. It is far superior to anything else that we are acquainted with in the way of ancient oriental historical writing," *ut sup*. p. 486. But when Meyer proceeds to pass a very much less favourable verdict on the other parallel Source, K^1, with its prophetic judgement upon history, describing it as belonging to a wholly different world (*ib*. p. 487), the author of K would certainly have protested vigorously against this verdict, and would have recognized in K^1 a true interpreter of his own intentions in view of the circumstances of a later and a different period (cf. 1 Sam. 9. 16). But in respect of the historical trustworthiness of this later Source, it is of course certain that the earlier K is incomparably more reliable in its representation of the outward course of events. It is nevertheless deserving of serious consideration whether it is not possible that objections to the innovation of the kingship may have at once arisen in prophetic circles (cf. the old antagonism of Shechem against this institution, Jg. 9, and Ahijah of Shiloh), and the memory of this opposition may well have remained alive, more especially in the Benjamite towns in the immediate neighbourhood of Samuel's former home, whereas in Court circles, from which K takes its rise, all recollection of it would naturally have disappeared, cf. I. § 7. And after all, the God of History has set His seal upon the view of the history taken in this Mizpeh Source—by the course of the history itself, as well as through its interpreters, the succession of the prophets whose written work has come down to us.

§ 4. *The Books of Kings*

Kittel, *Geschichte des Volkes Israel*, II. pp. 46-51, 278-94; Winckler, *Alttestamentliche Untersuchungen*, 1892, pp. 1-54; Gunkel, *Elias*, 1906; Erbt, *Elia, Elisa, Jona*, 1907; Brögelmann, *De fonte, qui est de Elia, quaestiones selectae*, 1910.

As has already been indicated in § 3, the Books of Kings were at one time most closely united to the Books of Samuel, and, like these, were not divided into two Books. The two chapters which stand at the head of these Books, as an Introduction, connect directly with 2 Sam. 20, and quite certainly belong (with the exception of 2. 1-4) to the Source which we found present there, K = J. They relate how through the efforts of Bathsheba, and of Nathan and Zadok, Solomon was designated as the successor of David, instead of his elder brother Adonijah, and how, after David's death, he ascended the throne and punished the former opponents of his candidature. The chapters close with the words (2. 46*b*) " and so the kingdom was established in the hand of Solomon" (or, if we follow the LXX, in v. 45 with a prayer for blessings upon Solomon)—a confirmation of our conclusion that this Source really was completed in the first half of Solomon's reign.

Cornill thinks he can trace J beyond this, especially in chapter 8, verses 12-13. But for these chapters another Source is named in 11. 41. And why should not this Source, if it was Judaean, have cited the " Book of the Valiant "[1] just as well as J? Again, the fact that 3. 16-28 might quite well have stood in J, is no proof that it did so. No further traces can be found.

In the whole of the rest of the Books of Kings, which narrate the history from the reign of Solomon down to the Babylonian Exile—from 1 K. 12 to 2 K. 17, the parallel history of the two kingdoms down to 722, in 2 K. 18-25 that of Judah alone—the hand of the *Deuteronomist* is to be observed. It is immediately recognizable by the fact that he passes judgement upon each of the Kings of Judah according to whether he offered sacrifices at the high-places or not (as all did except Hezekiah and Josiah), while in the case of the Kings of Israel it records whether they practised the worship of idols, the " sin of Jeroboam," and in general represents the fate of the people as determined by the religious attitude of the King; everywhere, in fact, it brings to bear a religious pragmatism. It offers also a definite chronological framework, and indeed synchronizes the history of the two kingdoms.

But the relation of the Sources is different here from what we found in the Books of Samuel. There we saw that the Deuteronomist had before him a detailed and complete work into which he has merely here and there interpolated a gloss ;

---

[1] The LXX has a reading at the end of verse 13 (LXX 53) which is probably a corruption for : " Is it not written in the Book of Jashar " (cf. Jos. 10. 13).—Translator.

here he is obviously the creator of the whole work; it was he who first combined together several other sources and worked them up under the guidance of a definite idea.

It is, however, clear that we have to distinguish in the Books of Kings the work of two Deuteronomists. One, who was the real father of the work, wrote very soon after the introduction of Deuteronomy, and looks to Deuteronomy to bring about the salvation of the State, while he knows nothing of the Exile, cf. 1 K. 8. 8; 9. 21, etc. Further data for the determination of his period are furnished by the fact that he had seen the fate of Josiah, 2 K. 23. 25, and cites for the last time the source from which he draws his material in 2 K. 24. 5, at the end of the reign of Jehoiakim; from which it appears that he must have written immediately after 596 B.C. Perhaps we ought to recognize him in Shaphan or his son Ahikam, from one of whom the narrative in 2 K. 22 and 23 must be derived, for the author of this is doubtless the author of the whole book.

The second Deuteronomist, a pupil of the first and the final redactor of the Books of Kings, wrote during the Babylonian Exile. The last incident which came within his experience— it is related by him in 2 K. 25—was the liberation and admission to favour of Jehoiachin, in 561. Of the Return in 538 he knows nothing. He is even more severe in his judgements than the first Deuteronomist (cf. the different attitude towards Solomon's offering at the high-place in Gibeon, 1 K. 3. 2 and 3. 3, 15), and repeatedly inserts references to the Exile as a coming judgement, 1 K. 8. 44-51; 9. 1-9; 2 K. 21. 7-15; 22. 15-20; 23. 26 f.; 24. 1-4, etc.

The first Deuteronomist made use of a whole series of older, and for the most part more trustworthy, Sources—in the first place, in 1 K. 3–11, of a *biography of Solomon*, which is expressly cited in 11. 41.

This biography has a distinctive literary character as compared with J and E. It divides the reign into two parts, one of light (4-10) and one of shadow (11), and, in chapter 3, places an introduction at the head of the work, borrowing verses 4-14 from $K^1 = E^2$. Whence it drew the remainder of its material we cannot determine, but we may distinguish between annals derived directly from Solomon's own period (4. 1-20; 4. 21-28; 15. 24-32, the kernel of 6. 1-7, 51, etc.) and popular narratives about him, such as 3. 16-28; 4. 29-34; 10. 1 ff. As regards the date of origin of the biography, it may be said that not only must it, in view of 9. 13; 10. 12, be separated by some little interval from the reign of Solomon, but, further, that in view of the borrowing from K[1] in 3. 4 ff. it can hardly have been written before the eighth century, though it may very well have been written then.

In addition to it, there fall to be considered, as the most important and continuous Source, a " History of the Kings of Israel " and " History of the Kings of Judah," 1 K. 14. 19, 29.

This *Book of the Histories of the Kings* must have contained not merely annals, such as were kept at every oriental Court— not merely short notes about wars, commerce, alliances, and the like—but also more detailed narratives of important events which happened at the Court. But I can see at present no possibility of distinguishing the two kinds of material in the Books of Kings as they have come down to us—*e.g.* marking off 1 K. 12. 2-24; 20; 22; 2 K. 3; 9. 1—10. 27 as a separate Source consisting of popular narratives—so long as we do not know how far narratives of that kind were admitted to the annals. For these too give a quite objective report. On the other hand, the statements made about the Kings of Northern Israel contain no more than any prophet in Shechem-Gilgal, Bethel, etc., would be in a position to know, so that here it is questionable whether we have to think of *annals* at all. The main point is that the source cited by the Deuteronomist is not a mere collection of annals, but, more or less like the Solomon biography, a historical work, itself based upon Sources. All data are so far lacking which might enable us to assign a date for its composition, or to explain how and when the North-Israelitish Source-material came to Jerusalem. It is only by guess-work if we suggest the age of Hezekiah. The Deuteronomist was content to give mere excerpts from this great historical work; what interests him especially are the notices and episodes which touch the domain of religion. His purpose is simply to write a sacred history, and for all beyond that he is content to refer the reader to these Sources. We cannot sufficiently regret that this dual national history has been lost.

A further Source, separate from the above, which the Deuteronomist seems to have had before him, may properly be characterized as consisting of narratives, or legends, *of the Prophets*. We meet with it in 1 K. 13; 17-19; 21; 2 K. 1; 2; 4-8; 13. 14-21; 19. 9*b*-35; 20. 1-19.

These stories are neither all of the same age nor all of the same value. It is possible to distinguish four strata: (1) the earliest set of stories, which have also the greatest unity, have Elijah as their centre, (2) those concerned with Elisha, (3) the biography of Isaiah, and (4) the rest. The first three cycles, while containing legendary elaborations (cf. 2 K. 2. 9 ff., 23 f.; 13. 20 f.; 20. 8 ff., etc.), have a kernel of historical material (in proof see *e.g.* 2 K. 3. 11; 9. 1 ff.; 19. 2-7), but the last (*e.g.* 1 K. 13, cf. v. 2) are of quite late growth and, from the historical point of view, valueless. The first two cycles, which begin abruptly in 1 K. 17, are certainly of Ephraimitish origin, cf. 19. 3, and are probably earlier than E², *i.e.* they were fixed in writing in the second half of the ninth century. We find no trace in them of the ideas which are chiefly prominent in the literary prophets, polemic against star worship and the like, while a plurality of altars is accepted as legitimate, 1 K. 19. 14. As regards the date when the biography of Isaiah was written, cf. B. § 1, II. 5.

While the Deuteronomist generally allows his Sources to speak for themselves, and contents himself with putting in additions afterwards, which are as a rule easy to distinguish, in a few cases he has *worked up* the various Sources so thoroughly that we can no longer decide what is his own work and what is the older kernel. That applies, *e.g.*, to 1 K. 11. 29-39; 12. 26-32; 14; 2 K. 18. 17, etc. Generally speaking, however, the analysis of the Books of Kings is straightforward and is carried out by all scholars with a relatively high degree of unanimity.

Summary: *The Deuteronomistic historical work of the period of the Babylonian Exile.*—On the basis of the results arrived at in the foregoing, we come to the conclusion that during the Exile, at the hands of the so-called Deuteronomist, in continuation of the work begun about 600 B.C., a single great and imposing historical work took shape, beginning with Gen. 2. 4*b* and ending with 2 K. 25. In this there was still lacking, as we have seen in the discussions above, the whole Priestly Writing in the Pentateuch and Book of Joshua, Jos. 24 ; Jg. 1 ; 9 ; 17-21 ; 1 Sam. 15 ; 28. 3-25 ; 2 Sam. 9-24 ; 1 K. 1 (in place of the latter, 2. 1-4, 12*b* was inserted). That in these passages new sections have taken the place of the old is often apparent even on the surface from the " catch-word " which points back to the original section, cf. Jg. 2. 8 ff. (continuation of Jos. 23. 16 ff.) with Jos. 24. 28 ff. ; 2 Sam. 8. 16-18 with 20. 23-26 ; 1 K. 2. 12*b* with 2. 46*b*.

That it was not the intention to offer an exhaustive history is at once made clear by the repeated references to the Book of the Histories of the Kings of Israel and Judah. But the question must be raised whether the work did not actually owe its origin to lectures on the nation's history given at public worship, or perhaps in schools ; in the sense that, while the earlier presentations of the history continued to be read (with some omissions), they were modified, sometimes by way of glosses and sometimes by the substitution of new sections, and sometimes, again, were enriched by the addition of wholly new material of earlier independent origin, such as the legends of the prophets. The purpose of the work is clear. The intention is to give a sacred history, which shall make manifest that the history of the world is the judgement of the world, and that the fate of Israel and Judah has been brought upon them by their own sins, and more particularly by the sins of sacrificing at the high-places and worshipping idols and false gods. But as some sections appear to be the immediate transcript of edifying comments upon the ancient history, or of suggestions for these (cf. Jos. 23 ; 1 K. 8. 14-53, etc.), the whole work possesses at the same time a didactic tendency— it aims at showing how to do better in the future. The call to repentance predominates, but it has as its counterpart the promise of salvation ; for the sake of David, the Servant of the Lord, much is forgiven to Israel and long patience exercised towards her (cf. 1 K. 8. 25 ; 11. 34 ff. ; 15. 4 ; 2 K. 8. 19, and, for the designation " Servant of God," 2 Sam. 7. 5 ff. ; 1 K. 3. 6 ; 8. 25 ; 11. 32 ff. ; etc. (already in the Elohistic writer, Ex. 14. 31 ; Num. 12. 7 ff. ; Deut. 34. 5). And for his sake the Divine mercy can never permanently depart from Israel (cf. 2 Sam. 7, the whole history of the patriarchs, etc.). We can thus understand how the " lifting up of the head " of Jehoiachin after his 35 years' imprisonment is placed at the conclusion of the work ; it is, for the author, the dawn of the day of deliverance, the return of the Davidic, which is also conceived as the Paradisaic, period.

With this great work there was amalgamated, in Ezra's time and after, the Priestly Writing, and at this period, first the Pentateuch, with shortly afterwards the Book of Joshua, which was provided in chapter 24 with a magniloquent close, was divided off as a separate Book. Next followed the Book of Judges, which now received, in chapter 1, a separate introduction taken from the Yahwist, chapter 9 being re-inserted, and 17-21—the latter section somewhat worked over—attached at the end. Similarly in the Books of Samuel there were restored, by another redactor, the chapters previously excised by the Deuteronomist 1 Sam. 15 ; 28 ; 2 Sam. 9-24—it may be that these had merely been put in brackets to indicate their omission from public reading and that all that was now done was to remove the brackets—and a division was made after the account in chapter 24 of the purchase of the Temple site, so that 1 K. 1 and 2, which originally were immediately connected with it, might be used as an introduction to the Book of Kings. This last redaction (dating in the case of Samuel and Kings from about 400 B.C.) left the individual sections practically intact (though there are traces of working-over in 1 K. 7. 48-50 ; 8. 1-18, and 12. 32 f. ; but probably from a still later hand). The redaction was free from " tendency," being purely objective, its interest lying in the preservation of the ancient literature, which was now regarded as in all its stages adapted to religious instruction. These books did not permanently satisfy those strictly Levitical circles which regarded the world and its history solely from the angle of vision represented by the Priestly Writing. They substituted for them a wholly new work, which was intended to serve as a continuation of the Book of Judges, viz. the Books of Chronicles, cf. III. *infra.*

B. The " Later Prophets," or Prophets
PROPERLY SO CALLED

Kuenen, *De profeten en de profetie onder Israel*, 1875 ; Duhm, *Die Theologie der Propheten*, 1875 ; Orelli, *Die alttestamentliche Weissagung von der Vollendung des Gottesreiches*, 1882 ; Koenig, *Der Offenbarungsbegriff des A.T.*, 1882 ; W. Robertson Smith, *The Prophets of Israel*, 1895 ; Cornill, *Der israelitische Prophetis-*

mus[7], 1910 ; Giesebrecht, *Die Berufsbegabung der alttestamentlichen Propheten*, 1897 ; Gressmann, *Der Ursprung der israelitisch-jüdischen Eschatologie*, 1905 ; Staerk, *Das assyrische Weltreich im Urteil der Propheten*, 1908 ; Koenig, *Das alttest. Prophetentum und die moderne Geschichtsforschung*, 1910; Sellin, *Der alttestamentliche Prophetismus*, 1912 ; Wilke, *Die politische Wirksamkeit der Propheten Israels*, 1913 ; Hölscher, *Die Propheten*, 1914 ; Caspari, *Die israelitischen Propheten*, 1914 ; Duhm, *Israels Propheten*, 1916.

§ 1. *Isaiah*

Guthe, *Das Zukunftsbild des Jesaja*, 1885 ; Giesebrecht, *Beiträge zur Jesajakritik*, 1890 ; Hackmann, *Die Zukunftserwartung des Jesaja*, 1893 ; Meinhold, *Jes. und seine Zeit*, 1898 ; *Studien zur israelitischen Religionsgeschichte*, I. p. 89 ff., 1903 ; Brückner, *Die Komposition des Buches Jes.* (chaps.) 28-33, 1897 ; Wilke, *Jesaja und Assur*, 1905 ; Küchler, *Jesajas Stellung zur Politik seiner Zeit*, 1906 ; Meinhold, *Die Jesajaerzählungen Jes.*, 36-39, 1898.

On Deutero-Isaiah : Seinecke, *Der Evangelist des A.T.*, 1870 ; Ley, *Historische Erklärung des 2. Teils des Jes.*, 1893 ; Koenig, *The Exile's Book of Consolation*, 1899 ; Sellin, *Studien zur Entstehungsgeschichte der jüdischen Gemeinde I. Der Knecht Gottes bei Deuterojesaja*, 1901 ; *Das Rätsel des Deutjes. Buches*, 1908 ; Stärk, *Die Ebed Jahwe-Lieder in Jesaja 40 ff.*, 1913 ; Gressmann, *Die literarische Analyse Deuterojesajas*, ZAW, 1914, p. 254 ff. ; Fischer, *Jesajas 40-55 und die Perikopen vom Gottesknecht*, 1916 ; Beer, *Die Gedichte vom Knechte Jahwes* in the " Festschrift " for Baudissin, 1918, pp. 29-46 ; Sellin, *Mose*, 1922.

On Trito-Isaiah : Gressmann, *Über die Jes. 55-66 vorausgesetzten zeitgeschichtlichen Verhältnisse*, 1898 ; Littmann, *Über die Abfassungszeit des Tritojesaja*, 1899 ; Cramer, *Der geschichtliche Hintergrund von Jes. 56-66*, 1905.

On the whole Book : Cheyne, *Introduction to the Book of Isaiah*, London, 1895 (German translation by Boehmer, 1897).

The earliest citation which clearly implies the existence of the Book of Isaiah in its present form is Sirach (Ecclus.) 48. 20-25. The ascription by the Chronicler in 2 Chr. 36. 22 f. of Isa. 44. 28 to Jeremiah is to be explained by a slip of the pen, or of memory, rather than by supposing that chapters 40-66 had not at that time been attached to the Book.

The Book as we now have it obviously falls into the following divisions: (1) Introductory Discourse, chapter 1 ; (2) prophecies of Isaiah concerning Judah and Jerusalem, 2-12 ; (3) utterances (each of the ten being introduced by the word Massa, *i.e.* utterance—A.V. and R.V. "Burden") regarding the foreign nations, 13-23 ; (4) Eschatological Discourses, 24-35 ; (5) Narratives about Isaiah, 36-39 ; (6) A Book of Consolation, 40-66, which in turn falls into three parts marked by the repetition of the same refrain, 40. 1–48. 22 ; 49. 1–57. 21 ; 58. 1–66. 24.

The basis of this work is formed by the writings of a man who, according to 1. 1, lived and worked in the reigns of the Jewish kings, Uzziah, Jotham, Ahaz and Hezekiah. According to 6. 1 ff. he was called to be a prophet by a vision which affected the whole current of his life, in the year of Uzziah's death, that is to say, about 740, and his first commission was to be a prophet of Judgement and of hardening of the heart. According to 1. 1 ; 2. 1, he was the son of an otherwise unknown Amoz, who was, however, certainly an inhabitant of Jerusalem, 7. 3 ; 22. 15 f. ; 28. 7, and of a family of standing, 7. 3 ; 8. 1. According to 8. 3, Isaiah was the husband of one wife, and the father of several sons, to whom he gave names symbolical of future happenings. He followed with a keen eye all the political events of his day, and shed upon them the light of Divine revelation ; indeed, in a critical moment he intervened with energy in the policy of the Court.

Under Jotham he worked undisturbed. But in the case of Ahaz there was an open rupture, because the king, in spite of the prophet's opposition, called in the aid of the Assyrians and voluntarily became tributary to them, 7. 3 ff.

In consequence of this, Isaiah withdrew from public life for several years and confined his activities to the narrow circle of his disciples, 8. 16 ff. Under Hezekiah, however, he at first acquired great public influence, but there is not a trace of evidence that he was in any way responsible for the religious reformation which this king, under the powerful impression made by the break-up of the Northern Kingdom, took in hand (2 K. 18). The explanation must simply be that there were, among those who were " faithful to Yahweh " at the Court, different circles with different ideals. And Isaiah had certainly a different conception of the future development of the people from that presented in the legislative scheme of Deut. 12—26; 28.

In any case his influence at the Court was soon ousted by that of a pro-Egyptian party which, in spite of all his warnings, persuaded the king to refuse, in reliance upon Pharaoh, to continue to pay tribute to the Assyrians. But Isaiah's warnings were justified by the event. Egypt gave no help. Sennacherib invaded the country and overran it. Yet, in consequence partly of a plague which broke out in his camp, partly of unfavourable political news from East and West, he was obliged to raise the siege of Jerusalem and make a hasty retirement, which had a distinct suggestion of flight about it. The influence of the prophet must have been extraordinarily enhanced by this event. We know nothing further as regards his fate. There is a legend that he was sawn asunder in the reign of Manasseh. Cf. the Ascensio Isaiae, 5. 1, and Heb. 11. 37.

K

I. The Genuine* Parts of the Isaian Book

This, like all other prophetic writings, has had its history. As the three separate superscriptions, 1. 1; 2. 1; 13. 1, and chapters 36-39, of which the prophet is the subject, show, the book was not written as a single whole by Isaiah himself, but has grown up gradually from the combination of separate sayings, discourses and poems of Isaiah, or of collections of Isaiah's prophecies. That, in the case of a compilation of this kind arranged by later hands, some non-Isaian material might easily find its way in must be admitted to be *a priori* probable.

The following portions have, however, stood the test of criticism and been generally admitted to be genuine : 1-12 ; 14. 24—20. 6 ; 22 ; (23. 1-14 ?) ; 28—33. Although absolute certainty is not in every case attainable, these sections may nevertheless be assigned with considerable probability to the various periods of the life of Isaiah as follows :

To the period before the invasion of the Syrians and Ephraimites, *i.e.* before 735, belong 2. 6—6. 13 ; 9. 8—10. 4 ; 17. 1-11 ; to the time of this invasion belong 7. 1—9. 6 ; 11. 1-10 (7, like 20 at a later point, is taken from a biography of Isaiah) ; shortly before the Fall of Samaria in 722, 28. 1-6 ; 14. 24-27 ; about 711, 20. 1-6 ; 14. 29-32 ; 15 and 16 ; shortly before, during, or after 701 ; (23 ?) 1. 2—2. 4 ; 10. 5-34 ; 17. 12-14 ; 18 ; (19 ?) ; 22 ; 28. 7—33. 24.

---

* " Genuine " is used in the strict technical sense which it bears in criticism, meaning that a book is by the author whose name it bears. Genuineness is in this sense distinguished from " authenticity," which refers to the trustworthiness of the contents.—Translator.

(To this period belong also perhaps 37. 22-29, 30-32, 33-35, cf. II. 5.)

From the time of the vision at which he received the call which determined the whole subsequent course of his life, God was for Isaiah "the Holy One of Israel." The word "holy" is an ancient word, but Isaiah understood it in quite a different sense from the people generally (8. 11 ff.). For him it meant the supreme greatness of God, absolutely exalted above everything creaturely, which reduces man to nothingness and forces him to cast himself down into the dust. The fundamental religious attitude which answers to this conception is therefore the absolute renunciation of all that is merely human, an absolute casting of oneself upon God, of grasping His unseen Hand, of believing, 7. 9 ; 28. 16 ; 30. 15 ; on this basis ethical conduct is determined by the principle "the Holy One shall be sanctified through righteousness," 5. 16, cf. 1. 16 ff. ; 10. 2, etc. This innermost kernel of his preaching remained at all periods unchangeably the same, but the form which it assumed altered according to the circumstances of the historical situation. He hailed Assyria as the chosen instrument of God, and again at another time launched curses against it. (To find a definite temporal dividing line between the two attitudes, say in the year 704, as Wilke has done, does not seem to me possible, although obviously most of the prophecies hostile to Assyria fall after this date.) Sometimes he announces the future destruction of his People to its absolute roots, sometimes he assumes the salvation of a remnant, sometimes the conversion of the whole People, sometimes the impregnability of Zion. Sometimes he sees nothing but defeat and destruction, sometimes he pictures the time of salvation, when the nation shall be led and pastured by the Prince of Righteousness, who is also the Prince of Peace, on whom, from of old, the fathers set their hopes. Isaiah is thus no logician or systematic thinker, but the messenger of an unseen world, the herald of an eternal ethical world-order which will in the end realize itself, it matters not by what historical means ; and withal he is a master of speech, the king among all the prophets.

Many critics of recent times have denied the Isaian authorship of a number of the sections which we have enumerated as firmly established ; but for

reasons which are likely to find less and less acceptance the more a truly historical spirit gains ground.

The following are the sections which are chiefly questioned :

(*a*) The promises of salvation in 2. 2-4 ; 4. 2-6 ; 9. 2-7 ;
11. 1-10. The arguments brought against the genuineness of
these by Stade, Hackmann, Marti and others (contradiction
with the ideas of Isaiah elsewhere, want of logical connection,
unintelligibility in his own time, and the like), lose their force
if only we hold fast to the principle that Isaiah, like all the
prophets, did not newly create the expectation of salvation and
a saviour, but assumes it to be already familiar to his hearers ;
that, in fact, he has taken them over from tradition, but transformed them in the process. Cf. Amos 5. 18. In reality, to
think of them as originating after the Babylonian exile would
be much more difficult ; 9. 4, 5 ; 11. 1, 3, 4 absolutely demand
the Isaian age. Cf. in regard to the first, 14. 24-27, and, further,
Bertholet, *Stellung der Israeliten zu den Fremden*, pp. 97-99 ;
Gressmann, *Eschatologie*, p. 279 ff. ; 288 f. ; Caspari, *Echtheit*,
etc., *von Jes.* 9. 1-6 (= E.V. 2-7) ; Schmidt, SchAT, p. 112 ff. On
the other hand, it is true that such a dispersion as is described
in 11. 11 not only had not taken place in Isaiah's day, but cannot
even have been expected by him. But, as against this, the
mention of the jealousy of Ephraim in 11. 13, the boundaries of
the kingdom in verse 14, and the relations of Egypt and Assyria
(cf. Hos. 9. 3 ; 11. 5, etc.), support the view that in 11. 11-16
we have before us a prophecy of salvation, by Isaiah, which has
been worked over by a later hand.

(*b*) The utterance about Moab in 15 and 16. Here the
departures from Isaian diction are to be explained by the
explicit statement of 16. 13, that the oracles of 15. 1-16. 12 are
not derived from Isaiah but merely adopted by him, and given
a new application (to the Assyrian invasion). The reference
to the conquest of Moab by Jeroboam II., 2 K. 14. 25, is obvious.
We have here one of the earliest examples of literary prophecy.
A post-Exilic origin, which is to-day suggested by many (Guthe,
Marti, etc.), is absolutely excluded by 16. 5. That the enemy,
according to 15. 1-4, has invaded Moab from the south-east,
and that the reference must therefore be to desert nomads, is
an unproved assertion. It is quite natural that the chief towns
should be mentioned first as having been conquered, then the
seats of the cultus, at which, as in Jer. 41. 5, the national
catastrophe is bewailed (cf. ZEAT, p. 71 f. ; also Gressmann

in SchAT II. p. 317 ff.). Isaiah's purpose in reproducing this minatory oracle was to warn his contemporaries against a coalition with Moab.

(c) The utterance about Egypt, 19. The only arguments which can be brought against verses 1-17 are of a general aesthetic nature and of no great strength. The divided Principalities in Egypt implied in verse 2 ff. point, at least in the first place, to the period prior to Psammitichus I., that is to say prior to 663, and the inner dissolution of Egypt which forms the starting-point of this prophecy began as early as the latter part of the eighth century. Much more serious, no doubt, are the objections against the genuineness of verses 18-25, which seem to pre-suppose a different period from that of 1-17, and in which, in particular, the definite allusion to Leontopolis in verse 18 b* is impossible in the mouth of Isaiah. On this ground, and be-cause of the almost unparalleled universalism, some critics have proposed to transfer it to the Seleucid, or even to the Maccabaean era. But the mention of a mazzebah as a well-known feature of the cultus, v. 19, is decidedly in favour of a pre-Deuteronomic date. Cf. Deut. 16. 22. And since the Elephantine papyri have lately proved that there was a sanctuary in Egypt long before the time of Cambyses, and as it has become almost certain that the colony there had its beginnings as early as the time of Psammitichus (about 650), and verse 18 ff. accordingly refers entirely to pre-Exilic (cf. Assyria in v. 23 ff.) and pre-Deuteronomic circumstances, it will be advisable to be very cautious in pronouncing a categorical judgement, and to be content for the present with the probability that the first half was written by Isaiah and the second half about the middle of the seventh century; it is possible that passages like Hos. 9. 3; 11. 5; Deut. 17. 16 take us back to the time of Hezekiah and therefore to that of Isaiah himself. Verse 18c is of course in any case a gloss, even the form of the words is noticeable. The Maccabaean origin of verses 16-25 ought not to have been maintained, if only in view of Josephus, *Antiquities*, XIII. 3. 1-3, for this passage absolutely proves that Onias, when he built a temple in Leontopolis in 170 B.C., was acquainted with verses 18a, b, 19 ff. Cf. Steuernagel, *Bemerkungen über die neuentdeckten jüdischen Papyruskunden*, ThStKr, 1909, p. 1 ff.; Stärk, *Die Anfänge der jüdischen Diaspora in Ägypten*, 1908.

(d) The utterance about Tyre, 23. Duhm in particular

---

* See Hastings, *D.B.*, article " Ir-ha-heres," for a full discussion of this verse by Driver.—Translator.

has rightly pointed out that verses 1-14 of this chapter are based on an Elegy upon *Sidon*, which was only afterwards transformed, by the addition of verses 15-18 (and by small changes in verses 5 and 8), into an Elegy on Tyre. That this redaction is not Isaian is certain. Not only the seventy years of verse 15, in imitation of Jer. 29. 10, but more especially the contents of verse 18, exclude the Isaian authorship, for Isaiah would have cried out against such a use of the word holy. Presumably this verse is based on the destruction of Tyre by Alexander the Great. But there is no reason for doubting the Isaian origin of the original Elegy. Sennacherib did as a matter of fact conquer Sidon; if he did not destroy it, that does not prove that Isaiah could not have composed the elegy as a minatory oracle. Cf. Amos 5. 1 f.; Mich. 2. 4. Anything unusual about it is to be explained by the fact that the prophet is using a traditional style. To attain any higher degree of certainty we should need to be sure of the interpretation of verse 13, which appears to be glossed. Probably we should alter *Kasdim* into *Kittim* (cf. v. 12), and translate " Behold the land of the Kitians—Assyria has laid it in ruins " (then on this was superimposed the gloss : This People was not there, they founded it for ships, set up its watchtowers, towns and palaces). If we could be sure about this, the Isaian authorship would be certain. But this is all, it must be admitted, conjecture and hypothesis.

(*e*) The survey of the Last Times, 32 and 33. Its genuineness is rejected by Duhm, Marti and others, on general subjective grounds (as " insipid," " jejune," " didactic," " vapid," " verbose," " vague "), but is not disproved by historical arguments. Chapter 32. 1 takes us back to a time when kings are still reigning in Jerusalem (vv. 6-8 might be a later addition), and, above all, the address to the careless women, v. 9 ff., implies pre-Exilic circumstances (cf. v. 14 !). Chapter 33, too, contains eschatology, but the possibility that Isaiah could have made that the subject of his poems will be denied only by those who falsely assume that eschatology as a whole was an Exilic or post-Exilic literary invention. In refutation of that it is sufficient to point to 29. 1-10, which no doubt was, as 29. 11 expressly states, a " sealed book " to his contemporaries. Chapter 33 deals with the same deliverance from the great final onslaught of the nations upon Jerusalem to which 29. 1-10 or, again, 8. 9 f.; 17. 12 refer ; a very ancient tradition, which is here applied to the Assyrians. Where Marti finds the basis of his conclusion that 33. 18 f. refer to the Syrian tax-collectors and troops of mercenaries of the year 163 B.C., he does not inform us, but others will be more inclined to be reminded of 28. 11 ; 36. 2 ff. ; Nah. 2. 13*b*.   The " king " in verse 17 also points to the pre-Exilic period.   Of course, in chapter 33 slight traces of working over in verses 13-16, 21-24 are not excluded, but the difference of date between it and chapters 34 and 35 is obvious. (Cf. ZEAT, p. 72 f. ; also Kittel-Dillmann in Comm., and Stärk, *Das assyrische Weltreich*, p. 102 ff. ; Schmidt, SchAT, p. 119.)

II. The certainly Non-genuine Parts of the Isaian Book

1. A Prophecy against Babylon, 13. 1—14. 23

That this cannot be derived from Isaiah himself is now admitted by practically all critics.   The following arguments are decisive : (*a*) Babylon is not here announced as the future enemy of Judah ; it is taken for granted that she already is so, v. 11 ff. ; which was not possible in Isaiah's day.   (*b*) While in Isa. 1-12 Exile in Babylon is not so much as mentioned, here it is not merely threatened as something in the future, but it is announced that its end is approaching—the Fall of Babylon on the one hand, v. 19 ff., the Return of the Jews on the other, 14. 1 ff.   (*c*) The Medes, who lay outside the historical horizon of Isaiah, are definitely named as the destroyers of Babylon, indeed the author even has some knowledge of their characteristics, 13. 17. We are here, therefore, certainly in the closing period of the Babylonian Exile.

As Budde has well shown (in the Baudissin " Festschrift," 1918, p. 55 ff.), it must originally have been clearly stated in the opening verses of chapter 13 that Babylon is the subject, and not first in verse 19 * ; and that it was only at a later period that " the Day of Yahweh " was interpolated and

* *Sc.* apart from the title " the Burden of Babylon," etc.—Translator.

the historical characteristics of the above-mentioned period were so far as possible obliterated.

It is not, however, quite so certain that the vigorous Taunt-song of 14. 4*b*-21, composed on the death of a king, belongs to the Babylonian era. In verses 4*a* and 22 it is no doubt referred to the King of Babylon, but in the song itself Babylon is never mentioned. Now it has been felt that the last Babylonian king, the weakling Nabunaid, was hardly a fitting subject for the poem; that it requires an epoch-making historical personality. In looking round for such an one the eye naturally falls on the Assyrian King Sennacherib, whose fate awakens poetic echoes in 2 K. 19. 21 ff.; Nah. 1. 14 also. This possibility, which would involve the pre-Exilic (according to Winckler even the Isaian) origin of the poem, must be reckoned with. On the other hand, verse 17*b* does look like a reflection of the disappointed expectation which, after the ray of light in the reign of Amel-Marduk, fell to the lot of the Jews through the altered policy of Nergal Sarezer and Nabunaid. The actual king may be looked on by the poet merely as a representative of the powerful dynasty, and, moreover, the purpose of the poem, as with all these prophetic taunting elegies, is prophecy, not a review of the past (cf., on the one side, Winckler, *Forschungen*, I. pp. 193 and 414; Stärk, *ut sup.* 226 f.; on the other side, Lohmann, *Die anonymen Prophetien gegen Babel*, 1910, pp. 26-42).

2. An Oracle against Babylon, Oracles upon Edom and the Arabians, 21

Verses 1-10 are non-genuine on the same grounds as chapter 13, cf. esp. v. 2. As Cyrus is not yet mentioned, this too may belong to the period between 550 and 545. Regarding the two other short oracles, the best answer is a *non liquet*. The oracle upon Edom, v. 11 ff., is, strictly speaking, not an oracle at all, but nothing more nor less than a refusal to give one, clothed in a current form of answer given by a watchman to the question, "How goes the night?" And in the "Utterance" about the Arabians, vv. 13-14, a Bedouin song, which was likewise previously current, has been transformed into a prophecy against Kedar.

3. A Book of the Last Things, 24-27

These chapters contain a connected apocalypse which deals with the Judgement and the coming of the world-dominion of Yahweh, the punishment of the God-opposing heavenly Powers, and of the Powers of this world, with the fate of the Nations, the salvation and gathering of Judah amid this world-catastrophe, with the abolition of death and the resurrection of the just. This apocalypse, which is one of the finest and most powerful in the Old Testament and is written by a hero of hope, to whom it is hard to find a peer, who has himself overcome the world and death, is contained in 24. 1-6, 13-23 ; 25. 6-8 ; 26. 12-19 ; 26. 20—27. 1, 7-9, 12, 13. Interspersed with these passages is a cycle of poems, *viz.* 24. 7-12 ; 25. 1-5, 9-12 ; 26. 1-3, 4-6, 7-11 ; 27. 2-6, 10-11. These have no direct connection with the apocalyptic sections by which they are surrounded, their theme is in general the triumph of the City of God over the World-City. They may be later, or they may be earlier than the apocalyptic sections. (For an analysis, see Lohmann in ZAW, 1917–18, pp. 1-58.)

That this little Book is not derived from Isaiah is certain. Not only does the language diverge completely from that of the Isaian discourses (*lamo, bal, bemo, ade*), there is also a whole set of religious ideas which are wholly foreign to this prophet (cf. 24. 21 ; 25. 8 ; 26. 16 ff.). Above all, Babylon appears here also as an enemy of the Kingdom of God, 27. 1, Israel is already dispersed to the ends of the earth, 24. 14-16 ; 26. 13 ; 27. 12, 13, there does not seem to be a king, we hear only of " elders," 24. 23, of priests and of people, 24. 2.

Although in view of all this it cannot be doubted that the Apocalypse (in the narrower sense) is of post-Exilic origin, it must be admitted that it is impossible to date it more exactly. It is true that recently Duhm, Marti and others have with great boldness proposed to place it in the late Maccabaean period, about 100 B.C., and have thought they could find reflected in it the events of this period. But their whole argument stands on a foundation of quicksand. The Apocalypse itself gives *no clue whatever* to the more exact determination of its date. The only datum which can serve the above-named writers as a starting-point is the repeatedly recurring mysterious reference to the *unnamed city* in the interspersed poems, 24. 10, 12 ; 25. 2, 12 ; 26. 5 ; 27. 10, which they without more ado interpret as Samaria, which was destroyed by Hyrcanus in 111-107. But any other application, whether to Babylon, cf. 47. 1 ff. ; 13. 19 ff., or to a Moabitish stronghold, cf. 25. 10 ; or to the Samaria of the period of the Diadochi, is just exactly as probable. (The only suggested reference which is perhaps possible is to connect 26. 1-3 with Neh. 12. 27 ff. ; cf. Lohmann, *ut sup.*) This " city " was originally an apocalyptic entity which it would be futile to seek upon this earth, but which has later been brought into connection with historical entities. Cf. 26. 5 ; Amos 1. 14 ; Jos. 6. 1 ff., etc. In any case the history of the language and that of the Canon place the gravest difficulties in the way of assigning to it a date in the late Maccabaean period ; and the so-called Zadokite Writing which has been edited by Schechter, and which, according to E. Meyer, belongs to the Seleucid era, several times quotes from chapters 24-27.

4. The Destruction of Edom and Redemption of Zion, 34 and 35

In these chapters we have also before us an apocalypse which deals with the Judgement of the World and the Deliverance of Judah from that Judgement. The dispersion of the People throughout the world is not foretold but is already a fact,

35. 10. The borrowings from Deutero-Isaiah, cf.
35. 1 with 41. 18 f. ; 35. 10 with 51. 3, 11, 61. 7 ;
35. 8 with 40. 3, 43. 19, 49. 11 ; 35. 6 with 43. 19 f.,
48. 21, etc. ; also the hatred against Edom, 34. 5 ff.,
cf. with 63. 1 ff., and finally the reference to the
" Book of Yahweh," 34. 16, make it certain that we
are already in the post-Exilic period. To date it
more exactly is impossible.

5. EPISODES FROM THE LIFE OF ISAIAH, 36-39

This section, which treats of the vindication
of Isaiah during the siege of Jerusalem by the
Assyrians in 701 B.C., the sickness and the restoration of Hezekiah in 711 B.C. through him — the
latter, with a view to the transition to chapter
40 ff. is placed after the siege, though really earlier
(39. 2 excludes the possibility of referring 38 and
39 to the year 701)—is found again almost word for
word in 2 K. 18. 13—20. 19. The narrative of the
payment of tribute by Hezekiah, 2 K. 18. 14-16, is
omitted, and the omission is balanced by the insertion of a psalm of Hezekiah, 38. 9-20, composed
after his recovery. That the section is not from
the hand of Isaiah himself is clearly evident, since
he is always spoken of in the third person, and
37. 38 cannot have been written until after Sennacherib's death (681 B.C.).

As chapters 7 and 10 show clearly that there
was an extant biography of Isaiah—perhaps based
on an autobiography—the redactor of the Book of
Isaiah, as well as that of the Book of Kings, may
very likely have drawn his material from it (at
least 37. 8—39. 8). On the possibility that some
genuine sayings of Isaiah may have been pre-

served in these chapters, *viz.* 37. 22-29, the vigorous taunt-song against the King of Assyria (verses 26-28 being perhaps a later expansion), 37. 30-32, the announcement of a sign, 37. 33-35, the prophecy of the inglorious retreat of the Great King, probably also, indeed, the prediction of the deportation of the royal family (not the People !) to Babylon, see Wilke, *ut sup.* pp. 91-94, also Schmidt SchAT, p. 122 ff.   In support of the genuineness of the first of these passages, I may add here that had the poem originated after 681 B.C. the death of Sennacherib could hardly have been passed over in silence.   Cf. Nah. 1. 14.   The whole pericope has obviously been used by the redactor of the Isaian Book with the purpose of making chapter 39 serve as a bridge connecting the two halves.   As this biography was known to the first Deuteronomist (cf. A. § 4), it must date from about the time of Manasseh.

6. The Book of Consolation, Deutero-Isaiah, 40-55

From the time when the question was raised by Eichhorn, in 1782, down to the middle of the last century, the authorship of chapters 40-55 was long and vigorously debated, but it has now become a universally accepted result of Old Testament Criticism that these chapters were not written by Isaiah, but by an unnamed author, who is usually designated Deutero-Isaiah, *towards the close of the Babylonian Exile.*

Here not only are there marked differences of language (*lamo, bal, ṣu, bemo,* etc.) alongside of a few deliberately adopted resemblances such as " Holy One of Israel," *yomar*

Yahweh, etc.), and of ideas (abstract religious universalism, theoretical monotheism, the belief in creation as a fundamental dogma, the idea of the Servant of God, etc.) from the genuine Isaian discourses in 1-33, but what is still more decisive are the *historical* arguments, the internal evidence of subject-matter. Jerusalem and the Temple are both already destroyed, 44. 26-28 ; 51. 3 ; 52. 9 ; the People are in a position of banishment and captivity in Babylon, 42. 22, 24 ; 43. 14 ; 46. 1 ; 47. 1 ff. ; 48. 14 ; 52. 2, 3, 5, and, moreover, this condition has already been for a long time in existence, 43. 28 ; 47. 6, and now the redemption is close at hand, 40. 1 f., 9 ; 46. 13 ; 51. 14. The oppression by Assyria—which was in the time of Isaiah—belongs to the past, 52. 4 f. The appearance on the stage of history of the Persian King Cyrus is not predicted in advance but lies already behind the speaker ; all his contemporaries know him and have already heard of his brilliant victories, 41. 2 f., 25 ; 44. 28 ; 45. 1-3 ; 48. 14.

The only point about which controversy continues is the *place* where the author himself was living. Many, especially in view of the way the words " from thence " are applied to Babylon, 52. 11, cf. 43. 14 ; 48. 20 (though as against this argument may be quoted the use in 1 K. 2. 36), have thought of Phoenicia, Egypt (on account of 45. 14 ; 49. 12) or even Jerusalem itself. But the " here " of 52. 5, the author's acquaintance with events in Babylon in the year 538, cf. 43. 14, with Babylonian religion and astrology, 40. 19 f. ; 41. 6 f. ; 44. 9 ff. ; 46. 1 ; 47. 2 f., but above all his language, which, as has been proved in the last few years, has a strong Babylonian colouring, lead to the conclusion that he himself lived in Babylon, indeed had grown up there (cf. Kittel, *Cyrus und Deutero-Isaiah*, ZAW, 1898, pp. 149-162 ; Gressmann, *Eschatologie*, p. 305 f. ; Sellin, *Rätsel*, p. 99 ff.). And, finally, the greater part of the sayings and poems of the book are addressed directly to the Babylonian *Golah* (captivity), Cyrus is directly addressed, the Babylonian divinities are challenged to a face-to-face disputation. Is it not in view of all this a case of neglecting what is directly under our eyes if we seek a place other than Babylon for its composition ?

The Book probably appeared in two parts ; at least the poems and prophecies proceed from two different periods. In those of the first period (40-48) Cyrus occupies the centre of interest, the conquest

of Babylon by him and a marvellously glorious
liberation of the Jews are expected to occur immediately.   In the consolatory prophecies and hymns
of the second period (chaps. 49-55) we hear not a
word more of the Persian King nor of the taking
of Babylon, and yet the Return is, according to 52.
1 ff.; 11 ff.; 55. 12 f., still delayed.   That can only
be explained by supposing that 40-48 were written
when Cyrus was first about to strike his final blow
against Babylon, immediately before or immediately
after the occupation of Sippar in the year 539 B.C.,
those of 49-55 after the conquest of Babylon in 538,
which happened in quite a different way from that
expected by Deutero-Isaiah and in which Cyrus
did not realize the prophet's hopes.   The edict of
liberation was issued not from Babylon but from
Ecbatana, cf. Ezra 6. 2, and on the Cyrus cylinder
the king professes allegiance to Marduk and says
nothing about the Jews.

The author often receives something less than justice. It
is indeed generally admitted that it was he, a Hero of Hope,
who for the first time, consistently and with full consciousness,
raised the religion of his People to the position of a world-
religion, but at the same time it is generally thought that in
working out his conceptions in detail he became an enthusiast
and a visionary.   But in thus judging him it is forgotten that
his whole Book is eschatological.   With the victory of Cyrus
there dawn for him those Last Times which for centuries
had been the object of a burning hope.   By this everything
is to be explained—the miraculous march through the wilderness, the picture of the New Jerusalem, the conversion of the
heathen and the overthrow of the world-power (cf. also 49. 26;
51. 6 ff.).   In the question whether his prophecies were only
circulated in writing, or also delivered orally, the second
alternative is to be accepted.   His theatre of action was, however,
no longer the Temple or the market-place, but some conventicle
of pious exiles meeting in a room.

The explanation of what are known as the " Servant of

God " passages or poems (42. 1-4 ; 49. 1-6 ; 50. 4-9 ; 52. 13—
53. 12) has been much debated in the last three decades. It
is quite clear that in these the Servant of God, who in the rest
of the book (41. 8, etc.) is the People of Israel, appears as an
individual, distinct from the People, who is to deliver, restore,
and by his sufferings redeem Israel. Cf. 49. 5 f. ; 53. 2-6, 8.
These passages cannot be disposed of by any exegetical sleight-
of-hand (as is attempted by Budde, *Die sogenannten Ebed-
Jahwe Lieder*, 1900 ; Giesebrecht, *Der Knecht Jahwes bei
Deuterojesaja*, 1902, and others). But when this is admitted,
the origin of the poems presents a very difficult problem.
Undoubtedly the great similarity of ideas and language points
to a single author for both Book and poems. As, however,
it is impossible that the author, if he wrote both at the same
time, meant by the Servant at one moment an individual, at
another the whole Nation, I formerly held that he first composed
the poems with an individual in view, later, however, wished
to make use of them in working out the present book, and in
doing so gave them a new interpretation as referring to the
People (cf. 42. 19 ; 51. 4 f. and the parallel Babylonian and
Old Testament psalms). On this hypothesis we ought in all
probability to see in the individual about whom they were
first composed that Jehoiachin, of David's line, who, after
innocently suffering imprisonment for 36 years, was in 561
raised to a splendid eminence and hailed as the long-expected
deliverer of his People. Cf. 2 K. 25. 27 ff. ; also Josephus, *Ant*. x.
7. 1 ; *Bell*. vi. 2. 1, and Sellin, *Rätsel*, pp. 110-113 ; *Die isr.-jüd.
Heilandserwartung*, pp. 51-60. In many respects the very
thorough examination of the problem by Stärk led him to a
similar result, except that he was inclined to see several poets
where we thought of different periods in the life of one and
the same poet. The essential difference between the Servant
of the first three passages and that of the last passage was
very clearly brought out in his essay.

Lately, however, I believe I have been able to prove with
certainty that this individual Servant of God is none other
than Moses himself, who, according to the prophetic tradition,
suffered a martyr's death in Shittim, cf. Hos. 5. 2 ; 9. 7-14 ;
12. 13 ; 13. 1, and Num. 25. 1-15, who for that reason was
traditionally described as the meekest of men, Num. 12. 3, and
is always designated as pre-eminently the Servant of God,
Num. 12. 7 ff., Deut. 34. 5, Jos. 1. 2, 7, etc. As the Book of
Malachi (4. 5 f.) sets its hopes on the return of Elijah, so Deutero-
Isaiah hopes for the return of Moses, cf. Mt. 17. 1-13, and

assumes that he will lead back to their home the Jews liberated by the favour of Cyrus, and in their homeland will establish a Kingdom of God for all the nations of the earth. This is in fact the only interpretation which solves the great enigma that he who is the subject of the prophetic poems is at once a personage belonging to the historic past and at the same time is only now about to be glorified. Cf. Sellin, *Mose*, pp. 81-113.

7. THE SO-CALLED TRITO-ISAIAN BOOK, 56-66

These chapters used always to be immediately connected with Deutero-Isaiah, though even then it was often remarked that 56. 9—57. 21 would be more appropriately placed at Jerusalem. We are indebted to Duhm for pointing out that there is a deep division after 55, that after 55. 13 there is no further mention of the Return from Babylon, that the whole book, 55-66, points to Jerusalem. Cf. 56. 8*b*; 57. 5 ff., 19; 58. 6; 60. 3 ff., 17 f.; 62. 8; 64. 10 f.; 66. 1 ff., 6, 7-9, 24. Duhm therefore ascribed these chapters to a Trito-Isaiah, to be distinguished from Deutero-Isaiah, who wrote shortly before the advent of Ezra and Nehemiah, being perhaps a contemporary of Malachi, and in whose book the coming schism of the Samaritans— to whose cultus, or perhaps to the temple which they were then planning, 57. 7 ff.; 66. 1 ff., 17 ff., are to be referred—is constantly alluded to. This view has found acceptance in many quarters, except that many critics have questioned the unity of 56-66, and, on the ground that the personality of this Trito-Isaiah would have too chameleon-like a colouring, have suggested a Deutero-Isaian or Trito-Isaian School. But all positive statements rest so far on an insecure foundation, for, after all, our knowledge of the post-Exilic community is very incomplete.

Against Duhm's hypothesis we have to note that the two points which formed the foci of interest in the Ezra-Nehemiah period, and even already in Malachi's day, the Law and mixed-marriages, are not touched on here at all. And, conversely, there is here (especially chapters 57 and 65) a polemic against the worship of false gods, of which we find no trace in Malachi. Three passages in the book point with certainty to a time when the Temple was not in existence, 63. 18; 64. 8 f.; 66. 1-5. There are therefore two possibilities. *Either* the writing is a unity, in which case it must date from the period 537–520 B.C., the time when the Temple was not yet built and when the controversies with the Samaritans must have assumed the sharpest form (cf. also Rothstein, *Juden und Samaritaner,* p. 30, etc.). In this case they might have been written by Deutero-Isaiah, who had come back with the returning exiles; and the differences in language and ideas from chapters 40-55, which, in spite of all the striking affinities, undoubtedly exist, would be explained by the complete change of local, social, and religious circumstances. Nevertheless, it is perhaps better to think of them as the work of a disciple of the latter. *Or,* on the other hand, the writing is not a unity. In that case we could only quite hypothetically suggest that here perhaps a man of the post-Exilic period had combined a section of Deutero-Isaian eschatology, 60-62, with the work of a Jerusalemite prophet of the period between 586 and 520, 56. 9—57. 13; 63. 7—66. 5, and enlarged it with additions of his own, 56. 1-8; 57. 14—59. 21; 63. 1-6; 66. 6-24 (similarly Budde in HSAT). Marti's attempt to assign a Maccabaean date to 63. 18; 64. 8 ff. is open to grave objection, if only on account of the necessity which it involves of violently detaching these passages from 66. 1 ff.

The combination of 40-66 with 1-39 to form one book is usually explained either as purely fortuitous, or as due to the fact that among the Jews the prophets were originally placed in the order, Jeremiah, Ezekiel, Isaiah, and the Minor Prophets, and the anonymous writing, chapters 40-66, might in this way easily become attached to Isaiah. In view, however, of the linguistic affinity which certainly exists between 1-39 and 40-66 (" the Holy

L

One of Israel," *e.g.*, occurring there twelve times, here seventeen times, and elsewhere only five times), it is much more probable that Deutero-Isaiah originally caused his book to appear under the name of Isaiah, or at least intentionally attached it to the latter's work. To this points also the repeated emphasis laid on the idea that " the former things," *i.e.* the destruction of Babylon and the victorious campaign of Cyrus, had been prophesied "from of old." Cf. 41. 26 ; 44. 7 ; 45. 21 ; 46. 9, 10 ; 48. 7, 16.

The author is certainly here alluding to his own earlier prophecies, cf. 41. 25, 48. 14*b*—for his present writing deals with " new things," *i.e.* the liberation of the *Golah* by Cyrus and the Return— but he puts them into the mouth of his great Teacher, Isaiah, finding a connecting link in what is in all probability a genuine prophecy of Isaiah, 39. 6. If this hypothesis is correct, we have to see in Deutero-Isaiah at once the brilliant last repre- sentative of the older prophecy and the pioneer of the later prophetism which wrote anonymously or under a pseudonym—the first representative, in fact, of Apocalyptic.

§ 2. *Jeremiah*

Schwally, *Jeremias Weissagungen gegen die Völker*, ZAW, 1888, p. 177 ff. ; Marti, *Der Prophet Jeremia von Anatot*, 1889 ; Sellin, *Jeremia von Anatot*, NKZ, 1899, p. 257 ff. ; Erbt, *Jeremia und seine Zeit*, 1902 ; Kieser, *Das Jeremiabuch im Lichte der neuesten Kritik*, ThStKr., 1905, p. 479 ff. ; Jacoby, *Zur Komposition des Buches Jer.*, ThStKr, 1906, p. 1 ff. ; Workman, *The Text of Jeremiah*, 1889 ; Wilke, *Das Skythen-problem im Jeremiabuch*, ASt, 1913, p. 222 ff. ; Mowinckel, *Zur Komposition der B. Jeremia*, 1914 ; Volz, *Der Prophet Jeremia*, 1918.

The Book of Jeremiah as we now have it seems to have been composed on the following plan.

(1) The call of the prophet, chap. 1.   (2) Minatory and hortatory discourse to Judah under Kings Josiah, Jehoiakim, Jehoiachin and Zedekiah, 2-35 (with the exception of 25).   (3) A historical account of the activities and experiences of Jeremiah, 36-45. (4) Prophecies against the Foreign Nations, 46-51. (5) Conclusion : the carrying away of Zedekiah to Babylon, 52.

The basis of the book is certainly a writing of Jeremiah, son of a Priest Hilkiah of Anathoth.   In the year 626 B.C.—that is, four or five years before the discovery of Deuteronomy in Josiah's reign—he was, when still a youth, called by a vision to be a prophet.   In his own city, it appears, his preaching had no success, and brought him only persecution, 11. 18 ff. ; 12. 6.   In Jerusalem he worked in Josiah's reign without opposition.   But under Jehoiakim began his martyrdom.   His threat that the Temple should be destroyed like the sanctuary of Shiloh, brought on him the charge of blasphemy ; he was rescued with considerable difficulty by lay friends, but forbidden to visit the Temple for a term of years, 26. 1 ff. ; 36. 5.   He then endeavours to bring his influence to bear upon the people by writing.   He succeeds in getting read, by his disciple Baruch on a fast-day in the Temple, a declaration that the executant of justice, whom he had formerly foretold more vaguely, is Babylon. This makes a great impression on the people, and the writing is brought to Jehoiakim, who, however, burns the book-roll, chap. 36.

When, in 597, Nebuchadnezzar was really approaching and the prophet was repeating his former threatenings he was put in the stocks and ill-treated by Pashhur, the overseer of the Temple, chap. 20. Under Zedekiah he formulated his political programme with increasing definiteness, in the single injunction to be and remain obedient to Babylon. He symbolized it also by going about publicly with a yoke upon his neck. To Hananiah, the prophet who opposed him, he predicted a speedy death, chap. 28. He brought every possible influence to bear to win over Zedekiah to his view, and he also wrote a letter to the exiles in Babylon, who were inciting him to revolt, chap. 29. When, however, all this proved of no avail, and the King nevertheless revolted, he openly predicted his terrible destruction, 21. 1-10.

Nebuchadnezzar came, and during the siege Jeremiah's martyrdom reached its climax. Accused of attempted desertion to the enemy and treacherous conduct, he was first thrown into prison and afterwards into a pit, although the King in his weakness constantly felt secretly drawn to him, chaps. 37 and 38. With the Fall of Jerusalem the hour of Jeremiah's outward deliverance had struck. The Babylonians treated him with respect; he was allowed to remain in the land, 39 and 40. After the assassination by Ishmael of the governor Gedaliah, whom Nebuchadnezzar had appointed, he warned the remnant of the people against a flight into Egypt, but was himself compelled to take part in it, chaps. 42 and 43. There, even in his old age, he sought to influence the souls of his fellow-countrymen, chap. 44.

There is no prophet whose career is better known to us than his. And among them all he comes nearest to us in his humanity. We are given a deep insight into his inner develop-

ment, into the fearful struggles which arose between the word
of Him who sent him and his own natural thoughts and wishes,
8. 8—9. 2 ; 15. 10-21 ; 18. 21-23 ; 20. 7-18. But God had
the victory within him and made the naturally weak and
tender-hearted man into a pillar of iron and a wall of brass,
1. 18.

In his preaching he most resembles Hosea, and for him
too God's innermost being is love, 2. 5 f. ; 3. 1 ff. ; 31. 3.
But he deepens the thought of Hosea. He sets the God " who
trieth the heart and reins," 17. 10, in the closest relationship
with the *heart* of the individual, looks on this as the proper
seat of religion, and places, in opposition to the Temple services
and sacrifices, obedience and prayer as its highest expressions.
His whole relation to God is one of a constant dialogue with
Him. Cf. 4. 4 ; 7. 4 ff., 22 ff. ; 8. 18—9. 1 ; 12. 1-4 ; 14. 8-22 ;
31. 33 ; 32. 39. He thus gave a unique inwardness to the
religion of Israel, and so assured its existence for a time in
which there was no Temple, sacrifice, or priesthood ; and
became the prophet of a New Covenant.

The key to the analysis of the Book of Jeremiah
is given to us by chapter 36. It there appears
that, in the fourth year of Jehoiakim, Baruch wrote
out carefully, at the Prophet's dictation, all the
discourses delivered by his master in the previous
twenty-three years (v. 18). This roll was thrown
into the fire by Jehoiakim, whereupon the prophet
once more dictated its contents to his disciple
(v. 28). This roll must form the basis of our Book.
To this, new material was added later, partly by
Jeremiah himself (all the passages which are in the
first person, cf. 36. 32), partly by Baruch (most of
the passages—with the exception of superscriptions—which speak of Jeremiah in the third person,
for these contain things which only Baruch, in
addition to the prophet, can have known, cf. 45.
2-4), and, finally, by later hands ; so that in the
book, as we have it, three categories of passages
are to be distinguished.

I. Directly Jeremian portions, 1. 1—9. 26; 10. 17–17. 18; 18; 20. 7-18; 21. 11-14; 22—25. 11, 15-26; 27; 30-32; 35. Of this, the original roll no doubt contained 1. 1—17. 18 and probably also 31 (in its original form). But even while Jehoiakim was still reigning other chapters were added: 18; 20. 7-18; 21. 11—22. 9; 25; 35. From Jehoiachin's reign date doubtless only 13. 18 f. and 22. 20-30; from Zedekiah's, 23; 24; 27; 32; from the period after the Fall of Jerusalem, 30.

II. Portions written by Baruch, 19; 20. 1-6; 21. 1-10; 26; 28; 29; 33. 1-13; 34; 36-45; 47, and the kernel of 46; 48; 49. We have a highly important criterion for judging these predominantly narrative sections in the fact that we have the discourse about the destruction of the Temple both as dictated by Jeremiah, in chapter 7, and in Baruch's version, 26. 1-6. We see from this that while Baruch has accurately preserved the main ideas, he is on the whole more interested in the events which followed upon the discourse.

When and by whom Baruch's memoirs were worked up together with Jeremiah's discourses we do not know. But the most probable hypothesis is that Baruch himself wrote them from the first with a view to supplementing and elucidating the discourses, and, accordingly, that here it is not necessary to assume a special redactor. The direct transition from material dictated by Jeremiah to material narrated by Baruch, and conversely, which is frequently found (25; 27; 32; 35, etc.), is best explained in this way.

III. Portions added by later redactors: 10. 1-16; 17. 19-27; 25. 12-14, 27-38; 33. 14-26; 39. 1-13; parts of 46; 48; 49; the whole of 50-52.

The arguments for the non-genuineness of these sections are either that they are mere centos of phrases from other

parts of Jeremiah or from Deutero-Isaiah, or that they are
lacking in the LXX (so, *e.g.*, 33. 14-26; 39. 4-13), or, again,
that, like the Sabbath discourse, 17. 19-27, they are in direct
contradiction with Jeremiah's views as expressed elsewhere.
That 52 is not from the hand of Jeremiah follows at once from
51. 64*b*; the chapter is simply taken from the Book of Kings.
But, again, the prophecy about Babylon, 50; 51, cannot
possibly be Jeremian, because Jeremiah did not expect an
immediate deliverance from Babylon such as is here predicted.
Cf. chap. 29. Further arguments in Budde JDTh, 1878, p. 420 f.

There are, however, two critical problems about which
opinion is still somewhat divided : (*a*) regarding 30 and 31.
While Stade and Smend reject chapter 31 *in toto*, Giesebrecht
and Cornill have shown that this chapter must have at least a
genuine kernel (say, verses 2-6, 15-20, 27-34), a poem referring
to Northern Israel from the prophet's earliest period. But similarly, in regard to chapter 30, it must be recognized that verses
5, 6, 12-17, 18-21 are genuine, cf. ZEAT, p. 76 ; (*b*) regarding the
Discourses on the Foreign Nations, 25 ; 46-49, which are rejected
especially by Schwally and Stade. The position is much the
same as in the case of (*a*). According to 1. 10, cf. 36. 2, Jeremiah
had also a commission to the heathen, and no material arguments are brought against verses 25, 1-11, 15-26 and 47, only
false assumptions of a religious-historical character. As against
these, it may be pointed out that the image of the cup of the
wrath or poison-cup of Yahweh, chap. 25, was not indeed newly
invented by Jeremiah but must have become generally current
just in his time. Cf. 8. 14; 9. 15; 23. 15; Ezek. 23. 32 f., etc.
In chapters 46, 48 and 49 there are no doubt traces of a
redactor's hand, but here too there is certainly a genuinely
Jeremian basis of considerable extent (46. 3-5, 7-12, 13-25;
48. 1-3, 6-9, 11 ff.; 49. 7-11, 13, 28-33). See Giesebrecht,
Cornill and Rothstein in HSAT.

Duhm's criticism, which applies to the Book a purely
aesthetic and stylistic criterion, and leaves the prophet only
some sixty short prophetic poems (quatrains of alternate three-
stressed and two-stressed lines), may often be right in detail,
but the principle is unsound. There is not a shadow of proof
that some of the prophet's discourses were not delivered in
rhythmic prose ; chapters 1 and 16, in fact, are certain proof
to the contrary.

One special problem presented by the Book of
Jeremiah is that in it LXX and MT differ from one

another in a way unparalleled elsewhere in the Old Testament. Not only is the position of whole portions different in the two, but the LXX text is shorter by about 2700 words than the MT. The question which text is to be preferred cannot be treated as a clear-cut alternative, it is rather the case that several principles have to be employed as criteria in coming to a decision in particular cases.

It is obvious that the Greek translator has often given a rendering which is not only very free, but, especially in the case of unusual words, absolutely wrong; and also that he was working from a badly-written text, so that it was easy for him to misread similar consonants. But at the same time the text of this MS. must have differed widely from the MT. And though these divergences are often seen to be intentional smoothings and abbreviations, nevertheless in many passages the text which lay before the Alexandrian translator was the more original; for many words, phrases, and whole sections which he has not got are clearly shown by internal evidence to be glosses and later additions. In the case of the divergence which most strikes the eye, the placing of the prophecies against the heathen nations, 46-51, between 25. 13 and 25. 15-38, the fact evidently is that in connecting 46-51 with 25 the LXX certainly gives the original connection, but in inserting the passage between verses 13 and 15 and also in altering the order of the Nations it has made arbitrary changes, while the MT is here the more original. The original position of 46-51 was therefore after 25. 26.

§ 3. *Ezekiel*

Cornill, *Das Buch des Propheten Ez.*, 1886; D. H. Müller, *Ezechielstudien*, 1895; Herrmann, *Ezechielstudien*, 1908; Jahn, *Das Buch Ez. auf Grund d. LXX hergestellt*, 1905.

The most important facts in the life of Ezekiel were, according to his book, the following. He was a priest, the son of a certain Buzi, 1. 3. As such he belonged to the aristocracy of Jerusalem, who, in the year 597 B.C., were deported along with

Jehoiachin to Babylon. Here he lived at Tell-Abib (3. 15) by the river Chebar (1. 1). He was the husband of one wife, and, it would appear, childless, 24. 16-18. His house served as a meeting-place for the Elders among the Exiles; he was evidently, therefore, a person of consideration, 8. 1; 14. 1; 20. 1. In the year 592 he was called, by an imposing vision, to be a prophet, 1. 2 ff.

His prophetic activities fall into two periods, divided by the Fall of Jerusalem in 586 B.C., 33. 21 f. In the first he was exclusively a preacher of repentance and judgement; in discourses and by symbolic actions he foretold the destruction of Jerusalem. Once the news of this event reached him, the character of his discourses changed. He became a consoler, a herald of salvation, nay, more, a reformer, looking to the coming period of Restoration. His last prophecy which has a note of time attached to it is 29. 17, which falls in the year 570.

Ezekiel is distinguished from the other Old Testament prophets by the special prominence of the *pathological* element in his prophecy. Visions, ecstasies, second-sight and striking symbolic actions bulk largely in his experience. Perhaps in addition to certain Babylonian influences (cf. some of the figures in his visions, the banning, etc.) some corporeal ailment is to be brought in by way of explanation, *e.g.* temporary dumbness with paralytic symptoms, catalepsy, as Klostermann (ThStKr, 1877, p. 391 ff.), on the ground of 4. 4 ff.; 24. 27; 29. 21; 33. 22, has argued. Herrmann (p. 75 ff.) has contested the literal interpretation of these passages as referring to physical conditions, pointing to 16. 63; 29. 21, where the "opening of the mouth" is meant symbolically. Cf. also Baentsch, *Pathologische Züge in Israels Prophetentum*, ZWTh, 1907, p. 52 ff.; Hölscher, *ut sup.*, p. 301 f.; the latter considers 4. 4 ff. to be a legend based on 3. 25 f.

The Book of Ezekiel falls into three main parts. After the Introduction, which is formed by the story of his Call in 1. 1–3. 15, the first part, 3. 16–24. 27 contains the most diverse variations upon the theme of the destruction of Jerusalem. The second part, 25-32, contains prophecies against seven of the surrounding nations, the third, 33-48, comprises the consolatory discourses after the destruction of Jerusalem, including (*a*) 33-39, Promise of the New Covenant, the Resurrection of the People, the Destruction of Gog, (*b*) 40-48, the Vision of the New Temple and New Law.

The diction of Ezekiel is apparently jejune and often offends modern aesthetic feeling, but beneath it there glows a fierce and sacred fire. It was this man who, humanly speaking, saved the exiles from a religious *débâcle*. And he also influenced the religious development of his People for the future, since, (1) as the spiritual guide of the exiles, he for the first time promulgated a doctrine of individual retribution, 14. 12 ff. ; 18. 2 ff., though not, indeed, without himself immediately coming into conflict with it, 14. 21 ff. ; 18. 2 ff ; (2) in spite of the national catastrophe, he held firmly by the Davidic dynasty, 34. 24 ; 37. 22 f. ; and (3) he gave fixed form, for the time of the restoration, to a Temple Law, and so became the real father of Judaism.

The widely prevalent idea that he is also—in contradistinction to the pre-Exilic Prophets—the father of *Apocalyptic*, rests in part on the evidence of passages which are not his at all (38. 8, 16), partly on a false conception of the origin of eschatology in general, which was in fact no literary creation, but rests upon a tradition that goes back for centuries and can be proved to have been known to all the pre-Exilic Prophets. Ezekiel is decidedly to be counted as one of the really great prophets, of whom he is the last. His inspiration is thoroughly authentic, although, like all the prophets, he has reproduced the word of God which flowed in upon him in the forms prescribed by his own personality.

It was long held that, while the text was in many places very corrupt, the Book itself raised hardly any critical problems, but was throughout genuine, and had proceeded as an ordered whole from the hand of the prophet, just as we now have it. As against this view Krätzschmar, on the ground of the two-fold superscription, 1. 1-3, the doublets in 7. 1-9, and frequently elsewhere (3. 4-9; 4. 9-17, etc.), has sought to distinguish two recensions, a shorter one which speaks of Ezekiel in the third person (1. 2 f.; 24. 24), and another fuller one in which he always speaks in the first person. Since, however, in point of fact the third person is only once used of Ezekiel (1. 2 f.), this view has been modified and corrected by Budde (*Geschichte d. hebr. Litt.*, p. 154 f.) to the effect that the book composed by Ezekiel himself was for a time circulated in various versions, which later on were reduced to unity by a redactor. The still more thoroughgoing analysis of Herrmann has given a better explanation of the inconcinnities detected by Krätzschmar by suggesting that, on the one hand, Ezekiel did not write his book all at one time, but put it together gradually by combining separate portions, and worked at it for a long time, correcting and revising; while, on the other hand, later interpolations have found their way into numerous passages.

Chapters 38, 39 and 40-48 have lately been felt to present a special problem. In 38, 39 Krätzschmar had earlier tried to show that there were two mutually exclusive parallels, viz. 38. 3-9, 16*b*, 17; 39. 1-8; and 38. 10-16*a*, 18-23; 39. 9-20. In this he received the support of Gressmann (*Eschatologie*, p. 180 ff.), who, however, maintained further the spuriousness of the whole Gog section, on the ground that Ezekiel's predictions of the future ended with chapter 37. As against this, Herrmann has shown that there is a homogeneous strand running through the two chapters which may well be derived from Ezekiel himself, a prophecy, namely, referring to the Fall of Babylon, of which, curiously, nothing is said in 25-32. This prophecy was framed on mythological models, and was glossed by later hands with the purpose of transferring events that Ezekiel expected in the near future to the End of the Days, 38. 5-6, 8, 14-16, 17-23; 39. 5, 16. We may suggest the question whether this last was not, on the contrary, an integral part of the mythological basis, and we hold, for example, that the excision of 38. 17-23 is unjustifiable, because the " through my servants the prophets " of verse 17 can be best explained, even in the mouth of Ezekiel, as spoken to a *heathen* king. But in the main the right solution will certainly be found in the line of investigation initiated by Herrmann.

A second point of far-reaching significance is that Herrmann, on the basis of a detailed analysis of 40-48, which have hitherto been held to be almost completely homogeneous, has arrived at the result that the genuineness of 43. 13-27; 44. 20-31; 45. 11-15; 46. 11, 13-15; 47. 13–48. 34 is doubtful. Further work will be needed to decide this point. (See also Steuernagel, *Einleitung*, p. 593 ff.)

Completely unsuccessful was the attempt of Winckler (*Forschungen*, III. pp. 135-155) to place this Book in the post-Exilic period, and to reckon all the dates in it from the return of Sheshbazzar, which requires the arbitrary alteration of all the figures

§ 4. *The Collection of the Twelve Minor Prophets*

Duhm, *Anmerkungen zu den zwölf Propheten*, 1911 ; Procksch, *Die kleinen prophetischen Schriften*, I., 1910, II., 1916.

These Books, denominated in the LXX simply " The Twelve," and in the Vulgate, on account of their smaller extent, "the lesser Prophets," were regarded from early times as a whole, bearing the sacred number twelve, as is evident from Sir. (Ecclus.) 49. 12. Since size was thus a determining factor in the making of the collection, the most various writings from the most various periods of Old Testament History are here set side by side. Writings in which we can trace almost more strongly than in any others in the Old Testament that breath of Divine inspiration which is exalted above all limitations of time and space (Amos, Hosea, Micah), have as their next-door neighbours others whose authors were not really prophets at all (Jonah).

The order, which however is not the same in the LXX (there : Hosea, Amos, Micah, Joel, Obadiah, Jonah), seems only to have been so far influenced

by chronological considerations that the three
writings which were then held to be post-Exilic are
placed in their historical order at the end (Haggai,
Zechariah, Malachi). But the order of the remainder has clearly been determined by other
points of view. (Hosea, *e.g.*, as the longest, was
placed at the head, a prophet of the Northern
Kingdom was paired with one of the Southern,
others are connected by catch-words, *e.g.* " the Day
of Yahweh" in Joel, Amos and Obadiah; Carmel,
Bashan in Micah 7. 14, Nah. 1. 4, etc.) The
collection of the Twelve into one Book, moreover,
was certainly separated by several centuries from
the writing of most of them. So that, if we wish
to assign a date to them, we are thrown back on the
superscriptions which most of them bear (Hosea,
Amos, Micah, Zephaniah, Haggai, Zechariah) and,
still more, on a careful historical examination of the
historical circumstances which the books imply.

§ 5. *Hosea*

Valeton, *Amos en Hosea*, 1894, German translation by Echter-
nacht, 1898 ; Oettli, *Amos und Hosea*, 1901 ; Volz, *Die Ehegeschichte
Hoseas*, ZWTh, 1898, pp. 321-35 ; Riedel, *Alttestamentliche Unter-
suchungen*, pp. 1-18, 1902 ; Meinhold, *Studien zur israelitischen
Religionsgeschichte*, I. 1903; Baumgartner, *Kennen Amos und
Hosea eine Heilseschatologie ?*, 1913 ; Peiser, *Hosea*, 1914 ; Prätorius,
Bemerkungen zum Buch Hosea, 1918 ; Alt, *Hosea, 5. 8-6. 6*, NKZ,
1919, pp. 537-68.

Of Hosea (the name = God's Help) we know,
directly, only that his father was named Beeri.
For any further information we are thrown back
on inferences from the book itself. That he was a
citizen of the Northern Kingdom may be inferred,
if not from 7. 5, certainly from 10. 3*b*, in conjunction with linguistic considerations; his acquaintance

with the special sins of the priests (cf. chap. 4) hardly warrants the conclusion that he belonged to priestly circles ; but according to 9. 8 ff. he certainly belonged to the fellowship of the *Nebiim*. He is little moved by the social, but very strongly by the religious and political, troubles of his people.

In the superscription, 1. 1, it is noticeable that four Kings of Judah are named and only one of Northern Israel, Jeroboam II., who died as early as 743, whereas the line of Judah is followed for thirty years further. That would seem to indicate that the reference to Judah is made here simply on the analogy of Amos 1. 1, and is expanded in imitation of Isa. 1. 1. But in essence it is doubtless right. According to 1. 4 the first public appearance of Hosea did actually take place in the time when the House of Jehu, to which Jeroboam II. belonged, was still reigning, while, on the other hand, the greater part of his activity, 7. 3-7, 16 ; 8. 4 ; 10. 15, implies anarchical times and circumstances, with rapid changes on the throne, such as obtained during the succession of those transient and embarrassed phantoms, Zechariah, Shallum, Menahem, Pekahiah, Pekah. It can be said with something like certainty that the allusions to the payment of tribute to Assyria, 5. 13 ; 10. 6 ; 12. 1, refer to Menahem's payment in 738 B.C. (cf. 2 K. 15. 19 f.). Lately Alt has rightly pointed out that 5. 8—6. 3 refer to the Syro-Ephraimite war. And the rôle played by the Egyptians, 7. 11 ; 9. 3, 6 ; 11. 5 ; 12. 1, as the counterpoise to Assyria seems to take us down to the time of the last Israelitish King. Accordingly the career of Hosea must be placed between 750 and 725 B.C.

Hosea's prophecy is strongly influenced by an entirely personal experience, in the form of his marriage, of which he tells the story in chapters 1 and 3. He was obliged, by the Divine command, to take a harlot to wife, in order to set before Israel symbolically its own relation to Yahweh. And this commission to carry out a prophetic act, together with his efforts to lead his wife to faithfulness, and the birth of three children of the marriage, gave him the impulse to a series of prophetic discourses.

The old and much-discussed question—whether 1 and 3 are *allegory* or *actual fact*—is now rightly answered by the majority of critics in the latter sense. If the chapters did contain anything morally objectionable this would be as objectionable in an allegory as in actual fact; the name Gomer is not susceptible of an allegorical interpretation, the parallels in Isa. 7. 3 and 8. 3 demand a literal interpretation, and the number of the children (3), as well as the little touch about the birth of the third after the weaning of the second, in 1. 8, defy allegorical interpretation.

A second question which has not yet been definitely solved is whether the wife spoken of in chapter 3 *is another or the same*. The majority of critics decide in favour of the latter alternative, and assume that we have to fill out the story by supposing that between 1 and 3 Gomer has fallen into slavery, but that Hosea's love for her is not dead and he therefore purchases her freedom. Cornill has sought to simplify the matter by suggesting that in accordance with Ex. 21. 7 the wife would naturally return to her father's house, and that the father sold her a second time to Hosea—who did not at first wish to have her back as a legitimate wife—as a slave. But there are very serious difficulties in the way of this interpretation. We should thus get a twice-repeated separation of the wife from her husband, and that ought to mean, as reflected in the facts, a twice-repeated Exile. But the main point is that the plain wording of 3. 1 in the text as we have it almost compels us to think of another wife. Of the adultery and dismissal of Gomer we do not in fact hear a word. Marti and others propose to strike out chapter 3 as a later interpolation, but verse 4 cries out against this. See below. Steuernagel sees in chapter 3 a second fragmentary account and interpretation of the same event as in chapter 1, which was wrongly taken by a later editor to be a second event. This editor then definitely imposed his interpretation upon it by inserting the words " Beginning of the speaking of Yahweh with Hosea " in 1. 2, and " once more " in 3. 1. My own view is that, in the first place, there was a homogeneous narrative in the first person, according to which Yahweh twice made the hard demand of Hosea that he should take to wife a harlot, 1. 2 ; 3. 1 ; 3. 3-5a (read, in verse 3, the imperative *weemor*, " and say " instead of " and I said ") ; 1. 3a ; 3. 2 (cf. the twice-repeated command to Ezekiel, 4. 9 and 14). A redactor then by a misunderstanding interpreted this of two separate marriages, detached 3. 1-5 from 1. 2, 3a, and transferred the " once more " to 3. 1.

Hosea has rightly been called the Minnesinger among the Prophets. As he himself loved faithfully and intensely, but unhappily, so too the Husband of Israel. God is *love*, that is the evangel that he brought into the world, 3. 1 ; 11. 1, 3, 8, 9. And from this he drew the conclusion that God demands nothing else than faithfulness, love and " the Knowledge of God "—that is, the surrender of the heart, 4. 1 ; 6. 6. The chief of sins is for him the whole cultus of his own time, in which he sees Canaanitish heathenism, the worship of images and at the high-place the sacrificial offerings, through which the search for God has gone astray out of the right path, 5. 6. In view of 9. 9 ; 10. 9, cf. with 13. 10, it is sometimes said that he places the kingship alongside of this as a main form of sin, but these passages ought not to be interpreted as referring to Saul's kingship, but to the shameful deed of Gibeah, Jg. 19-21 (cf. 10. 9b with Jg. 20. 13 ff.) ; in reality he condemns only the kingship *of his own time*, 7. 3 ff. ; 8. 4.

While it is certain that Hosea expected a temporary suspension of the marriage between God and His People, and some terrible form of judgement, cf. 9. 15; 10. 5-8; 13. 1, 5, 16; yet it is equally certain that it was as impossible for him as for any of his contemporaries to think of this judgement as final; he looked beyond it to a time of conversion and Divine favour and blessing; in short, he has *an Eschatology of Salvation.*

Even if chapter 3 is not a continuation of chapter 1, each by itself implies that the punishment will only be temporary (cf. 3. 3, 5 and 2. 16 ff. as a supplementary poem to chap. 1); and this is also implied by the whole conception of the Divine character in Hosea 11. 8, 9. In fact, the expectation of a final deliverance runs like a red thread through the whole book.

That, however, is at present disputed in many quarters. Of course the Book of Hosea, like the other Books, has a history behind it; and it is not to be denied that after 722, when it was doubtless brought to Jerusalem, here and there a stronger reference to Judah may have been interpolated. The mention of Judah in 1. 7; 5. 13; 6. 11; 8. 14 and 10. 11 is clearly foreign to the original connection, and consequently of secondary origin. But whether the same should be said of 4. 15; 6. 4 is highly questionable; and in 5. 10—6. 3 if the " Judah " is removed all possibility of rightly understanding the passage disappears. All these passages, however, are struck out by Marti, Volz and others on another ground as well, viz. that they contain promises. With them go 1. 10—2. 1, 2. 13b-23; 3. 1-5; 5. 15—6. 3, 5b; 11. 8-11; 12. 6; 14. 1-9.

But this whole criticism rests on completely false premisses. The expectation of deliverance is no new spiritual invention of the prophets, but a tradition which they inherited (cf. Amos 5. 18, etc.), and therefore the argument that it conflicts with the threatenings of disaster is not relevant. At the very least, it is wholly impossible to deny that Hosea in his first period cherished the hope of a spiritual re-birth of his People, and thought of the judgement as of a purifying character, but on this hypothesis it might still be argued that the compiler of the Book for literary reasons took sayings from this period and inserted them at the end, thus giving a false impression

M

that these were the last words of his public ministry (so *e.g.* Staerk, *ut sup.*, pp. 36-45).

Coming to detail, the following falls to be said. The fact that Yahweh is, at a later time, never called by the people " my Husband," 2. 16 (cf., on the other hand, Jer. 3. 19 !), the idea, which doubtless dates from long before the prophets, of a Covenant with the animals, 2. 18, and above all the whole of verse 4 of chapter 3 which, with its mention of the *Mazzebah* and the Elohistic-Ephraimitish *Ephod* and *Teraphim*, cf. 1 S. 15. 23; Jg. 17. 5 ff., and also the parallel *King* and *Prince*, cf. 7. 3; 8. 4, is not only pre-Deuteronomic but demonstrably Hosean, are arguments in favour of the genuineness of 2. 14—3. 5, which are not easily to be set aside. Verses 6 and 7 and 14-23 of chapter 2 are independent poems which Hosea added later to the chidings of 2. 2-13. Chapter 1. 10*b* and 2. 1, which refer prematurely to the change of the children's names, betray themselves as an interpolation between 1. 10*a* and 1. 11 and are to be struck out. The denial of the genuineness of 5. 15—6. 3 entirely ignores the inner connection of thought with 5. 14 (the allusion to the Adonis myth) and overlooks the parallel with 13. 1, where the death of the People is similarly spoken of. In regard to 11. 8, 9, even Marti has the feeling that it is genuine, but he changes the meaning into one of threatening. But that is excluded not only by verse 10 f. but also by 8*b*, and אֵיךְ almost always indicates that the thought of the verse is incredible or impossible (Jer. 3. 19; in 9. 6 the text is corrupt). Finally, 14. 1-8 must, if the linguistic argument is to have any force at all, be from the hand of Hosea (esp. vv. 2, 3, 8): they are presupposed already by Jer. 3. 22. That verse 3 might be understood, on the analogy of Isa. 30. 16, of an alliance with Egypt is perfectly true, but all the same it does not refer to that, but to an alliance with Assyria. Cf. 5. 13; 10. 6. In short, though the text of Hosea no doubt in many passages stands in need of correction, elimination of glosses and transposition of many verses (for example, 1. 10*a*, 11 should perhaps come after 5. 10—6. 3), a radical criticism is out of place. Cf., recently, Baumgartner, *ut sup.*, and Sellin, *Mose*, where positive arguments are adduced in favour of the genuineness of all the prophecies of salvation in Hosea, who expected their realization to take place at the Mount of God in the wilderness.

§ 6. *Joel*

Merx, *Die Prophetie des Joel und ihre Ausleger*, 1879 ; Holzinger, *Sprachcharakter und Abfassungszeit d. B.J.*, ZAW, 1889, p. 88 ff. ; Gressmann, *Eschatologie*, p. 91 ff. ; Stocks, *Der " Nördliche " und die Komposition d. B.J.*, NKZ, 1908, p. 725 ff. ; Knieschke, *Die Eschatologie des Buches Joel in ihrer historisch - geographischen Bestimmtheit*, 1912 ; Budde, OLZ, 1919, esp. p. 104 ff.

This short Book deals (*a*) in chapters 1 and 2 with a plague of locusts, bringing famine in its train, which has been devastating the land for years (2. 25), in which the prophet sees an approach of the Day of Yahweh (1. 15), but which is averted by a great day of repentance ; (*b*) in chapter 2. 28–3. 2 it deals with the outpouring of the Divine Spirit upon all flesh (in Judah), with which are to be associated signs in heaven and on earth ; (*c*) in chapter 3 with the Judgement upon all Nations, whom God brings together in the valley of Jehoshaphat and there destroys them, because they have scattered Israel.

The superscription tells us only that the Book is derived from a certain Joel, the son of Pethuel. (Whether there is any allusion in the name to Elijah, cf. 2. 23, must be left an open question.) Its date has therefore to be determined entirely by internal evidence. On this point the variation of opinion is extraordinarily wide. At an earlier period it was usual to date it, as perhaps the earliest of the prophetic writings, during the minority of Joash (so Delitzsch, etc.). Others, on account of many linguistic and other affinities with Jeremiah, placed it in the reign of Josiah (König, Stocks, Knieschke). Now, however, the most widely-held view places it in the post-Exilic period, after Malachi and Ezra (Merx, Wellhausen, Nowack,

Marti). And a division of the Book has also been suggested, dating chapters 1 and 2. 2-27 in the time of Joash, 2. 28-32 and 3 in the post-Exilic period (Vernes and Rothstein).

A certain datum for determining the time when the Book was reduced to writing is furnished by 3. 2, 3, 6, 17, 19. According to these passages both the destruction of Jerusalem and the dispersion of Israel-Judah lie behind the author, who is therefore writing in the post-Exilic period. And the circumstances of 1. 9, 13, 14; 2. 15-17 (no king, priests the only leaders of the people, Tamid-sacrifice) are also appropriate to it. The ideas also confirm this view. The Day of Yahweh is no longer, as for the pre-Exilic prophets, primarily a day of judgement for Israel, but a day of punishment for the heathen, 3. 2 f., 4, 19.

To determine the date of origin more exactly is not possible. All that we can say is that the Book as a whole is later than Malachi (cf. 2. 23 with Mal. 3. 23 f.), but earlier than the Macedonian period (cf. 3. 4 ff., 19, where the real enemies are not as yet the Greeks).

The Book, however, small as it is, presents yet another peculiar literary problem. Vernes and Rothstein were not without solid reasons for their hypothesis; indeed no reader can avoid the impression that chapters 1 and 2 on the one hand, 3 and 4 on the other (this is the Hebrew chapter-division; in the English Version the first part would be 1—2. 27, the second 2. 28 to the end), are two portions of diverse character which have been coupled together. Duhm has therefore rightly revived this hypothesis in a special form of his own. He distinguishes, first, a post-Exilic poetic writing, 1. 1—2. 17, which has for its subject a historical visitation of locusts and the means by which it was arrested. (Into this were worked later the references to the Day of Yahweh, 1. 15; 2. 1*b*, 2, 3*c*, 11*b*, which in every case disturb the metre.) Secondly, a long prose expansion of this, of apocalyptic character, dating from a later period (according to him from the Maccabaean age), 2. 18—3. 21. The fundamental idea here seems to me to be right, but the hypothesis requires modification in two directions. In the first place, the poem dealing with the locusts cannot possibly have ended with 2. 17, for in that case it would have lacked all point. The point is surely in 2. 18-27, only that here the poetical basis has been almost completely overlaid by the later eschatological expansion. To the former belong, probably, 2. 18, 19*aa*, 21*a*, 22, 23*aa*, *b*, 24, 26, which, when certain glosses have been removed, can easily be read rhythmically. Secondly, in the Locust poem some further excisions have to be made in addition to Duhm's, especially 2. 10, which is taken from 3. 15, 16.

On this hypothesis, Joel has taken an earlier poem on the subject of a historical plague of locusts and its merciful withdrawal—which doubtless dated from the first century after the Exile—and by interpolating the announcement of the approach of the Day of Yahweh, of the destruction of the eschatological Foe from the North (2. 20), of the coming of the (post-Exilic) Messiah (2. 23*aβ*, cf. Mal. 4. 5) and the addition of 2. 28–3. 21 transformed it into an Apocalypse.

The suggestion, however, came to him from a much older tradition, according to which locusts, pictured as a kind of demonic army, formed one of the eschatological plagues (cf. Gressmann, *Eschatologie*, pp. 91 ff.; 187 f.). Similarly, in 2. 28—3. 21 he is working for the most part on older material; the manifestation of the Divine Spirit in dreams and visions, 2. 28, the signs in heaven and on earth, 2. 30, the idea of the assembling of the nations for a day of Judgement, 3. 2, 9, 12, the coming of Paradise and the welling-up of the fountain of life, 3. 18—all these belong to the period before Amos and are presupposed by him, as also by Isaiah, Zephaniah and others of the prophets (cf. Am. 5. 18; 8. 9; 9. 13 ff.; Isa. 2. 12 ff.; 3. 13; 5. 26 ff.; 7. 18 ff., etc.). Moreover, in 2. 32 there is an express reference to former words of Yahweh.

§ 7. *Amos*

Cf. § 5. Löhr, *Untersuchungen zum Buch Amos*, BZAW, 1901 ; Baumann, *Der Aufbau der Amosreden*, BZAW, 1903 ; Sievers and Guthe, *Amos, metrisch bearbeitet*, 1907 ; Winter, *Analyse des B. Amos*, ThStKr, 1910, pp. 323-74 ; Budde, *Zur Geschichte des B. Amos* in the Wellhausen " Festschrift," 1914, p. 63 ff. ; H. Schmidt, *Der Prophet Amos*, 1917 ; Köhler, *Amos*, 1917 ; Marti, *Zur Komposition von Amos, 1. 3–2. 3* in the Baudissin " Festschrift," 1918, p. 323 ff.

According to 1. 1 the prophetic work of Amos falls in the reigns of Uzziah of Jerusalem and Jeroboam (II.) of Israel. The contents of his book entirely confirm that statement. The prophet directly addresses a threat to the House of Jeroboam in 7. 8, 11, and the outwardly prosperous reign of this king and his successful campaigns, 6. 13, everywhere find their reflection in the discourses of this prophet.

We might date the period of his activities more exactly, if we could be sure about the earthquake mentioned in 1. 1 (cf. Zech. 14. 5), or could decide whether the eclipse, which perhaps supplies him with his imagery in 8. 9, was that of the year 784 or the year 763. It is safest to place him somewhere about 750 B.C.

According to the superscription, he belonged to the herdmen, or flock-masters, of Tekoa, a village in the wilderness near the Dead Sea, and perhaps his origin and the nature of his Call are still better illustrated by his own saying, " I was no prophet nor of the guild of the prophets, but a shepherd was I, and a tender of sycomore figs, and the Lord took me from the flock and said unto me, Go prophesy against my People Israel," 7. 14. There, in the lonely wilderness, perhaps under the terror

of a storm (cf. 1. 2 ; 3. 8, so Bertholet in the
Bonwetsch " Festschrift," p. 1 ff.), the shadow fell
upon his soul which made him aware of the coming
judgement, and forced him to raise his voice in a
song of lamentation over his people, 5. 1.   For
the most part his prophecies were uttered on the
occasion of a visit to a feast at Bethel, 3. 14, 4. 4 ;
5. 6 ; 7. 10 ff. ; 9. 1 ; but before that he had been
acquainted with Samaria, 3. 9 ff. ; 4. 1 ff. ; 6. 1 ff.
A prophecy spoken in Bethel against the House of
Jeroboam (7. 9) gives occasion for his expulsion from
the precincts of this national sanctuary by the
High Priest Amaziah ; and the historical episode,
7. 10-17, was accordingly attached immediately to
this saying by a later redactor.

In reality, of course, 7. 1-9 ; 8. 1 ff. ; 9. 1 ff.
must have been spoken consecutively, and the
episode should be placed at the end of this whole
discourse.   (Unconvincing and contrary to all
analogy is Budde's hypothesis that the Book
originally began with the narrative portion.)   That
Amos, in spite of his protest in 7. 17, had to obey
the edict of expulsion, and returned (via Jerusalem)
to his home is naturally to be understood ; we are
not directly told anything about it.   And it was
there, at Jerusalem, no doubt, that he collected his
prophecies into a book.   The legend, in 1 K. 13, of
the man of God who came to Bethel, is perhaps a
later echo of his work.

That Amos was a man of Judah follows not only from 7. 12
but also from 7. 10, "in the midst of the house of Israel,"
implying that he did not himself belong to it.   He is one of
the most powerful preachers of repentance and a coming
judgement among all the prophets.   The very essence of the
Divine nature is for him an absolute righteousness, 3. 2,

9. 1 ff. ; he therefore demands of men nothing else than justice and righteousness in the fullest sense of the word ; in short, ethical good, 5. 7 ff., 14 ff. Consequently he condemns not only the whole secular life, but also the whole religious life of his time, 5. 5, 21-27. Judgement must come ; how, is inessential, though the burden of his prophecy is that it will take the form of a carrying away into exile by an unnamed enemy, 6. 7, 14 ; 7. 17 ; 9. 4 ; according to 5. 27 Assyria is already in the background of his thought.

It was long the fashion to see in Amos the creator of ethical *monotheism* and the initiator of the view that Yahweh is the God of the whole world. That is no doubt an error ; he was only the deepest, the most uncompromising and most eloquent herald of a truth that had long been known. In the very utterances which deal with this subject he implies that what he proclaims is already known, 1. 3—2. 3 ; 5. 18 ; 9. 7. In this path he had many predecessors (Nathan, Elijah, the Yahwist, the Elohist, Moses). But we have reason to be thankful that we have here for once the authentic utterances of one of these " troublers of Israel " (1 K. 18. 17).

The Book is obviously composed of three parts : (1) The Introduction, chapters 1 and 2 : the judgement which first sweeps like a storm over the seven surrounding nations and finally discharges itself upon Israel. (2) Chapters 3-6, a collection of minatory discourses. (3) 7. 1–9. 6, visions, with the interpolated historical episode, 7. 10-17, fragments of exhortations to repentance, 8. 4-14 ; 9. 7-10, and an appended promise, 9. 11-15. The most probable hypothesis is that Amos himself wrote his book in this general order (at Jerusalem) or had it written for him. But some parts of it have fallen out of order. The position of 8. 4-14 ; 9. 7-10 is surprising, for these passages would naturally come after chapters 3-6. And the narrative section, 7. 10-17, must originally have stood just before 9. 11-15.

This shows that later hands have been at work upon the book, a fact which has long been recognized in regard to the inter-related *doxologies*, 4. 13 ; 5. 8 f. ; 9. 5 f., which now interrupt the connection of thought in an intolerable way. These were probably written down at one time, by one and the same hand, originally, no doubt, in the margin, and their author must have been acquainted with the Book of Job. It is to be noted that they always stand at a point where there has been a reference to a destruction of the sanctuary of Bethel by Yahweh personally (3. 14 originally followed 4. 12*a*). Apart from doubts cast upon some less important sections, like 1. 6-12 ; 8. 11*b*, 12*b*—the genuineness of which must be admitted to be doubtful—by Wellhausen, Stade, Marti and others (though Bertholet has lately offered proof of the genuineness of 1. 2), objections are raised by the majority of critics against the prophecy of a judgement against Judah, 2. 4, 5, and the prophecy of salvation in 9. 11-15.

But the denial of the *genuineness* of the first-named section is not so strongly based as is usually assumed. The reason generally given is that here we do not find, as in other threatenings against the nations, specific sins named, but merely a censure clothed in general Deuteronomic phrases. But as Israel in 2. 6 ff. is treated differently from the surrounding nations, it is not surprising that Judah, which likewise stands in contrast with these, should also be treated differently, and as regards the so-called Deuteronomic phrases, it cannot be denied, in view of passages like Ex. 18. 16 ; Hos. 4. 6 ; 8. 12 ; Isa. 5. 24, that such phrases were possible as early as the days of Amos. The thought and language of 2. 4 are not specifically Deuteronomic, but Elohistic (cf. Jos. 24. 2 ff.), and by this source the prophet is influenced elsewhere (cf. Procksch, *ut sup.*, 256 f.) ; it is also possible that " lies " has been substituted for an original " gods." And would it not have been very surprising if Judah had been ignored in this connection by the Judaean Amos ? On the other hand, it is certainly not to be denied that the standard of judgement which Amos here applies is foreign to his practice elsewhere and that this oracle conflicts decidedly with Amos' expectation regarding the future of Judah in 9. 11-15. The objection, however, which has been taken to the *close of the Book*, with its promises, is invalid. It is evident, of course, that Amos cannot have spoken these words immediately after 9. 1-4, but all objections vanish as soon as we realize that they formerly stood immediately after 7. 10-17, *i.e.* that we have here a continuation of the prophecy of judgement against Amaziah. The glorious future of Judah signifies for Amaziah as for all Northern Israel, a crushing condemnation; it is a rejoinder to the contemptuous reference to Judah in 7. 12. It is certainly quite possible, in view of the political preponderance of the Northern Kingdom, that Amos might speak of the "falling tabernacle of David" and refer to the Davidic era as "the days of old." And this promise does not destroy the force of Amos' exhortations to repentance, any more than 3. 1 f. and 9. 7 mutually exclude one another. He has already, in 3. 12; 5. 2, 6, 14, 15, recognized the possibility of the deliverance of a part of Israel, and, moreover, the promises here given did not first spring to birth from the mind of Amos, but were taken over by him from the traditional eschatology of salvation, purified, however, in their ethical implications by the preaching of judgement which precedes them. Cf. 5. 18; Gen. 49. 10 ff.; Num. 24. 5 ff. The reference to Edom in verse 12 is in favour of genuineness; during the Exile the Kingdom of the Future would not have been confined to the boundaries of the former Davidic Kingdom but extended to include all nations. Cf. ZEAT, p. 65 ff., and Baumgartner, *ut sup.*; H. Schmidt, p. 103 ff.; Köhler, p. 32.

Again, 5. 26 is not as a whole an interpolation, but at a later time some one has read into it, with a reminiscence of 2 K. 17. 30 f., an allusion to the Samaritan gods *Sakkut* and *Kewan* = (*Nergal*). It originally ran, " And ye shall be taken away " (read *nissatem*) " with the tabernacle of your king and your god, whom ye have made for yourselves." Cf. Ex. 32. 1.

The *Egyptian* parallels to the schematism of the discourses of the Israelitish prophets (calamity—salvation) which E. Meyer (*Die Israeliten*, p. 451 ff.) believes that he finds even as early as the second millennium B.C., and which seem at first sight to suggest the idea of a borrowing from that source, must for the present be regarded with a certain scepticism, since it is disputed whether the Egyptian texts in question are of a prophetic character at all (cf. Ranke in Gressmann's *Altorientalische Texte*, I. p. 209 f., and Gardiner, *The Admonitions of an Egyptian Sage*, 1911. The prophetic character can only apply, if at all, to the Golenischeff Papyrus. And a still stronger reason for caution is that in that case we should expect to find the same scheme in the Israelitish popular prophets (cf. Isa. 29, 10, 14; Jer. 6. 13, 14, etc.). Cf. Koenig, *Prophetentum*, p. 62 ff.; Sellin, *Prophetismus*, p. 236.

§ 8. *Obadiah*

On a first glance the little book of Obadiah—of whose date nothing is said in the superscription—appears to fall into two parts: 1-14, 15-21. The first deals with the judgement which is coming upon Edom for having exalted itself in word and deed against Judah ; the second with the Day of Yahweh, which is coming upon all nations—only in verses 18*b* and 21 is there any special allusion to Edom—and it ends with the glorious restoration of Israel and the beginning of the reign of Yahweh.

But on a closer examination, it becomes evident that the first part is again divisible into two parts, the first of which, 1-10, treats in detail of the judgement upon Edom, only making brief mention of murder and violence against his brother Jacob as the grounds of this, while the second, 11-14, refers to this violence specifically as Edom's conduct at the destruction of Jerusalem, and describes, with a nine-fold repetition of the phrase, what happened "in that day." As regards these two sections it is possible, though not necessarily the case, that they originated at different times.

Small as the book is, the critical question connected with it is very complex. We have a definite point of departure in the circumstance that 11-14 refer to the Fall of Jerusalem in 586 B.C., and from this it follows that verses 15-21—which are not, however, themselves a unity (vv. 17*b*, 19, 20 are a second strand)—come from a later, therefore certainly a post-Exilic, time.

But what are we to say of 1-10? The answer depends, in the first place, on the relationship of these to Jer. 49. This chapter obviously borrows from Ob. 1-10; cf. especially 49. 16 with Ob. 3, 4. From that would follow at once the pre-Exilic origin of Ob. 1-10, were it not that recently it has been shown, especially by Giesebrecht, that in Jer. 49 the Edom prophecy is not as a whole derived from Jeremiah, but only the core of it, say verses 7-11, 13. But the resemblances are almost all in 49. 14 ff. and subsequent verses ; which are therefore to be considered as later additions to Jeremiah, taken from Obadiah, and can prove nothing as regards the date of the latter. But the relationship between Ob. 5 and Jer. 49. 9 is undeniable, and it is equally certain that Jeremiah is here quoting from Obadiah and not *vice versa*.

Since then in the redaction of Jeremiah 49 only Ob. 1-10 was made use of, and not 11-14, we have reason to assume that the former at one time existed separately, and is earlier than 11-14. But in that case it cannot have been written with reference to the events of 586. It must, rather, have stood in more or less close connection with the revolt of Edom against Judah under Jehoram, 852 ; cf. 2 K. 8. 20-22. The language and style have affinities with those of Isa. 15 ; 16. It cannot unfortunately be absolutely determined who the faithless confederates of Edom (v. 7) were. Verse 1 may be from the hand of the editor who expanded the section.

While we have therefore, with high probability, in verses 1 (or 2) to 10 one of the oldest of prophecies, this was expanded during, or immediately after, the Babylonian Exile by the addition of 11-14, so as to refer to the destruction of Jerusalem ; and at a later period, perhaps that of Malachi or Joel, the whole was transformed by the addition of verses 15-21 into a little apocalypse, in which Edom plays the part elsewhere assigned to " Gog," " the Foe from the North," " the Locusts," and so forth.

§ 9. *Jonah*

Böhme, *Die Komposition des B. Jona*, ZAW, 1887, p. 224 ff. ; H. Schmidt, *Absicht und Entstehungszeit d. B.J.*, ThStKr, 1906, p. 180 ff. ; and, by the same author, *Jona, eine Untersuchung zur vergleichenden Religionsgeschichte*, 1907 ; Döller, *Das Buch Jona*, 1912.

The Book of Jonah differs markedly from all the others in the prophetic canon. It does not profess to be written by a prophet at all, but only to tell the story of a prophet, and does so with a didactic purpose, as is sufficiently obvious (cf. 3. 7; 4. 2, etc.). What the lesson is that he wishes to teach he tells us quite clearly in 4. 11: God's mercy is not confined to Judah; it has no limits, but extends to all men, and even to the animal creation.

This *motif* in itself suggests that the date of the book, in its present form, is probably subsequent to Deutero-Isaiah, and that is confirmed by 3. 3. Nineveh here belongs to a hoary antiquity and is already the centre of a growth of legend. And above all the language demands the fifth, if not the fourth, century as the time when the story was reduced to writing; cf. esp. the Aramaisms in 1. 4, 5, 6, 12; 2. 1 (Heb.=A.V. 1. 17); 3. 7, etc.

But the subject-matter has a long history behind it, and is doubtless centuries older. The hero of the narrative is a *historical personage* who lived in the time of Jeroboam II., shortly before Amos, 2 K. 14. 25.

Even his mission to Nineveh may be historical, like that of Elisha to Damascus; and, strangely enough, we hear—as Winckler was the first to point out—in the time of the Assyrian King Ramannirari III., with whom he was contemporary, of a monotheistic reform in Nineveh. But this historical kernel has been elaborated in legendary fashion, on the one side by way of parallel to the story of Elijah under the juniper bush in 1 K. 19, and on the other has been brought into connection with a folk-tale, based on a mythological foundation, which is found among many nations in different parts of the world—Indians, Egyptians, and others.

Böhme has attempted to divide the book between two sources, but the attempt must be regarded as unsuccessful. Almost the only disturbance of the text is that 4. 5 has been displaced from its original position after 3. 4. "Yahweh," which is used predominantly in the earlier part, later usually gives place to "Elohim," but in 4. 6 remains alongside of it. In the main the book is *a unity*; only Jonah's psalm of praise, which he is said to have uttered in the belly of the fish, 2. 2-9, but which, according to the wording of verses 5 and 6, knows nothing of a fish, but only of deliverance from the waters of affliction or the jaws of *Tehom*, cf. Ps. 18. 5 f., is a later addition. That the book is derived from a passage in that Midrash on the Book of Kings which is mentioned in 2 Chron. 24. 27, relating to 2 K. 14. 25-27, as Budde concludes from the continuative formula " *wayehi* " in verse 1 and the absence of a mention of Jonah's home, is in view of the whole spirit of the book not probable (for the use of the phrase at the opening of a narrative, cf. Ezek. 1. 1 ; 1 S. 1. 1, etc.). Still more improbable is the conjecture of Schmidt, that the book dates from the latter part of the Exile, and that Nineveh is a " covering name " for Jerusalem.

This little Book is, in virtue of its universalistic teaching, which is so strongly opposed to the post-Exilic exclusiveness, and of its childlike faith in the Father and Bestower of mercy upon man and beast, one of the most precious jewels of Hebrew literature. It is inspired by a truly prophetic spirit, and thoroughly deserves, in virtue of its content, the place which those who formed the canon have given it, not, as is sometimes said, merely in order to make up the number twelve—they could have done that by simply dividing off Zech. 9 ff.—but because they traced in it " a breath of His Spirit."

§ 10. *Micah*

Stade, ZAW, 1881, p. 161 ff. ; 1883, p. 1 ff. ; 1884, p. 291 ff. ; Nowack, ZAW, 1884, p. 277 ff. ; Ryssel, *Untersuchungen über die Textgestalt u. d. Echtheit d. B. Micha*, 1887 ; Budde, *Das Rätsel von Micha I.*, ZAW, 1917–18, p. 77 ff.

According to 1. 1 Micah's home was in Moresheth, and he prophesied in the reigns of Jotham, Ahaz, and Hezekiah, being thus a contemporary of Isaiah. This statement is confirmed by Jer. 26. 18, where the contemporaries of Jeremiah quote a passage from his prophecy (3. 12) and say that he prophesied in the days of Hezekiah.

The first chapter of his book must, in view of both verse 1*b* and verse 5 ff., certainly date from before 722 ; the second and third chapters are not to be dated with certainty ; the prophecy at the end of the latter, however, must, in view of the quotation in Jer. 26. 18, date from the reign of Hezekiah ; and 3. 11 and 12 would in fact be most intelligible after the centralization of the cultus which Hezekiah undertook. As to the personality of Micah, which is directly referred to only in 3. 1 and 8, and 7. 7, we know nothing further, except that he was obviously a simple countryman, who saw in the great cities of Samaria, Jerusalem (1. 5*b* is no doubt to be deleted, but cf. 3. 10 ; 6. 9), and Lachish, 1. 13, the roots of evil, and whose wrath was primarily directed against men of high position. His exhortations to repentance addressed to the rich, the judges and the prophets are inspired by the deepest moral earnestness ; he is in this respect an Amos *redivivus*.

The book, which during the last decades has been subjected to a very thorough criticism, falls into four parts : (1) Calls to repentance and prophecies of judgement, 1-3 ; (2) Eschatological prophecies, 4 and 5 ; (3) Exhortations to repentance combined with a lamentation of the prophet over the corruption of his people, 6. 1 – 7. 7 ; (4) Prayer and announcement of salvation, 7. 8-20. Of these not only (1) but also the kernel of (2) are to be ascribed to the contemporary of Isaiah, (3) belongs perhaps to the time of Ahaz, perhaps to a prophet of the time of Manasseh ; (4) to the Exilic or post-Exilic period.

1. The genuineness of 1-3 is almost universally admitted. A characteristic point is that Micah addresses his hearers as *Jacob* and *Israel*, cf. 2. 9 ; 3. 1, 8, 9, also 2. 12 ; 5. 7 ; 6. 2, which is doubtless a consequence of the Fall in 722 of the Northern Kingdom, of which Judah wished to constitute itself the heir. But as early as 1. 5*a* his subject is Israel as a whole (cf. also 1. 13-15). Marti's attack upon the word-plays in 1. 9-16 is not justified. A later editor would have chosen more familiar names than these, which are in some cases quite obscure, and a post-Exilic glossator would certainly never have chanced to hit upon the " chariot-town " Lachish, 1. 13, which has been so surprisingly confirmed by the excavation of the royal stables there (cf. also v. 14*b* !). And verse 9 by itself can certainly not be the whole of the lament announced in verse 8 ! More often attacked are 2. 12, 13. These cannot certainly be the words of the lying prophet mentioned in 2. 11, for they contain something very different from a " prophecy of wine and strong drink," and they cannot in fact have originally stood at this point, for they interrupt the sequence of thought in 2. 11 and 3. 1 ff. in an intolerable fashion. But, on the other hand, it is not correct to say that they presuppose the Exile. Verse 12 does not refer to Israel as a whole, but to Judah after 722, cf. 3. 9, and not to the Exile, for an assembling of Israel during the Exile is an absurdity, and verse 13 obviously speaks of a breaking forth from Jerusalem, in which Judah, attacked by enemies, has been obliged to concentrate. Cf. Isa. 22. 2. The two verses therefore go with 4. 6 f. and have been transferred here from that point. If any one had intended to interpolate a promise, he would certainly not have chosen to place it in such close connection with the prophet of lies !

2. There has been much controversy in regard to the eschatological chapters 4 and 5. Wellhausen, Nowack, Giesebrecht, and others admit in these only a small genuine kernel ; 4. 9, 10, 5. 1 ; 5. 10-14 ; others, like Stade, Cornill and Marti, reject this also and distinguish only between two non-genuine strata, an earlier one, 4. 1-4 ; 4. 11—5. 3 ; 5. 7-15, and a later, 4. 5-10 ; 5. 3, 4. But the only one of their arguments which is at all impressive is the mention of the Babylonian Exile in 4. 10*b* ; and in this we have certainly to see a late gloss, the glossator having wrongly understood the " going forth into the field," 10*a*, as a reference to the Exile, for the words " there shalt thou be delivered " do not refer to " Babylon " but to the " field."

None of the other arguments is sound. The " Deuteronomic

colouring " (by which is meant the imagery of casting off, halting and sickness, etc., 4. 6 f.) is found in Babylonian and Egyptian prophecies as early as the second millennium B.C. The " abruptness," " want of connection," " desultoriness " are characteristic features of the eschatological style. That the designation of " Bethlehem Ephratah," 5. 2, could be used even in pre-Exilic times follows from 1 Sam. 17. 12, that it was in pre-Exilic times the smallest of the " thousands " of Judah is quite possible, and the purpose here is to lay stress upon that unpretentious origin of the deliverer which is a standing element in the expectation of salvation, in contrast with the great Jerusalem. Verse 3 of chapter 5 presupposes, not the Babylonian Exile but the Deportation of 722. That 5. 10-14 points to a time of reformation is no doubt true, but there is no reason why this should not be the reformation of Hezekiah.

And as against these arguments for a later date, the circumstances of the writer's time are clearly evident in 4. 8 ; 4. 9, 10*a*, 5. 1, 3, 5. According to these passages Judah has a king—there is no getting away from that—and this king is, according to 5. 1, not God but an earthly king. For the present the People is forced to concentrate in the city, and is there besieged, and the hosts of the heathen (according to 5. 5, Assyria) are gathered together against it. But this time of trial is to become the beginning of the time of salvation, 4. 6, 7. Judah is to " break forth," 2. 13 ; 4. 10*a*, the heathen will be miserably put to shame before the walls of Jerusalem, 4. 12 f. ; 5. 8 f. The dominion of Judah, 4. 8 ; 5. 7, which is also the dominion of Yahweh, 4. 1-7, and of the Deliverer, 5. 2-6, is about to begin. For all these thoughts exact parallels are to be found in Isaiah. Cf. esp. 29. 1-10. In 5. 10-14, too, the post-Exilic period in general is excluded by the reference to " horses," " chariots " and " strongholds," and the Maccabaean period, in particular, for which Marti contends, by the " witchcrafts," " *asherahs*," etc., of verses 12 and 14.

We have here, therefore, a document of the *pre-Exilic Eschatology of Salvation*. But if the prophecy is pre-Exilic, then the author is most probably Micah himself, in spite of its apparent inconsistency with 3. 12. It shows us how Micah regarded the approaching peril, of the year 701, in the light of eschatology.

It begins with a quotation from his greater contemporary, Isaiah, which has deeply influenced him, to which he adds in 4. 4 a touch characteristic of his own interests as a countryman, and it shows how he, exactly like Isaiah, Amos and Hosea,

N

looked beyond all the judgements of the near future to the Time of Salvation, the New Age. Verse 15 of chapter 5 is a gloss, which no doubt shows that this was once the end of a book (cf. also Gressmann, *Eschatologie*, p. 178; Stärk, *Der assyrische Weltreich*, p. 132 ff.; Schmidt, SchAT, p. 145 ff.; and, with reference to the possible contemporaneousness with Jeremiah, Sellin, *Gilgal*, p. 74 ff.).

3. Two more discourses of judgement and a lamentation form the contents of 6. 1—7. 7. We have first a legal controversy between God and His People in which the latter offers hecatombs, human sacrifices and so forth, while God demands righteousness, love and humility—one of the most imposing passages of the Old Testament, before the spirit of which all other oriental religions hide their diminished heads. This section obviously implies a different period from that of chapters 1-3, 4 and 5; and the sins which here and in the next two passages characterize this period are different. See 6. 10 f., 16; 7. 5 f. There are also linguistic differences. For these reasons Ewald long ago denied the Mican authorship, and ascribed it to an anonymous writer of the days of Manasseh (cf. 6. 6 with 2 K. 21. 3, 6, 11, 15).

It is of course by no means impossible that Micah lived on into Manasseh's reign. But in the first place 1. 1, which says nothing of Manasseh, is against this, and in the second place it is most probable—in view of the analogy of the Books of Isaiah, Amos, Hosea and Ezekiel, that the Book of Micah originally closed with the eschatological chapters; cf. also 5. 15. But it is also to be noted that we miss in this section much that we should have expected in Manasseh's reign (*e.g.* polemic against worship of false gods). We must therefore decidedly keep in view the possibility of Mican authorship under Jotham or Ahaz (6. 1 would in this case be an eloquent exordium like Isa. 1. 1 f. Schmidt now also favours the time of Ahaz, *ut sup.*, 141, 145), indeed it is a matter for consideration whether the town to which Yahweh cries aloud in 6. 9 is not Samaria; cf. 6. 16 and Isa. 9. 9. The lamentation of the prophet which begins in 7. 1 ff. finds its close, not in verse 6 but verse 7. Cf. Isa. 8. 17, and see Duhm on that passage.

The attempt has lately been made to relegate this passage also to the post-Exilic period on account of the address " Oh, Man " in 6. 8 and of a few unusual words (so Marti). But the description of the condition of the People (where do we find in post-Exilic times any trace of human sacrifice in Jerusalem? Cf. also Amos 8. 5; Jer. 5. 6, 9) as well as the proclamation of the Day of judgement, 6. 13 ff. ; 7. 4, and the reference to the " Statutes " of Omri, 6. 16 (cf. 1 K. 21), an entirely *un*-Deuteronomic expression, all tell against this hypothesis.

4. This section consists of two interwoven *psalms* on the subject of Zion's redemption, 7. 8-20, one of which speaks of God in the third person, the other (7. 14-18*a*, 19*b*, 20) addresses Him directly (cf. Stade, ZAW, 1903, p. 168). It is everywhere implied that the judgement has already taken place, the walls of Jerusalem are already destroyed, v. 11, the People is scattered, v. 12 ff. The *enemy* is, as in Isa. 47. 1, 5 ; Ps. 137. 8, a personified World-Empire, probably the Babylonian ; " Assyria " and " Egypt " stand, as verse 12*b* shows, quite generally for North and South.

These psalms might well therefore date from the Exilic period, or from just after the Exile. Marti's Maccabaean hypothesis rests on just as insecure a foundation here as elsewhere. Probably this section was added in order that the now expanded and perhaps revised Book of Micah should once more close on a note of promise.

§ 11. *Nahum*

Billerbeck and A. Jeremias, *Der Untergang Ninives und die Weissagungsschrift des Nahum*, B. z. A. (Beiträge zur Assyriologie), 1895, p. 87 ff. ; Gunkel, ZAW, 1893, p. 223 ff. ; Bickell, Sitzungs-berichte der Wiener Akademie der Wissenschaft, 1884, V. ; Arnold, ZAW, 1901, p. 225 ff. ; Kleinert, *Nahum und der Fall Ninives*, ThStKr, 1910, p. 501 ff.

Of Nahum we learn from the superscription only that he came from Elkosh, a place in regard to which we do not even know whether it was in Galilee (so Jerome) or Judaea (so Epiphanius) or in the neighbourhood of Nineveh itself (so the recent attractive hypothesis of Lehmann-Haupt in *Die Geschichte Judas und Israels im Rahmen der Weltgeschichte*, p. 88).

As to the time at which his Book, which is a minatory oracle against Nineveh, was written, the only thing that we can say with certainty is that it falls between the conquest of No-Amon—that is, the Egyptian Thebes—by Assurbanipal in 663, to

which it looks back in 3. 8-11, and the conquest of
Nineveh in 606, to which its threatenings point
forward.

That Nahum, in speaking of the " Shatterer " in
2. 1, the executant of the Divine decree, had in
view a definite historical enemy, is, in face of 3. 13,
the more probable hypothesis ; but what enemy
is intended cannot be definitely inferred from the
description.   It is usual to think of Cyaxares and
Nabopolassar, 608 ; from 3. 12 it appears that the
frontier fortresses of Assyria have already fallen.
The complete silence of Nahum as to the sin of
Judah is in any case best explained by a date in
the period subsequent to 622.   The "writing"
(*sepher*), 1. 1, is perhaps also a message addressed
to those men of Judah whose fathers had been
carried away to Nineveh in 701.

While 2. 1, 3-13 ; 3. 1-19 present no difficult problems of
introduction, and their genuineness is undisputed, there has
been keen controversy about 1. 1-14, 15 ; 2. 2.   After Wellhausen had first pointed out that, 1. 12, 14 ; 2. 1, 3 ff., Nineveh
is addressed, but in 1. 13, 15 ; 2. 2 Judah, and therefore held
the latter to be glosses, Gunkel and Bickell believed that they
could trace in 1. 1-14, 15 ; 2. 2 a psalm (eschatological),
composed in alphabetical stanzas dating from a later period.
But while in verses 1-10, the letters א to ס, the thing goes, more
or less, from that point onward the alphabetical scheme can
only be recovered by the most violent methods.   And as, moreover, 2. 1 cannot possibly be the heading of the oracle proper,
Nowack, Marti, Arnold and others have taken from chapter 1
also verses 11 and 14, and in some cases also 9 and 10, to
serve this purpose.

The question is a very involved one.   My own view is that
the closing three-stress couplet of the psalm, beginning with
the letter ע, has somehow got into verse 12 : " So do tyrants
fall and so are the mighty destroyed."   With 1. 11 begins the
prophecy against Nineveh, but its real exordium is to be extracted from verse 10, where we should reconstruct with Duhm,

" Woe to the lion's lair" (thicket). 1. 11 should be followed by 2. 1 and 3 ff. But in 1. 12, 13, 15 and 2. 2 there has been inserted a prophecy addressed to Judah—also, however, from the hand of Nahum. There are no historical grounds for doubting the genuineness of the psalm in 1. 1-10; alphabetical poems are known with certainty to have existed only a few decades later (elegies, etc.).

According to 2. 3, 4 the whole undertaking against Nineveh appears as an expedition of the Apocalyptic host of Yahweh (with the " made red " of v. 3 cf. Isa. 63. 1 ff., and also Isa. 13. 3 ff.) ; but if we have here an eschatological poem—which does not exclude the possibility that its historical realization had already begun—the main ground for making a distinction between 1. 1-11 and chapters 2 and 3 falls to the ground. The former passage is the best possible prelude to the conflict between Yahweh and the *Ben Bellijjaal* (cf. 1. 2-6 with 2. 1 ; 3. 19 and 1. 11 ; 1. 15 with 2 Sam. 23. 6 f.). Especially in the " Behold, I am against thee," 2. 13 ; 3. 5 (cf. Ezek. 39. 1), we have the idea of a duel. Chapter 3 falls into three short poems, vv. 1-7 ; 8-17 ; 18, 19.

Chapters 2 and 3 in particular are of remarkable poetical beauty. And when once we interpret chapters 1, 2 and 3 eschatologically, as we ought to do, the Book acquires an incomparably higher religious value than is now generally assigned to it. It is not a mere product of national hatred, or even of a just desire for vengeance, but a hymn to that Nemesis, at once ethical and divine, which inexorably realizes itself in history, with the thought clothed in the primeval imagery of a conflict of the gods. (Cf. the Babylonian Epic of the Creation.)

§ 12. *Habakkuk*

Stade, ZAW, 1884, p. 154 ff. ; Budde, ThStKr, 1893, p. 383 ff. ; Rothstein, ThStKr, 1894, p. 51 ff. ; Peiser, *Der Prophet Hab.*, 1903 ; Duhm, *Das Buch Hab.*, 1906 ; Caspari, *Die Chaldäer bei Habaquq*, NKZ, 1907, p. 156 ff.

Regarding Habakkuk's personality we are given not the smallest shred of information, not even the name is absolutely certain (cf. LXX Ἀμβακούμ). Anything which we can say of him must be an inference from the position which we assign to his writing.

The Book presents the following problem: In 1. 5-11 we find the announcement of the coming of the Chaldaeans as the rod of the Divine chastening, and from verse 12 onwards judgement is called down upon a "Lawless One," over whom in chapter 2 there is pronounced a five-fold woe, and in whom one is inclined at a first glance to see the Chaldaeans themselves; which would make the Book contradict itself. Of this problem the most various solutions have been suggested. Either 1. 5-11 has been supposed to be spoken by another slightly later prophet (about 610; so Wellhausen, Nowack and others), or 2. 9-20 and 3 have been denied to Habakkuk, and the former (in spite of 2. 16!) has been taken to refer to some post-Exilic Jewish magnate (Stade, Schwally and others); others again have seen in the author a prince, belonging to Judah, who, as a prisoner in Nineveh, was present at the taking of this city by the Babylonians (Peiser), or, like Marti, detect in 1. 2-4, 12a, 13; 2. 1-4 and chapter 3, psalms from the Maccabaean period; that leaves seven whole verses over for Habakkuk!

But the above difficulty is solved in the simplest fashion imaginable if, with Budde, we place 1. 5-11 after 2. 4 (similarly Rothstein, who, however, more elaborately, refers the former passage to Jehoiakim's reign, but supposes it worked over later into an oracle against Babylon). When this is done everything runs perfectly smoothly and, so far as that goes, the whole of the first two chapters might be left to Habakkuk; the "Ruthless One" about whom he laments in 1. 1-4 and 12-17, and on whom he calls down the woes of 2. 6 ff., is the Assyrian; the Divinely appointed rod of chastening for him will in turn be the Babylonians; such is the content of the revelation which Habakkuk received in 2. 3 f. But this conception—according to the

theory—soon gave rise to difficulties, because of
the course of history, and was therefore weakened
down by the displacement of the passage. The
Book, on this theory, must have been written
between 620—the Deuteronomic reform is traceable
in the use of " righteous " and " godless "—and
606 B.C.

There is no doubt therefore that the first great
difficulty is very neatly solved by Budde's hypothesis. But there are three strong objections to it.
(1) Is 1. 5-11 at all appropriate to the Babylonians ?
The nation spoken of here appears unexpectedly
upon the stage of history, their movement is,
according to 1. 9, directed eastward, and they are
essentially a nation of horsemen. (2) If this date
be assigned to the passages in question, chapter 3
must be by a different author ; and yet the linguistic affinity is obvious ; 3. 2 and 16 connect
with 2. 2, " godless " in 3. 13 has exactly the same
shade of meaning as in 1. 4, 13 ; 2. 4. (3) 2. 4 and
2. 5 are torn apart by this hypothesis ; and yet,
though it is not generally recognized, they are very
closely connected ; 2. 4 is the premiss to 2. 5
(according to the regular use of *aph ki*, " yea also ").
These difficulties, however, all disappear if, with
Duhm, we see in the nation spoken of in 1. 5-11 the
Macedonians of Alexander the Great, and suppose
the imprecations of 2. 6 ff. and 3. 13*b* ff. to be
personally directed against him. The " anointed "
of 3. 13 is then the High-Priest. Cf. Dan. 9. 26, etc.

Here, too, of course we are dealing with what is, so far,
only a hypothesis, and in many particulars we diverge from
Duhm. We must leave it an open question whether *khittim*
really stood originally instead of *khasdim* in 1. 6, cf. Isa. 23. 13,

and we are also doubtful whether the Book should be divided
into six poems, and not, rather, into four or five. I should like
also to connect 3. 2 ff. with 2. 3 still more closely than Duhm
does. We have in the former passage the Vision of which
Habakkuk speaks in the latter. On the other hand, I am
inclined to see in 2. 4, 5 a still stronger confirmation of the
theory even than Duhm himself does. Here I propose to read
" Behold the blasphemer faints (surely, his life remains not
in him ?) while the righteous through his faith remains alive ;
how much more shall the robber Greek (reading *Jewani*), the
arrogant man, have no continuance ? " In any case this
whole view of the Book and the date which it implies deserve
the most careful consideration. Cf. also Procksch, *ut sup.*, and
observe the affinity of 2. 2, 3 with Daniel 8. 17, 19 ; 12. 9.

From the fact that its author was a continuator
of the central thought of Isaiah, and a forerunner
of the Apostle Paul, cf. 2. 4—although he, as a
child of his time, applied the word " righteous " to
the Jewish people, therein differing widely from
these two—he has acquired a great and abiding
significance in the history of religion.

§ 13. *Zephaniah*

Schwally, ZAW, 1890, p. 165 ff. ; Budde, ThStKr, 1893, p. 393 ff.;
D. H. Müller, WZKM, 1905, p. 263 ff. ; Cornill, *Die Prophetie
Zephaniahs*, ThStKr, 1916, p. 297 ff.

Zephaniah prophesied probably under the impression of the Scythian invasion, which in 630 B.C.
burst upon Western Asia like a storm, but, as
appears from 1. 5 ff., before the reforms of Josiah
(622), who is mentioned in verse 1. A contrary conclusion in regard to this last point cannot be drawn
from the textually uncertain " remnant of Baal "
(LXX reads " name "), for this phrase means,
" Baal to the last remnant." Cf. Isa. 14. 22.

It is noteworthy that the superscription gives the
prophet's genealogy, which is followed for four

generations and ends with a certain Hezekiah. As there seems at first sight to be no rational grounds for giving this information unless the Hezekiah in question is the famous King of Judah, Zephaniah is generally held to have been a prophet of royal blood. But in view of chapter 2 and 2 K. 21. 1 chronological difficulties arise; at the least Amariah must have been a considerably older brother of Manasseh. And it would certainly be remarkable that Hezekiah's royal dignity was not mentioned. It may therefore be conjectured that the three names compounded with the name Yahweh are mentioned in order to make it clear that Zephaniah, in spite of his father's name Kushi, which means " Ethiopian," fulfilled the requirement of Deut. 23. 8 f., cf. Jer. 36. 14.   The subject of his Book is " the Day of Yahweh."

This Book, like others, was long the object of an *exaggerated criticism* (especially at the hands of Stade and Schwally, but also of Budde). It has been proposed to deprive the prophet of everything from 2. 4 onwards, including the minatory pro- phecies against the nations, as well as the promises of salvation. But chapter 2 is led up to by 1. 2, 3, and Cornill has rightly pointed out that 2. 13, 14*a* must have been spoken before 606, precisely because they were not fulfilled in this form.   Verses 8-11 of chapter 2 alone betray, by the mention of the revilings with which Moab and Ammon reviled Israel, and more especially by the phrase " the residue of my people shall spoil them," a different, and a post-Exilic period ; the metre also betrays a different origin.

But the genuineness of 3. 1-13 also is to be maintained. As D. H. Müller has shown, verses 1-4 are presupposed by Ezek. 22. 25-29 ; and lately Cornill has convincingly shown that in view of verses 5-7 the catastrophe of Megiddo in 608, not to mention that of 586, cannot as yet have happened, and that in this chapter, in spite of the surface appearance to the contrary, the same circumstances in Jerusalem are implied as in chapter 1.   The difficulty presented by verses 8 and 9 he gets rid of by reading in verse 8 *chakki* with the LXX, striking out clauses *ba* and *γ* of the verse, and emending in verse 9, with Grätz, " *my* people " instead of the " peoples." While verses 14 and 15 may also be from the hand of Zephaniah, verses 16 - 20 are certainly an Exilic or post-Exilic addition. They are in a totally different metre from the remainder of the Book, which exhibits throughout the *Ķinah* metre.

The Book of Zephaniah is of great importance for our knowledge of the Israelitish conception of the Day of Yahweh. It shows that even in pre-Exilic times, and, furthermore, even before Zephaniah himself, this was conceived as a world-catastrophe, sparing neither Israel, nor the nations nor the natural world ; but from it was to issue forth a new redeemed People of God. (Cf. Gressmann, *Eschatologie*, 136 ff.)

§ 14. *Haggai*

Sellin, *Studien zur Entstehungsgeschichte der jüdischen Gemeinde*, II. p. 43 ff., 1901 ; Budde, *Zum Text der 3 letzten kleinen Proph.*, ZAW, 1906, p. 1 ff. ; Rothstein, *Juden und Samaritaner*, 1908.

The writing of this prophet is more exactly dated than almost any other. Almost every single word of revelation which came to, or through, him is dated by the year and month. He prophesied in the second year of Darius, that is 520 B.C. The insurrection against that monarch which broke out in the whole Persian Empire is reflected even in this little Book, 2. 6 ff., 21 ff. All his prophecies revolve about two main ideas : first, the time has come to build the Temple ; and second, the Messianic age is at hand, and Zerubbabel is the chosen Servant of God, 2. 6, 23. The prophet's work is mentioned approvingly in Ezra 5. 1 ; 6. 14.

The Book as we now have it cannot be direct from the pen of Haggai himself. It is, rather, taken from an account of his whole activity, especially in connection with the building of the Temple, as may be clearly seen from the entirely narrative sections, 1. 12-15 ; 2. 10-14, and the recurrent formula " by the hand of the prophet Haggai," 1. 1, 3 ; 2. 1. (So, rightly, Klostermann, Marti, Rothstein, pp. 33-41.) But this narrative was no doubt based on notes of Haggai himself. Rothstein has lately shown that 2. 15-19 (perhaps also 2. 10-19) should come after the displaced verse, 1. 15, which referred to the laying of the foundation stone on the 24th day of the 6th month (not 9th !) ; and that Haggai, by the decision mentioned in 2. 10-14, laid down the principle which led to the separation of the Samaritans from the Jewish community.

§ 15. *Zechariah*

Cf. § 14. Marti, *Der Prophet Sacharja der Zeitgenosse Zerubbabels*, 1892 ; Rubinkam, *The second part of the Book of Zechariah*, 1892 ; V. D. Flier, *Sach.* 1-8, ThStKr, 1906, p. 30 ff. ; Stade, *Sach.* 9-14, ZAW, 1881, p. 1 ff. ; 1882, pp. 151 ff., 275 ff. ; Stärk, *Untersuchungen über Sach.* 9-14, 1891 ; Grützmacher, *Untersuchung über d. Ursprung von Sach.* 9-14, 1892 ; Eckardt, *Der Sprachgebrauch v. Sach.* 9-14, ZAW, 1893, p. 76 ff. ; Rothstein, *Die Nachtgesichte des Sacharja*, 1910 ; Marti, *Die Zweifel an der prophetischen Sendung Sacharja's* in the Wellhausen " Festschrift," p. 279 ff.

Zechariah, who, according to 1. 1, was the son of Berechiah, and grandson of Iddo, or more correctly, according to Ezra 5. 1 ; 6. 41, the son of Iddo, and, as we learn from Neh. 12. 4, 16, a priest, was a contemporary of Haggai, and worked side by side with him ; and, as it appears, took a still more active part in dealing with the difficult religious and governmental problems which were raised by the new circumstances. The two fundamental ideas are the same for him as for Haggai, but it is still clearer in his writing that he saw in Zerubbabel the promised " Branch of David," 3. 8*b*; 4. 7, 9, 10, 14 ; 6. 9-15. The Book which has come down to us under his name consists of two quite disparate portions.

PART I. CHAPTERS 1-8

This part contains (1) an Introduction, 1. 1-6 ; (2) the " Visions of the Night" with the addition of a narrative of a symbolic action, the crowning of Joshua, by which the imminent exaltation of Zerubbabel to be the Messiah of the community represented by Joshua is symbolized (or, by an alteration of the text in 6. 11, the crowning of Zerubbabel himself), 1. 7 — 6. 15 ; (3) the answer to a question (probably put by the Samaritans—read in 7. 2 with Hoonacker, *Beth Yisrael*, " House of Israel " for *Beth El*, " House of God ") with reference to observing the Fast days, chapters 7 and 8. The genuineness of these chapters is unchallenged ; and in spite of the thrice repeated exact dating, 1. 1, 7 ; 7. 1, the Book is not a mere later narrative about the Prophet, like the Book of Haggai. It is all in the first person, which occurs as late as 8. 18.

But the widely prevalent view that the Book offers no problems of introduction is not justified. We must distinguish between the eight Night-Visions which are from the same mould, and of which an understanding is regularly communicated to Zechariah by an angelic interpreter, 1. 7-15 ; 1. 18-21 ; 2. 1-5 ; 3. 1-7 ; 4. 1-5, 10*b*-14 ; 5. 1-11 ; 6. 1-8 (whether the Vision in 3. 1-7, which is not on the same lines as the others, was inserted by Zechariah later, so that the number was originally seven, may be left an open question), and the Divine " sayings," which indeed are also directly Zecharian but were written in by him later on the free spaces of the roll, without having any immediate connection with the Night-Visions. The fifth Vision, for instance, is now broken in two by one of these passages. These " sayings " give evidence of attacks directed against his mission as a prophet, being characterized on the one hand by an anxious recurrence to the earlier prophets, and on the other by the repeatedly emphasized " Ye shall know that Yahweh hath sent me," 2. 8, 9, 11 ; 4. 9 ; 6. 15. These sections are 1. 1-6, 16, 17 ; 2. 6-13 ; 3. 8-10 ; 4. 6-10*a* ; 6. 9-15 ; 7 ; 8.

That the Night-Visions were originally published separately is shown by 1. 7; also the genuineness of 2. 8 (where I read: *asher kbodo schlachani, i.e.* " Whose majesty hath sent me "), etc., is wrongly called in question by Marti, for 4. 9; 6. 15 take us back to the time of the building of the Temple. But a good deal of disorder has doubtless crept into the roll. 3. 8-10 has become detached from 4. 6-10, and both have got into quite unsuitable positions. So, too, 1. 5, 6a, breaks off abruptly and is followed by a later narrative verse, 1. 6b, while the original continuation stands now at 8. 14 f., where they now merely interrupt the sequence of thought (in 1. 6 read: *ethkem* for *abothekem*, " you " for " your fathers "). And similarly, the last Night-Vision breaks off abruptly in 6. 8; its conclusion has been transferred to 2. 6 f.

The characteristic difference of the Night-Vision from the ordinary Vision has so far not been clearly established. Probably the former is seen when looking up to the star-sown heaven. This is most clearly suggested in chapter 4, but it is probable that many other hitherto enigmatic passages, like 1. 18 f., will ultimately find their explanation along these lines. (Cf. also Jaeger-Hommel in *Die Reformation*, 1909, pp. 210-213.) The order of the Visions is determined by an inner progress of thought (the outward and inward up-building of the Messianic community). In the interpretation of the Visions by the angel, which is always necessary before they can be understood, there betrays itself a weakening of the Divine revelation, which in the case of the earlier prophets wells up in the heart with a direct and self-explanatory power.

PART II. CHAPTERS 9-14

That these chapters are not derived from Zechariah has gradually come to be universally recognized. Of the building of the Temple, of

Zerubbabel and Joshua we hear nothing more; language and ideas are alike wholly different. But they do not in fact profess to have been written by him. Instead of the exactly dated superscriptions of Zechariah, we have in 9. 1 and 12. 1 the simple " Utterance " (A.V. " Burden ") or " Utterance of the Word of Yahweh."

From what period, then, do these chapters date? There are, speaking generally, two opposite views. The majority of recent critics, since Stade, place their origin in the Greek period in the time of the generals who divided Alexander's Empire (the " Diadochi ") or of the Maccabees (Duhm, Marti, etc.). Earlier critics, on the other hand (Kuenen, Dillmann and others), and also many of the present day, Koenig, Orelli, etc., defend the pre-Exilic origin. A third class (e.g. Baudissin, Steuernagel) takes an intermediate position, and refers 9-11, mainly at least, to the pre-Exilic, 12-14 to the post Exilic, period. I myself formerly attributed 9-11 to a contemporary of Hosea, or possibly of Isaiah, 12 and 13 to a contemporary of Jeremiah, and saw in 14 a post-Exilic Apocalyptic addition, but my present view is that the whole work is derived from an Apocalyptic writer of the third century B.C., who, however, wrote in the character of a pre-Exilic prophet. (Cf. Daniel, Enoch, etc.)

The Book falls into three main divisions, in each of which it is possible to make two subdivisions. (1) 9. 1—11. 3, the coming of the Divine dominion, the gathering of scattered Israel and the annihilation of the world-power (written in three-stress couplets), of which the subdivisions are (a) 9. 1-17, (b) 10. 1—11. 3. (2) Two symbolical actions of the author (in prose but concluding with a poetic imprecation), (a) 11. 4-14, (b) 11. 15-17; 13. 7-9. (3) The fate of Jerusalem in the Times of the End (in elevated prose) :

(*a*) 12. 1—13. 6 (*b*) 14. These parts cannot have been published simultaneously, they must have appeared one after another. It is possible also that some smaller units within them, like 9. 9 f. ; 10. 1 f. ; 11. 1-3 ; 13. 3 f. ; 14. 8 f., originally appeared separately. Whether the whole is by one author is not quite certain ; between (1) and (3) in particular there is the striking difference that while in the former great interest is shown in the Northern Kingdom, in the latter there is no trace of this ; but that, after all, might be explained by the difference of the subjects dealt with. Cf. Ezek. 37. 15 ff. ; 38 and 39. Again, the contradiction between chapters 13 and 14 (in the former Jerusalem impregnable, in the latter immediately taken) might well be explained by altered historic circumstances.

As regards the author's *date*, it cannot be denied that the first impression made by his work is certainly that of belonging to the pre-Exilic period. The implication that Hadrach, Damascus, etc., are independent kingdoms, 9. 1 ff., the reference to war-chariots and horses in Jerusalem and Ephraim, 9. 10, the very existence of the Northern Kingdom, 9. 13 ; 10. 6, 7 ; 11. 14, the allusion to the first deportation from the eastern and northern parts of it, 11. 1 f., the apparent reference in the " three shepherds " of 11. 8 to Zachariah, Shallum and Menahem, 2 K. 15. 8-19, in 11. 15 to Pekah, the *Teraphim* of 10. 2, of which we nowhere else hear anything in post-Exilic times, the expectation of a personal Messiah in 9. 9 f. (cf. Ex. 49. 10 f.), the implication in 12. 7, 8, 10, 12, that the Davidic dynasty is still reigning, in 13. 2 f. that idolatry is still practised in the land, the opposition to the professional prophetic guild in 13. 2*b* ff., cf. Jer. 23. 9-40, and, finally, the antithesis between Judah and Jerusalem, 12. 2 ff., cf. 2 K. 23. 30*b*—all this makes it thoroughly intelligible that for almost a century the assumption of pre-Exilic origin was the prevailing one, especially as according to 10. 3 ; 13. 7 ff., the judgement of destruction on Jerusalem is apparently for the writer still in the future.

To confront this formidable array of evidence we have at first sight only a single argument which tells in favour of a post-Exilic origin, the mention of the " sons of Javan," *i.e.* the Ionians, as the opponents of Ephraim in 9. 13, and this phrase, which has not the very best textual confirmation (cf. LXX and Targum), is shown by metrical reasons to be probably a gloss. Nevertheless, when we come to close quarters with the Book, it must be confessed that its general air of pre-Exilic origin disappears, and circumstances and conceptions which belong to the later post-Exilic age force themselves upon our notice.

It is implied in 9. 11 that Judah also is already dispersed,
while the fact that the conversion of a heathen nation takes the
form of observing the Levitical dietary laws, cf. 9. 7, and,
above all, the conceptions of conversion and holiness in 14.
16-21, point to a time in which the dominion of the priestly
codex had already degenerated, prophetism as a whole is
included in one general condemnation, 13. 2 ff., true *Nebiim*
of Yahweh therefore no longer exist, the House of Levi stands
beside the House of David, and on the same footing with it,
12. 12, and Uzziah, " the King of Judah," is looked back to
as a figure of the past, 14. 5. Finally, at every step, but
especially in 10. 3 ; 11. 1-3 ; 11. 4-15 ; 11. 16 ; 13. 8 ff., a literary
dependence upon Jeremiah and Ezekiel can be proved.

In view of these facts the hypothesis which first suggests
itself is to suppose, with Kuenen, Baudissin and Steuernagel,
that pre-Exilic material has been worked up by a later hand.
But these critics have not succeeded in disentangling the pre-
Exilic material. Again and again we find the antithesis, which
takes a particularly pointed form in 9. 9 f. (where the Messiah
bears the title of King, but is in fact the Torah-teacher of
Isa. 42. 1 ff.) : the pre-Exilic *form* is preserved, but the *content*
is wholly post-Exilic. But that means that we have here to do
with an Apocalyptic writer, who, like Daniel, causes a Divine
messenger of earlier days to proclaim the ills of his own
time and the deliverance which was at hand in the coming
Times of the End. This characteristic has not yet been
sufficiently recognized, and that explains how it is that critical
opinion is here so widely divided.

The question whether the author lived on into the times of
the Maccabees, or at least witnessed its prelude, the treachery
and revolt of Jason and the murder of Onias, at first sight
forces itself upon us in 11. 4-17 ; 13. 7-9 ; 12. 10 ff. But, on
the other hand, it has to be emphasized yet once more that
there is no trace here of an inner division of the community
according to its attitude towards the Law (as in Daniel). The
Martyr, whose fate forms the subject of 11. 4-14 ; 13. 7 ; 12.
9-17, is in reality none other than Moses. Cf. Sellin, *Mose*, pp.
113-124.

If our view regarding the origin of 9-14 is correct,
it gives at the same time the best explanation of
the way in which these chapters came to be attached
to the Book of Zechariah. For now the old

hypothesis of Berthold appears to us in a new light,
viz. that there formerly stood at the head of chapter
9 the name of the " Zechariah ben Jeberechiah "
who is mentioned in Isa. 8. 2. That may well
have been the name behind which the apocalyptic
writer concealed himself. Afterwards, when in
consequence of the name the two " Zechariah "
writings had been mistakenly combined into one
by a redactor, the mention of Berechiah was
transferred to 1. 1 (whence the discrepancy with
Ezra 5. 1, where Zechariah the prophet is said to be
the *son* of Iddo).

§ 16. *Malachi*

Bachmann, *Alttestamentliche Untersuchungen*, 1894, pp. 109-12;
Winckler, *Altorientalische Forschungen*, ii. p. 531 ff., 1901.

The last Book of the Prophetic Canon bears the
superscription " Utterance of the word of Yahweh
to Israel through Malachi." This becomes more
intelligible from the fact that it is found also in
Zech. 9. 1 and 12. 1, where in the former passage
it is obviously original : " Utterance ; the word
of Yahweh comes down," and here, accordingly,
is derivative. Taking in conjunction with this
the curious "through Malachi," it has been rightly
suggested that the name is only a conjecture from
" My messenger " of 3. 1.

Though we thus learn nothing from tradition as
regards the writer, yet he stands before us, on the
ground of his book, as a clear-cut and characteristic
personality. He is an intensely earnest preacher
of repentance. Yet the form of his book shows us
that his period was no longer patient of such
preachers ; he has to have recourse to argument,

O

cf. 1. 6, 7, 13 ; 2. 4, 17 ; 3. 7, 13, 14.   There are
two special objects of his censure, the unworthy way
in which the cultus was practised, for which the
priests are above all to blame, and the putting away
on frivolous pretexts of Jewish wives, with its
correlative of mixed marriages with the heathen.
On account of these he sees the day of Yahweh's
judgement drawing near.

As it has not hitherto been recognized that 3. 6-11 is the
immediate continuation of 1. 2-5, the skilful arrangement of
the Book which has been obscured by later changes of order,
suggested by catch-words, has escaped notice.   The divisions
are : (1) Two exhortations to repentance addressed to the
whole People, 1. 2-5 ; 3. 6-11 and 2. 11-16 ; (2) two passages
in which the priesthood are called to account, 1. 6-13 and
2. 1-9 ; (3) two replies to the doubts of the godly, 2. 17—3. 5
and 3. 13-21.   It is pretty clear that the book is written in four-
lined strophes (generally consisting of two three-stress couplets).

As regards the author's date, difference of
opinion is hardly possible.   The Temple is standing, 1. 10 ; 3. 1, 10 ; a Governor is ruling, 1. 8 ;
the circumstances of the community exclude the
possibility that Ezra and Nehemiah had already
carried out their reforms.   And in point of fact
Malachi still keeps referring to Deuteronomy,
1. 8 ; 2. 11 ; 3. 8-10, 22.   He has also a conception
of sacrifice which is scarcely compatible with the
ideas of Ezra, 1. 11 f. (translate : " and in every
kind of place " ; Malachi is thinking of the then
widely prevalent belief in " the God of Heaven,"
cf. Neh. 1. 4 ; Ezra 1. 2, etc.).   Moreover, he is in
many ways a pioneer of that belief.   He is therefore to be placed about 470 B.C.

The only point in which the genuineness of the book has
been seriously disputed is in regard to the last three verses,

the prediction of the sending of Elijah, 4. 4-6. While the absence of any mention of this in 3. 1, and the abrupt change in the persons addressed between verses 3 and 4 tell against them, their Deuteronomic character and Sirach (Ecclus.) 48. 10 are in their favour. In essence the expectation here is the same as in 3. 1; it is simply added that the " messenger " there announced is no other than Elijah, the great prophet, the teacher of the law, on whom the Jewish community after the fall of Zerubbabel set its hopes. It is possible that the prophet himself added the verses at a later date than the rest of the prophecies.

III. THE KETHUBIM OR " SACRED WRITINGS "

§ 1. *The Psalms*

Ehrt, *Abfassungszeit und Abschluss des Psalters*, 1869 ; Giesebrecht, *Über die Abfassungszeit des Psalters*, ZAW, 1881, p. 276 ff. ; Sellin, *Disputatio de Origine Carminum, quae primus psalterii liber continet*, 1892 ; Stärk, *Zur Kritik der Psalterüberschriften*, ZAW, 1892, p. 91 ff. ; Stade, *Die messianische Hoffnung im Psalter*, ZThK, 1892, p. 369 ff. ; Jacob, *Beiträge zu einer Einleitung in die Pss.*, ZAW, 1896, pp. 129 ff., 265 ff. ; 1897, pp. 48 ff., 263 ff. ; Köberle, *Die Tempelsänger im A.T.*, 1899 ; Büchler, *Zur Geschichte der Tempelmusik und der Tempelpsalmen*, ZAW, 1899, pp. 96 ff., 329 ff. ; 1900, p. 97 ff. ; Kautzsch, *Die Poesie und die poet. Bücher des A.T.*, 1902 ; Gunkel, *Ausgewählte Psalmen*[3], 1911 ; Smend, *Über das Ich der Psalmen*, ZAW, 1888, p. 49 ff. ; Beer, *Individual- und Gemeindepsalmen*, 1894 ; Coblenz, *Über das betende Ich in de Psalmen*, 1897 ; Roy, *Die Volksgemeinde und die Gemeinde der Frommen im Psalter*, 1897 ; Balla, *Das Ich der Psalmen*, 1912 ; Mowinckel, *Psalmenstudien*, i. 1921 ; ii. 1922.

Numerous specimens of the religious lyric, of various kinds, are, as we have seen in Parts I. and II., scattered through the prophetic and historical books, including the Pentateuch. But there is one great Book in which a collection consisting exclusively of these was purposely undertaken, viz. the Psalter. This is the designation given to the Book in the LXX; it signifies primarily the stringed instrument, the " psaltery," and then, by metonymy, the songs sung to the accompaniment of this (*psalmoi*). In the superscription of the MT they are less appropriately called " *Tehillim*," hymns of praise, for the greater part of them are not hymns at all, and the only individual psalm which bears this title is Psalm 145. From 72. 20 it appears that one great collection originally bore the title " *Tephilloth*," prayers, but this again does not correspond exactly to their essential character, and in that collection only Psalm 17 is so denominated in its superscription. The most common designation for the individual psalms is *mizmor*, which comes from *zamar*, meaning to cut up, then to articulate, and finally to play and sing at the same time, *i.e.* to sing to the accompaniment of a musical instrument.

In reality, therefore, the collection includes hymns, prayers and poems, and in these three kinds various sub-species are to be distinguished, *e.g.* processional, festal and liturgical hymns, and hymns of victory, etc. (cf. Stärk in SchAT, 1911). The widely prevalent impression that by an oversight (!) a secular poem has found its way into this collection in Psalm 45 is due to a false interpretation of this psalm. It is no doubt a marriage ode, but it is composed for the marriage of a king who is thought of as a Divine Deliverer.

As was long ago recognized by the Fathers of the Church, the Psalter is divided, obviously in imitation of the Pentateuch, into five books, the close of each being marked by the recurrence of a similar doxology. These books are, 1-41 ; 42-72 ; 73-89 ; 90-106 ; 107-150. The identity of 1 Chron. 16. 36 with the doxology in Psalm 106. 48 might seem to suggest that this division was already made before the time of the Chronicler, *c.* 300 B.C. ; but that cannot be safely inferred, for it might quite well be that Psalm 106 ended from the first with verse 48 and was for that reason chosen to round off a book of the psalms, cf. Deut. 27. 16 ff. ; Neh. 8. 6 ; and another possibility is that 1 Chron. 16. 8-36 has been interpolated between verses 7 and 37. All that we know with certainty is that the LXX found the division already made.

That the whole collection was not made at one time, but represents the gradual amalgamation of several smaller collections, is proved with certainty by a variety of arguments.

(*a*) We find in the Psalter certain psalms twice over in only slightly varied form. Cf. 14 with 53; 40. 13-17 with 70; 57. 7-11 and 60. 7-14 with 108. (*b*) In 72. 20 we find at the close of the psalm " The songs of David are ended "; and, nevertheless, there follow in our Psalter many other Davidic psalms, and conversely in the earlier portion there are many Korahitic, *e.g.* 42-49. It would appear, therefore, that Psalm 72 must have formed the close of an earlier collection of exclusively Davidic psalms. (*c*) Similarly it may be concluded that the Korahite psalms, 42-49, 84-89; the Asaphite, 50, 73-83; the Maschil, 52-55; the Michtam, 56-60; and the Ma'aloth psalms, 120-134; the Hallelujah psalms, 105-107, 111-118, 135, 136, 146-150, represent older collections. (*d*) Psalms 42-84, again, must have formed a separate collection, and so must 3-41, for, whereas in the latter Yahweh is used 272 times, Elohim only 15, in the former Yahweh is used only 48, Elohim 208 times. That can only be explained by supposing that 3-41 formed an earlier collection, 42-84 a later one, which was prepared by a redactor who endeavoured to eliminate the name Yahweh so far as possible (cf. Ps. 14 with 53).

We see, then, that the collections noticed under the headings (*b*) and (*c*) above represent the earliest stage, that these were followed by the Elohistic redaction of 42-84, which separated the Korahite and Asaphite collection, and that the final redaction, certainly in two places (41 and 72; perhaps also in 89), used the close of an earlier collection to form the end of a book. Within the collections the individual psalms are arranged, as has been especially pointed out by Delitzsch (*Symbolae ad psalmos illustrandos isagogicae*, 1846), on a very arbitrary basis—similarity of phrase, catchwords and the like (cf. 34. 7 with 35. 5 ff.).

Regarding the date of the various psalms, we seem at first sight to be very well informed, for most of them, to the number of about 100, bear the name of their author upon their forehead, in the form of a superscription (73, that of David; 2, Solomon; 12, Asaph; 11, the sons of Korah; 1, Moses; 1, Etham; 1, Heman; 1, Jeduthun). That the prepositional ל prefixed to these names signified always and everywhere, in the intention

of the redactor, the author, and not the subject of
the song, the model on which it is based, or the
choir by which it was to be sung, ought not to be
denied. Cf. Ps. 72. 20 ; Hab. 3. 1, and above all,
the statements added in the case of thirteen of the
psalms regarding the circumstances in which David
composed them. But these superscriptions are not
to be regarded as trustworthy statements of historic
fact.

The first thing that throws suspicion on them is that some of
them are taken almost word for word from the Books of Samuel,
and therefore are not derived from the poet but from a later
redactor. (In regard to the one apparent exception, Ps. 7, title, 8,
cf. 2 Sam. 18. 31 in LXX.) But, above all, we find in some of
these psalms elements which absolutely exclude the possibility
of the superscriptions being correct, cf. esp. 63. 2 and 11.
And the proved incorrectness of some shakes the trustworthiness
of the rest. And another circumstance that weakens our
confidence in these attributions is that they are often textually
uncertain. The LXX names David as the author in twelve
additional psalms, in one Jeremiah, in four Haggai and Zechariah
alongside of David, and makes no mention of Solomon in 127.
The Chronicler (1 C. 16) ascribes to David two psalms which
the Hebrew text does not assign to him. The Peshitto, again,
contains superscriptions which diverge widely from the Hebrew
and Greek texts, cf. Acts 4. 25 ; Heb. 4. 7.

But, on the other hand, both the Asaphite and the Korahite
psalms show a common characteristic language and circle of
ideas, and thus the trustworthiness of the inscriptions does appear
to be so far vindicated that the psalms of these collections
did really proceed from a particular circle of writers. On this
analogy we are justified in assuming, in the case of the psalms
attributed to David also, that they are derived from a great
collection containing poems of similar type, which bore the
name of the royal Singer as their superscription. In this
collection, however, there came to be included, in the course
of centuries, poems which had some affinity with his or were
imitated or elaborated from his, just as it came about in the
case of the crystallisation of laws about the nucleus of the laws
of Moses, or of proverbs, about those of Solomon. Thus, in
the last resort, the decision regarding the date of particular

psalms rests simply on internal evidence as interpreted by historical criticism.

In recent decades the criticism of the Psalms has, however, in many quarters, got upon wrong lines. And that in two directions. 1. It has been contended that the speaker, the " I " of the Psalms, is never this or that particular poet whom we might expect to trace, but *the whole Jewish Community*, assembled for prayer in the Temple (Reuss, Olshausen, Smend). As a consequence the whole of the psalms must be a creation of the community ; that is to say, of the post-Exilic period.

The supporters of this theory point to the immediate transition in many psalms from persecution to trouble, pain, sickness, death and the misery of sin, in others to the strong conviction of salvation, and finally to the curses directed against enemies, which, it is held, exclude the idea that the speaker is an individual. But the fact is that exactly the same phenomena are to be observed in the prayers of Jeremiah, Job, the Son of Sirach, and frequently also in Babylonian and Egyptian psalms which are certainly of an individual character (cf. esp. Balla, *ut sup.*). And, on the other hand, there is lacking in these poems any indication of the basis of the consciousness of salvation, such as we find expressly stated in real communal prayers, in the Covenant of Sinai and elsewhere. Moreover, the kind of personification supposed would be a wholly unnatural one, cf. 27. 10 ; 35. 11-14 ; 41. 5, 9, etc., and, most conclusive of all, the poet, or the offerer of the prayer, frequently and quite expressly distinguishes himself from the community, cf. 4. 2-5 ; 22. 25 f. ; 34. 3 ; 35. 18 ; 62. 8 f. ; 69. 6 ff., etc. This theory has, therefore, rightly been gradually abandoned again in all quarters.

2. Equally mistaken is the view, which is still widely prevalent, that because the Psalter was the hymn-book of the post-Exilic community, every one of the hymns in it must necessarily be post-Exilic (Wellhausen, Stade and others), a view which the analogy of any hymn-book one chooses

to name would be sufficient to disprove. Cf.
ZEAT, p. 80 f.

The following special points have still to be noticed : (*a*)
The references in the titles to musical accompaniment, which
we find especially in 1-89, prove only that these psalms were
at one time or another adapted to musical use in public worship ;
their composition may have taken place long before that. (*b*)
Many psalms, such as 1 ; 3 ; 4 ; 6 ; 7 ; 8 ; 11-13 ; 18 ; 19 ; 25 ;
34. 11-22 ; 37 ; 39 ; 41, etc., are clearly shown by their content
to be written with quite other aims than to be used in public
worship. (*c*) It is clearly proved by passages like Ex. 15. 1 ff. ;
32. 18 ; Jg. 5. 1 ff. ; Amos 5. 23 ; Isa. 30. 29 ; Ps. 137. 3, 4 ;
Ezek. 40. 44 (? cf. Köberle, *ut sup.* p. 17 ff.) ; Neh. 7. 44, that
even in pre-Exilic times there was singing with musical accompaniment at processions, festivals and divine service ; just
as we have religious hymns and penitential psalms from Egypt
and Babylon as early as the second millennium B.C.

I. A sounder criticism of the Psalms must start
from the certainty that the Psalter must in any
case contain a nucleus of pre-Exilic psalms.

A simple and inexpugnable argument for this is at once
furnished by the so-called Royal Psalms, 2 ; 18 ; 20 ; 28 ; 45 ;
61 ; 63 ; 72 ; 110 ; 132. The desperate attempts, there is no
other word for it, to interpret these as referring to a future
Messiah, a foreign king, or a Maccabaean prince, must be
regarded as, one and all, complete failures. The prince is
always a real personality of the present world, though, no
doubt, in 2 ; 21 ; 45 ; 72 ; 110, a personality in whom the
poet also celebrates the expected Saviour, the Divine Deliverer.
This excludes a foreign king, as completely as the title *king*,
the communication of Divine oracles regarding him in Ps. 2 and
110, and the language, exclude a Simon, or other prince, of
the Maccabaean family.

But if these psalms are pre-Exilic, then the two strongest
motives for giving a post-Exilic date to all the rest are disposed
of at a stroke. These motives are (1) their *spiritual* character,
and (2) the absence of reference to them in pre-Exilic prophets
and histories (in spite of Ex. 15 ; 1 S. 2. 1 ff. ; 2 S. 22. 1 ff. ;
Deut. 32 ; Isa. 12. 1 ff. ; 38. 9 ff. ; etc.—which, however, are
all similarly relegated in the most high-handed fashion, in spite
of 2 Sam. 1. 10, etc., to the post-Exilic period). The question

may be asked, would it have occurred to any one, simply on the basis of these passages, that a pre-Exilic king could already be celebrated in such strains as those of, *e.g.*, Psalm 21 as a wholly spiritual sovereign? The fact is, we do not possess in the pre-Exilic literature which has come down to us sufficient material to give us that kind of acquaintance with the religious currents and impulses of the time, which would warrant us in attaching much weight to the *argumentum e silentio*.

Alongside of the Royal psalms we ought probably also to place those in which the authors take up, in regard to the animal sacrifices, the same position as the pre-Exilic prophets, in contrast with the period after Ezra when the Priestly Writing was the dominant influence; thus giving us grounds for regarding them as contemporaries of the prophets (cf. Ps. 40. 6 f.; 50. 8 f.; 51. 16 with Isa. 1. 10 ff., Micah 6. 8, etc.); and cf. also Ps. 15 and 24. In the case of the latter, verses 7-10 take us, further, into a period when the ark was still carried in procession to the sanctuary. The decision is no doubt not so certain in these cases as in the Royal psalms, as it is also possible that they might have been composed in post-Exilic times in the bosom of conventicles in which the ancient prophetic type of piety was still preserved, in defiance of the official religion.

Finally, we may point out that the free use of quotations from petitionary psalms which we find in Jeremiah, and his own prayers couched in the style of these, prove to demonstration that poetry of the type of the psalms was already at home in pious circles of the pre-Exilic period, cf. Jer. 11. 18—12. 6; 15. 15-21; 17. 12-18, etc. Gunkel has rightly pointed out that the prophet implies in 20. 13 the whole category of the " songs of the poor," and in 33. 11 liturgical hymns of praise. And, moreover, we find constant evidence that he is not creating a new style of prayer, but only introducing into the prophetic discourse one which already existed, as was natural enough, since he makes prayer the centre of the religious life. He follows the analogy (as Hosea also did, 6. 1-3; 14. 1 ff.) of already existing penitential and elegiac psalms, cf. 14. 7-9; 17. 12 f.; his dependence on the psalms of the first part of the Psalter permits in many cases of proof, cf. Sellin, *Disputatio*, pp. 118-122; ZEAT, p. 84 and Baumgartner, *Die Klage-gedichte des Jeremia*, 1917.

Speaking generally, there is between the pre-Exilic psalms just mentioned and those by which they are surrounded so close a relationship in ideas and language that we are warranted in concluding that the nucleus of the Davidic collection, 3-41, 51-72, belongs to the pre-Exilic period, and was the book of prayers and hymns which Judah took with her into Exile (no doubt along with others).

But in this connection two points have to be kept in mind. The first is that, just as a psalm from this collection might by a later redactor be detached from its surroundings and inserted in another collection (cf. 45 ; 50 ; 110 ?), so a certain number of Exilic or post-Exilic psalms may have found their way in here (22 ; 69 ? ; etc.). And the second point is that even the pre-Exilic psalms have a history behind them, they lived prior to their enrolment in collections, " on the lips of men," and this or that detail in them may well be the reflection of a later period. Not only do our own hymn-books show us analogies for such vicissitudes in the case of religious lyrics, but a quite obvious direct example is furnished by the relationship of Psalm 14 to 53 ; and again in 60 a later setting enshrines an oracle which is centuries older, vv. 7-10 ; the same applies to Ps. 68, v. 22 f. ; and 51. 18 f. is a later addition to 51. 3-17, etc.

A question subsidiary to the problem of pre-Exilic psalms is whether the collections 3-41 ; 51-72 contain actual Davidic psalms.

We have already seen that the tradition embodied in the superscriptions is uncertain. That in many psalms it is quite untenable admits of proof. It is impossible that psalms can be by David which (a) address the king directly, or speak of him in the third person, 20 ; 21 ; 61 ; 63 ; 72 ; 110 ; (b) imply that the Temple is already in existence, 5 ; 27 ; 28 ; 63 ; 68 ; 69 ; 101 ; 138 ; (c) are composed in a strongly Aramaizing style, 139 ; (d) imply a purely religious opposition to the godless enemies who are in power in the land, whereas in the enmities of David religious opposition was combined with either private (cf. 1 S. 26. 19 f.) or political conflict (2 S. 8. 1 ff., etc.). Contrast Ps. 9 ; 12 ; 14 ; 27 ; 35 ; 38 ; 101, etc.

On the other hand, the tradition which pointed to David as the religious poet *par excellence* must obviously have had some kind of historical starting-point; and a collection of Davidic poems could crystallize only round a really existing nucleus. And we know from unimpeachable historical evidence (1 S. 16. 18; 2 S. 1. 17; 3. 33 f.; 6. 15; 23. 1 ff.) that he was skilled in playing the harp and versed in the lyric art. And the Books of Samuel also avouch that he was deeply religious. Though the Chronicler certainly idealized him, it is equally certain that the picture of his religion which is often formed nowadays (on the basis of a false interpretation of the ephod, false inferences from 1 Sam. 26. 19 f., etc.), and which is held to exclude him from the list of writers of psalms, is a mere caricature.

Of course, what was said above regarding pre-Exilic psalms in general applies to the Davidic psalms in particular; their century-long history must have left unmistakable marks on them also. Here, too, we have a concrete example in a case in which a psalm has been preserved to us in twofold form, viz. the relationship of Ps. 18 to 2 S. 22. What a multitude of variants! And yet this is the one single case in which we can assign a psalm to him with some approach to scientific certainty. Here we have not only the double evidence of the tradition, not only the later subscription in verse 50, which itself must from its content date from pre-Exilic times, but verses 37-48 compel us to think of a victorious king, in the height of his prosperity, as the poet. And the antique language, the characteristically primitive circle of ideas (the theophany, vv. 6-15; the spirit of vv. 29 and 42 with its suggestion of the period of the Judges, not to speak of the naïve conception of retribution in 24-26) confirm the correctness of the tradition (vv. 21-23 are later glosses of the type which a mention of righteousness at once suggested to a later editor). Elsewhere we can only speak of possibilities.

As psalms in which early *Davidic* material is perhaps to be found, the following, in addition to 18, have claims to consideration: 3; 4; 7; 8 (in the last named it is not necessary to suppose that the Priestly Writing is the basis, but only the centuries-older *material* of its creation story); 19 (vv. 1-6); 23 (the " House of Yahweh " of verse 6 may, in view of 4*a*, be Palestine); 24 (vv. 7-10); 29 (an eschatological psalm); 32 (there are in existence penitential psalms by King Assurnasirpal about 1100 B.C., and still more from Assurbanipal) ; 60 (vv. 9-12).

II. In the same general sense that Ps. 3-41 ; 51-72 may be asserted to be pre-Exilic, it may be affirmed that 42-50 ; 73-150 date from the Exilic and post-Exilic periods. But even these are only in part originally composed for liturgical use ; to a considerable extent they had their source in conventicles of the godly.

In the psalms of these collections we have either explicit references to the deportation, the destruction of Jerusalem, the rebuilding of the City and Temple, cf. 42 ; 43 ; 44 (46 and 48 are to be understood eschatologically) ; 74 ; 79 ; 80 ; 84 ; 85 ; 89 ; 102 ; 118 ; 126 ; 137 ; or the position taken up towards the other nations corresponds with the ideas and language of Deutero-Isaiah, 47 ; 49 ; 93-99 ; or they show traces of being originally composed for a Temple use such as we know to have existed in post-Exilic times, cf. 95 ; 96 ; 100 ; 103 ; 104-7 ; 111-13 ; 117 ; 118 ; 135 ; 136 ; 146-50, with 1 Chron. 16. 8, 36 ; Neh. 1. 11 ; 9. 5 ; Ezra, 3. 10. But again in this collection it is not impossible that a wandering pre-Exilic psalm may have found a home here. In addition to 45 ; 50 ; 110 and 132, others which suggest this origin are, e.g., 89. 1-37 and 101.

A subsidiary problem here is, whether any Maccabaean psalms are included in the Psalter, or whether it was definitely closed before that period.

The arguments adduced by Ehrt, etc., in favour of the latter alternative, 1 Chron. 16 ; Sir. 47. 8-10 ; 1 Macc. 7. 17 ; 2 Macc. 2. 13, do not prove what they are required to prove. They only show that prior to the Maccabaean period there was already a psalter in existence, not that particular psalms could not subsequently have been inserted into it. On the other hand, we must be very cautious about assuming the existence of such psalms. It is not merely the exclusion of the Psalms of Solomon, written about 60 B.C., nor the quotation of the certainly late Psalm 79 as Scripture in Maccabees 7. 16 ff. (i.e. about 100 B.C.), nor the improbability that the Pharisees would have tolerated

the admission of anything from the era of the hated Has-
monaeans; but, in addition to all this, the language warns
us to be cautious.

There is a pretty general consensus at present in favour of
regarding at least 44; 74; 79; 83 as Maccabaean. But these
certainly cannot, in view of 44. 17-22; 74. 8, 9; 79. 12, refer
to the catastrophe of 586 B.C.; and it is equally certain that
they are not really appropriate to the Maccabaean period, for
the most characteristic feature of this period, the division of
the people into those who were faithful to the Law on the one
hand, and those who apostatized on the other (cf. 1 Macc.
2. 44; 3. 5, 8), is wholly absent; we have here before us a
united community of the godly. We shall, therefore, with
greater probability, refer these psalms to an earlier catastrophe,
perhaps in the time of Artaxerxes Ochus (cf. Eusebius, *Chronicle*,
ed. Schoene, 113, and Solinus, ed. Mommsen, 34. 4). The
traditional argument against this date, viz. that we should
have no certain knowledge of such a catastrophe from any other
source, will no longer be found convincing by any one since
the discovery of the Elephantine papyri.

We have to conclude, therefore, that while there
is in principle no reason why there should not be
a few Maccabaean psalms in the Psalter, their
presence has certainly not yet been proved. If
there are any, the most probable place to look for
them is among the Hallelujah psalms of the last
book (cf. esp. 118).

We may sum up by saying that the Psalter may
be described as the Response of the pious community to the Divine acts of revelation, from the
days of David up to the threshold of the Maccabaean period, or perhaps going just beyond that
threshold. The literatures of Ancient Egypt and
of Babylon show us that in respect of religious lyric,
as of prophecy, the People of the Revelation reached
a height absolutely unique among the nations of
the Ancient East. In spite of all the formal
affinities of style, imagery, etc., it is here alone that

the ethical is set free from the bondage of the natural (cf. 40; 50; 51); it is here alone that a consciousness of salvation is attained which in places already bears an almost New-Testament character (73. 23 ff.); it is here alone that the keynote is the hope of a Kingdom of God which is to embrace all nations, along with the heavens and the earth, a kingdom where " mercy and truth are met together, righteousness and peace have kissed one another " (85. 10, cf. 22; 72; 93-99, etc.).

§ 2. *The Proverbs of Solomon*

Oort, *Spreuken, 1-9,* Theol. Tijdschr., 1885, pp. 379-425 ; Franken-berg, *Prov. 1-9,* ZAW, 1895, p. 104 ff. ; Mühlau, *De proverbiorum quae dicuntur Aguri et Lemuelis origine atque indole,* 1869 ; Pfeiffer, *Die religiös-sittliche Weltanschauung des Buches der Sprüche,* 1897 ; Friedländer, *Griechische Philosophie im A.T.,* 1904 ; Sellin, *Die Spuren griechischer Philosophie im A.T.,* 1906 ; Meinhold, *Die Weisheit Israels in Spruch, Sage und Dichtung,* 1908 ; Volz, *Sprüche der Weisen,* SchAT, 1911.

The Proverbs form the first book of that literary *genre* which is known as the *Ḥokhmah,* or *Wisdom Literature* (it in-cludes also Job, Ecclesiastes and some of the Psalms ; and, in the Apocrypha, Sirach (Ecclesiasticus) and the Wisdom of Solomon).

" Wisdom " in Israel is not to be placed in the same category as the " philosophy " of other nations, for it everywhere assumes as axiomatic the fundamental ideas and primary demands of religion (cf. Prov. 1. 7 ; Ps. 111. 10), and only in its latest exponents (Ecclesiastes, Wisdom of Solomon) does it show a definite influence from Greek philosophy. In Prov. 8. 21 ff. (read, in v. 30, *amun,* foster-child, instead of *amon,* master-workman), and in Job 28. 1 ff. wisdom is thought of as personified, and so represented, just as, in Prov. 9. 13 ff., Folly is personified as a woman ; but it is not a hypostasis in the same sense as the Greek νοῦς.

But as the Wisdom literature, on the other hand, applies itself to the observation of human character, and makes almost no reference to the special national interests (the Covenant of Sinai, the cultus, the eschatological and Messianic hopes), it is best thought of as the " Humanism " of Israel. It is clear that this humanism was especially cultivated among certain circles in the capital, particularly at the Court. While it is not unfriendly towards the priests and the prophets, it takes up a neutral position in regard to them, and shows us that the intellectual life of Israel was much richer and more many-sided than we are apt to imagine it from attending too exclusively to the evidence of the prophetic and historical writings. The aim of the Wisdom literature is primarily practical and ethical ; it aims at educating, and it seems indeed as time went on to have devoted itself more and more to the education of youth (Prov. 23 ; 24 ; 30. 1-9 ; chaps. 1-9).

This kind of Wisdom, as the subject of a technical study, existed in Israel from the days of Solomon onwards (cf. 1 K. 4. 30 f., 34 ; 10. 1 ff.). That it began systematically with elementary instruction we see in Isa. 28. 9 f. Jeremiah recognizes " the wise " as a distinct class, alongside of priests and prophets, 18. 18. From the first the international character of Wisdom was consciously apprehended. Cf. 1 K. 4. 30 ; Isa. 19. 11 ; Jer. 49. 7 ; 50. 35 ; 51. 57 ; Ob. 8., etc. And it becomes more and more probable that Solomon brought the first teacher of it from Egypt, where a recognized form of poetic composition inculcating in short aphorisms practical wisdom in the conduct of life, was already flourishing in the second millennium B.C., cf. the aphorisms of Amen-em-het I. (? = Heman of 1 K. 4. 31), Ptah-hotep, Ani, etc. ; see Gressmann, *Altorientalische Texte*, i. p. 201 ff. That it would, for this very reason, appear somewhat suspicious to the prophets, and that we should hear little or nothing of it from them, is quite intelligible. In spite of its serious ethico-religious purpose, it would too easily incur the verdict pronounced in Isa. 5. 21. It was only when, after the end of the fifth century B.C., the imposing advance of Greek culture threatened to overwhelm the ancestral Jewish ethics and religion, that even priestly circles learned to value this Wisdom more highly as a means of maintaining the hold of the ancient religion upon the cultured members of the community. But even as late as the Book of Chronicles we see the reluctance to recognize this cultivation of the humanities ; the Chronicler makes no mention of it in the case of Solomon or Hezekiah.

The Proverbs fall into three main divisions : I. Introductory Discourses, chapters 1-9. II. The collection proper of Solomonic proverbs, 10. 1 — 22. 16 (all in couplets, mainly antithetic, but some parallel), with two appendices of proverbs from anonymous sages, 22. 17 — 24. 22 and 24. 23-24 (not in pure *Mashal* style, but in form more closely allied to chapters 1-9 ; in addition to couplets there are also triplets and quatrains). III. Solomonic proverbs collected by the " men of Hezekiah," 25-29 (couplets, almost always real similes), with three appendices, viz. (*a*) sayings of Agar, 30 ; (*b*) sayings of the mother of King Lemuel addressed to her son, 31. 1-9 ; (*c*) the eulogy on the virtuous woman, in the form of an alphabetical poem, 31. 10-31.

These appendices are themselves sufficient evidence that the superscription " Proverbs of Solomon " is not to be understood literally, but that here as in the so-called " Psalms of David " the date of origin of each different group calls for a separate historico-critical investigation. Chapters 1-9 certainly belong to the post-Exilic period.

Budde, in particular (*Geschichte der hebräischen Literatur*, p. 269 f.), has shown, from 1. 1-8, that chapters 1-9 are not by Solomon at all, but are simply intended to serve as an introduction to the proverbs of Solomon, which begin with chapter 10. These chapters are placed by their language (the un-Hebraic long periods in 1 and 2, the Greek loan-word *etūn* in 7. 16), by the stage of culture implied (cf. 6. 24 ; 7. 5 ff., 16 ; foreign culture, but not polytheistic religion, threatens to ensnare the Jewish community, 2. 16 ff. ; 5. 3 ff. ; 9. 13 ff.), by the ideas (especially the personifying of wisdom, with its mildly speculative quality, which is intended to take the wind out of the sails of a godless speculation, 8. 22 ff.), and, finally, by the close affinity with Sirach, quite unmistakably in the post - Exilic period, and, more definitely, in the time when Greek influence was extending its sway in Palestine, *i.e.* about the fourth century B.C.

The completely different spirit which animates the central part of the Book points to an earlier period ; and, moreover, a pre-Exilic period, as is shown by the proverbs which refer to the King.

While in 1-9 the King is never mentioned—and in Sirach only once or twice and then either as something undesirable, Sir. (Ecclus.) 7. 4-6 ; 8. 2, or at least as something remote, 10. 1-5—here the existence of the Israelitish Monarchy is everywhere implied. Moreover there is a remarkable confirmation of the division of this collection into the two parts 10. 1—22. 16 and 25-29—the latter of which, with its carefully worked out comparisons, represents a higher stage of the formal development of poetry—that we cannot help allowing that tradition is right. This confirmation is that in the first collection enthusiasm for the Monarchy and confidence in it is everywhere apparent, cf. 14. 28, 35 ; 19. 12 ; 20. 2, 8, 26, 28 ; 21. 1 ; 22. 11 ; and especially 16. 10-15 ; in the second there is scepticism, 23. 2-6 ; 28. 15 f. ; 29. 4, 12, 14, 26 ; in 28. 2 there is perhaps even a side glance at the rapid changes on the throne of the Northern Kingdom. It is exactly the same kind of relationship as between the two sources of the Books of Samuel.

Yet another confirmation : in 10. 1—22. 16 we find the word *Torah* only once, and then with the express addition " of the wise," 13. 14 ; but in 25-29 we find it in the sense of Divine guidance, 28. 4-9 ; 29. 18, as in the days of Isaiah, cf. Isa. 8. 16, 20 ; 28. 9-13 ; 30. 9 ; also Jer. 8. 8.

But if we thus find that not only the pre-Exilic origin of the central part of the Book, 10-29, but also the division into two collections is fully confirmed by internal evidence, we are justified in giving credence to the tradition in a further point, viz. that the nucleus of 10. 1 – 22. 16 goes back to the Solomonic era, while the kernel of 25-29 owes its origin to a collection set on foot by Hezekiah, the Jewish Assurbanipal, as a royal patron of literature.

In 1 K. 4. 32, after an express comparison of the wisdom of Solomon with that of wise men of other nations, it is stated that he composed 3000 proverbs. The attempt has been made to deprive this statement of any bearing on our problem, either by asserting that these proverbs must according to v. 13 have

P

referred to natural objects—whereas this verse says nothing about proverbs, but alludes to his fame as an exorcist (for " cedar and hyssop " as charms against demons, cf. Ex. 12. 22 ; Lev. 14. 4 ; Num. 19. 6)—or, that we have in this collection only 935 verses, that is to say, not a third of the 3000 ; as if that was an argument of any force at all, and as if in other cases great historical works, collections of Israelitish songs, etc., had not also disappeared. To suppose that the curious little discovery made by Behnke (ZAW, 1896, p. 122) that 10. 1—22. 16 contain 375 proverbs, which number, expressed in letters = šlmh = Solomon, serves to explain the origin of the superscription, makes the impression of being a bad joke. The utmost extent to which it could have any bearing on the problem would be that 10—22 might later have been rounded off to this number of proverbs.

Of course, as we have seen in similar cases, the tradition is not to be pressed too far. In the first place the King, as so often in antiquity, stands as the representative of his Court ; his wise men and poets, who composed their poems in his honour —in Egypt too this branch of poetry is in part a Court product —are included under his name. In the second place, the superscription of 25. 1 itself shows that the technical term " Solomonic proverbs " had become established as the designation for this form of didactic poetry in general, so that a collection of " Solomonic proverbs " could be compiled at the Court of Hezekiah. Finally it has to be kept in mind, here as in the Psalms, that in the course of the repeated redactions, extending down into the Greek period—to which the numerous doublets bear witness, cf. 14. 12 with 16. 25 ; 11. 13a with 20. 19a ; 25. 24 with 21. 9, etc.—older proverbs might be recast, or replaced by others more appropriate to the times. This would explain the proverbs against riches, 15. 16, those implying monogamy, 12. 4 ; 18. 22 ; or those that give evidence of a knowledge of God deepened by prophetic teaching, 16. 2 ; 20. 27 ; 21. 3 ; 28. 13 (that *zedakah* in 10. 2 ; 11. 4 already meant " alms-giving " is, however, not the case, cf. 11. 5 f.).

Finally, four other reasons have led to the rejection of the tradition by most modern critics (Stade, Frankenberg, Cornill, etc.). One is that too low an estimate is still formed of the culture of the Solomonic Court and the influence exercised upon it by the older civilizations. Secondly, it is said that prophecy and law lie behind the Proverbs as closed and complete entities. But in general nothing further is presupposed than the Divine demand of a pure morality, with which ancient

Israel was already acquainted in the Decalogue, and which Amos, Hosea, etc., also take for granted (the thought of 15. 8 ; 21. 27 was already known to the Yahwist, Gen. 4. 4 f., 7). There is in fact not a single reference to " The Law." In the third place it is asserted that the proverbs imply a monogamic and a trading nation, and that both these characteristics point to the post-Exilic period. But though polygamy was doubtless perfectly legitimate in pre-Exilic times, the practice was nevertheless rather different, cf. Gen. 2. 24 ; the Egyptian collections of proverbs of the second millennium always in exactly the same way refer to one wife, and as regards trade in Israel in pre-Exilic times cf. Amos 8. 5, Micah 6. 10 f., Ezek. 27. 17, etc. And finally, although the parallel between these aphorisms * and the so-called proverbs of other nations has rightly been generally given up, the idea of the *popular wisdom* embodied in the ordinary popular proverb, still exercises its influence (cf. Budde, pp. 289, 295 *et al.*). And starting from the axiom that this is the last thing to find expression in a national literature, its codification in Israel is placed in the post-Exilic period. But once more, that is a complete misapprehension of the character of this definite poetic form, with its foreign origin. And how could aphorisms like 16. 10-15 have been preserved in the popular mouth alone throughout the Exilic and early post-Exilic periods ?

The appendices 22. 17 — 24. 34 are in form later than 25-29 ; but in view of 22. 29 ; 24. 21 they also are probably pre-Exilic, and perhaps date from the time of Jeremiah. The form of direct address " my son " which meets us here and again, later, in chapters 1 — 9 belongs to the aphoristic style in Egypt as early as 1000 B.C. (cf. the aphorisms of Ani). As Agur and Lemuel are completely unknown to us, the dates of the last three appendices

---

* The German word " Spruch," used in the title of the Book of Proverbs, is of much wider connotation than the English word. It can mean anything between a " saying " and an " oracle," by which words it might quite properly in certain contexts be translated. Since it is the title of the Book it seems proper in the discussion of the Book to represent it by " proverb," but here, where it is directly contrasted with " Sprichwort," a (popular) proverb in the ordinary sense, I have suggested the difference by using aphorism.—Translator.

cannot be determined. The only thing that seems to be certain is that the *Massa* of 30. 1 ; 31. 1 (rendered " prophecy " in A.V.) is to be understood as the name of a place or people, cf. Gen. 25. 14 ; 1 Chron. 1. 30, and that therefore the persons in question are foreign, probably North-Arabian, princes.

§ 3. *Job*

Merx, *Das Gedicht von Hiob*, 1871 ; Budde, *Beiträge zur Erklärung des Buches Hiob*, 1876 ; Giesebrecht, *Der Wendepunkt des B. Hi.*, 1879 ; Grill, *Zur Krit. d. Komp. des B. Hi.*, 1890 ; Cheyne, The Expositor, 1892, p. 245 ff. ; Laue, *Die Komposition des B. Hi.*, 1895 ; Strack, *Die Priorität des B. Hi. gegenüber Prov. 1-9*, ThStKr, 1896, p. 608 ff. ; Ley, *Die Abfassungszeit des B. Hi.*, ThStKr, 1898, p. 34 ff. ; K. Kautzsch, *Das sogenannte Volksbuch von Hiob*, 1900 ; Fries, *Das philosophische Gespräch von Hiob bis Platon*, 1904 ; Volz, *Das Buch Hiob*, SchAT, 1911 ; Sellin, *Das Problem des Hiobbuches*, 1919.

The Book of Job is a didactic writing of epic character which in places assumes an almost dramatic form. It is a tremendous work, and may be considered the finest flower of the *Ḥokhmah* literature, although it is also a declaration of bankruptcy by a Wisdom-teacher (chapter 28). The problem which forms its subject is : How can the suffering of a righteous man be reconciled with the existence of a righteous God ?

The arrangement of the Book is as follows :

I. The situation, 1 — 3. (*a*) Job's prosperity, 1. 1-5; (*b*) the Wager in Heaven, and Job's Misfortunes, 1. 6 — 2. 10 ; (*c*) the appearance of the Three Friends, Eliphaz, Bildad and Zophar, and Job's first complaint, 2. 11 — 3. 26.

II. The main " action," 4 — 31. (*a*) Three colloquies between Job and the friends, who, on the

basis of the current doctrine of retribution, en-
deavour, with increasing acerbity, to bring Job to
acknowledge his secret sins, while he emphatically
asseverates his complete innocence, and finally
rejects every attempt to explain his suffering,
declaring that wisdom is withheld from men, 4—28;
(*b*) Job's final appeal to God's righteousness, 29—31.

III. The *Dénouement.* (*a*) The Speech of Elihu,
who sees the purpose of the sufferings in purification
from spiritual pride, 32—37; (*b*) the "Answer" of
God, Who, by pointing to His own almighty power
and wisdom, silences Job's complaints, and demands
that all earthly things should submit to His supernal
wisdom and counsel, 38. 1—42. 6; (*c*) Job's self-
humiliation and renewed prosperity, 42. 7-17.

Even this general survey at once raises the
question : What is the solution which the author
offers of the problem which forms his subject ?
And it must be frankly admitted that, in spite of all
the labour which has been expended upon it, this
question has not been answered with certainty even
to the present day. There are in fact three solutions offered in III., and we may, if we choose,
regard chapter 28 as giving yet a fourth. But such
a result must mean that the Book is not a unity.

1. It is now almost universally admitted (it has lately been
contested only by E. and K. Kautzsch) that the prologue
1. 1—2. 10, and the epilogue 42. 7-17, are not by the same
author as the rest of the Book. There is in fact not merely
a contradiction between the purpose of the poet in 38. 1—42. 6
and the occurrence of an earthly reparation in 42. 7 ff., but,
moreover, in the whole Book there is never the slightest reference
to the wager with Satan, and the Job of the poem is (especially
in 22. 6 ff.; 29. 1 ff.) a different kind of person from the Job
of the prologue and epilogue—not a shepherd-prince but a
city ruler—and his sufferings in 16. 10 ff. are of a wholly different

character from those described in the prologue (the death of the children is alone alluded to, 8. 4; 29. 5; 19. 17 is not certain). The majority of critics rightly see in this framework an earlier popular book, which the author of Job has, with poetic freedom, made the setting of his great poem (so *e.g.* Duhm, Budde, Baudissin, etc.). It is also possible that the so-called Satan passages in this (1. 6-12; 2. 1-7*a*), and also the visit of the three friends (2. 11-13; 42. 7-9) were inserted by the author of chapter 3 ff., while the old folk-tale only narrated that God Himself had tempted Job (cf. Gen. 22, etc.), but that he, in spite of everything, in spite even of his wife's up-braidings, sustained the trial gloriously.

2. Again, the speeches of Elihu, 32—37, cannot have been written by the poet at the same time as the rest of the work. For (*a*) Elihu does not appear before or after 32—37, and no notice is taken of his arguments; (*b*) 38. 2 implies that Job, not Elihu, had spoken immediately before; (*c*) the Elihu speeches repeat, quite unnecessarily, much that has been already said by the friends, and anticipate, especially in chapter 37, much of the subject-matter of the Divine speeches; while on the other hand they directly contradict these, for the out-come of the Divine speeches is, that it is not for man to ask an explanation of the Divine counsel, whereas Elihu gives an explanation; (*d*) the language shows considerable divergence from that of the other chapters. In recent times only Budde, Cornill and Wildeboer have sought to defend the immediate and original unity of these speeches with the rest of the work, on the ground that without them the Book offers no solution whatever of the problem, and moreover that it leads up to precisely the solution here offered—the purification of the righteous from pride. But this assertion is not in accordance with the structure of 3—31; for, if it were correct, Job's pride ought to be more and more strongly emphasized, up to the time when it is cured by Elihu's lesson; which is certainly not the case. And, moreover, a literary postulate of this kind cannot override the positive arguments (*a-d*) against the original unity; and the ground is cut from beneath it as soon as it becomes evident that the original book did not propose to offer a solution of that problem at all.

3. Moreover, on close examination it appears that the hymn to Wisdom in chapter 28, in spite of the fact that it now connects with 12. 2, 13; 17. 10, etc., is equally in contradiction with 38. 1—42. 6, for, in the hymn, Job has already by his own insight perceived what in the latter passage he is represented as first

learning from the theophany and the Divine speech, viz. that wisdom and insight are denied to man, and that nothing remains for him but to fear God, cf. 42. 6 (so *e.g.* Duhm). It is said, of course that in this chapter Job is attacking only the false wisdom of his friends, but there is nothing to indicate that it is addressed to them, and the wisdom which they represent is quite other than the wisdom referred to here. It is remarkable also that Job never mentions his sufferings here. As moreover 27. 11-23, to which 28. 1 ff. are attached (the " for," however, only explains the refrain verse, 28. 12, 20, which has fallen out here), are quite inappropriate in the mouth of Job, since in speaking them he would be contradicting himself, this is most probably the last speech of Zophar. Accordingly chapter 28 had originally nothing to do with the Book of Job, and was simply inserted here at a point where it seemed to fit in more or less appropriately.

4. But we must go yet a step further. Though 29—31 fit on well enough to 27. 10, and come with sufficient appropriateness before 38, there is nevertheless a contradiction between this central portion and the solution given by the theophany. The defenders of the " genuineness " of the Elihu speeches have always pointed to this contradiction, but they have drawn a wrong conclusion from it. After the speeches of Job against his friends one would certainly not precisely expect that the solution of the problem would consist in an appearance of God in this fashion. Job has repeated again and again that such a confrontation with God would not help him, that in such a case God would only overwhelm him. More particularly in 9. 2, 3, 14-16, 20, 29-31 he anticipates precisely what is said by God afterwards in 38 ff. ; cf. also 10. 6 f. ; 13. 15-21. Indeed the very form of the theophany of 38 is anticipated in 9. 17 and declared to be worthless : " Nay more, he gnashed upon me in a tempest and multiplied my transgression without cause."

Now it is certainly worthy of notice that this thought, which reaches its maximum of emphasis in chapters 9 and 10, appears clearly for the last time in 13. 20 f., and that in the same chapter, 13. 16-19, another note, that of longing for a legal trial, appears alongside of it, and that the idea of God's overwhelming him by His might, is in 23. 6, if the text is correct, actually changed round into its opposite. In any case, from chapter 13 onwards, we observe a constantly increasing intensity in Job's demand for a day of judgement, a demand to see God face to face, come what may, 16. 18-22 ; 19. 23-27 ; 23. 3-10 ; 31. 35-37. But the meeting here contemplated is simply not that of 38—42, in which there is hardly a reference to Job's physical and spiritual suffering, to his sins or righteousness (cf. 38. 2 ; 40. 1-14), but only an exaltation of the Almighty Lord of Nature ; so that it would fall under the censure of 9 ; 10 ; and 13.

From this discrepancy Cheyne and Volz, SchAT, p. 23 ff., have drawn the conclusion that the Divine speeches also formed no part of the original work, and that this consisted originally only of the dialogue on the great question of suffering. This idea seems to me worthy of all consideration, but neither critic has discovered the actual theme. This is, in 3—27. 10 ; 29—31, *the testing of the righteous in suffering and death*. In point of fact we have here a self-consistent whole : Job who is by his sufferings tested to the uttermost has not wavered in his righteousness ; chapter 9 f. is, according to the original plan of the work, not a falling into sin, but only the first wild complaint, which, however, dies away gradually down to 23. 15 and gives place to the desire for a day of assize on which the righteous may appear before God, may appeal from a damnatory to a justly-judging God (cf. 16. 21 !), and may from Him receive, if only in the hour of death, in which he sees Him, his justification (19. 25). In this triumphant certainty the work comes to its conclusion in 31. 35-37. Is this faith, with its defiant " nevertheless," a worse solution than the resignation of 38—42. 6 ? The fact is, these chapters in which Job is blamed for his struggle for faith contradict the fundamental thought of the author of 3—31 not less than do the prologue and the speeches of Elihu. An external confirmation for the view that 38—42. 6 did not originally form the conclusion of 3—31— that the latter must in fact at one time have been followed by a quite different Divine speech as an answer to Job's complaint, is, I think, to be found in 42. 7, which must be from the original author. This verse certainly cannot have been originally preceded by the present dialogue between Job and God.

5. It is of less central significance, but still deserving of mention, that within the Divine speeches the extraordinarily detailed description of the hippopotamus and the crocodile, 40. 6—41. 34, is by some critics considered to be an interpolation after 38 and 39, a view which is supported by the doublets 40. 1-5 compared with 42. 1-6, and 40. 6 ff. compared with 38. 1 ff.

By most critics this analysis, according to which, of the 42 chapters only 3 — 27. 10—and

possibly 29—31, in which, however, a difference of
style is observable—are allotted to the original
Book of Job (while others delete also 7 ; 12 ; 14 ;
16 ; 17 ; 24 ; 26 ; 27. 1-10), is the final answer to
the question of " genuineness " or " non-genuineness." But this decision is not unchallengeable.
We have to ask ourselves whether the literary
standard which we have applied is not a mistaken
one, whether this analysis does not tear asunder
sutures which were perhaps made by the author
himself, whether we may not very well assume in
the life of an ancient poet *a repeated working-over*
of his book, resulting in a want of unity ; a two-fold
or even a three-fold treatment which we could not
accept from a modern poet without protest, but
which in the case of a poet of the ancient east we
must be content to take as we find it ?   It appears
to me that this question must be answered in the
affirmative.

Is it not really quite conceivable that the poet
might wrestle with his subject all his life long ?   On
this view, he originally composed only the dialogue
between Job and his friends as a *glorification of
the righteous man who proves himself in suffering*,
while his fellow men seek to brand him as a sinner.
It would be at once a protest against the vulgar
doctrine of rewards and punishments, and a poem
in which the good man triumphs by his faith,
refuses to allow the crown of righteousness to be
torn from his brows, does not, even to his last
breath, let go his hold on God, even though he can
find no righteousness in Him, and he knows that
finally, even though it be only in the hour of death,
he will behold Him as the God who justifies him.

Cf. 10. 20; 13. 3, 16; 16. 19 ff.; 17. 3; 19. 23 ff.; 23. 3 ff.; 24. 1; 27. 3-10; 31. 35-37—a poem which follows the same lines as Psalms 6; 7; 17; 88, and, especially, 73.

After a certain time the poet revised his view; his religious sensitiveness had become keener. In Job's asseveration of his righteousness, which had in it something of the Titan, he is now conscious of a danger of presumption, of an attitude towards God which is not clear of sin; so he now lets that for which Job always, in spite of all his trembling at the terribleness of God, longed with such intensity, viz. the vision of God, become a reality, but the God who now appears is not the righteous God to whom the Job of the original poem had appealed, but the Incomprehensible and Absolute, and the effect is quite other than he had expected—only condemnation. The hero, in whose fate the interest has perceptibly cooled, must now sink in nothingness into the dust, must simply surrender himself to God, cf. 38. 2; 40. 1, 8; 42. 6. The discrepancy between the earlier conception and the present is only unsatisfactorily bridged over by 42. 3, 5, and yet the language shows clearly that the author is the same.

Moreover it was only after he had reached the definite result that Job does not find his vindication, that the poet was gradually led on to another problem, that which we now think of as the essential problem of the Book: Why does the righteous God allow the righteous to suffer? To this question no positive answer is given in 3 — 27. 10; 29 — 31; 38 — 42. 6, which deal only with the faithfulness of the righteous amid suffering; the question is only occasionally touched on in the speeches of the friends, who, however, do not offer a solution of any problem whatever, but are solely concerned to deprive the righteous of his righteousness. The author is now obviously surrounded by a circle in which it is believed that all the problems and enigmas of the world can be solved by the aid of Wisdom. This solution by means of speculation, he has rejected as not leading to the goal at which he aims, and in chapter 28 he puts his rejection of it into the mouth of the virtuous sufferer, as a final protest against the friends, who indeed had said nothing of the kind, but he finds an external point of connection for it in 12. 2, 13 ; 17. 10, etc.

But once the problem had been definitely raised, its claim to a positive solution could not be denied. The only solution which the Book gives—in that Budde and those who take a similar line are absolutely right—is contained in the Elihu speeches : *The purpose of suffering is to purge the righteous from spiritual pride.* And I, for my part, cannot see any insuperable objection to the view that the original author inserted these speeches later as the ripest fruit of his own life of trial, thus softening down the hardness which lay in 38—42. 6; and skilfully connected them with 9. 34 and 13. 21 by means of 33. 7 (similarly, *e.g.* Kamphausen in Bunsen's *Bibelwerk*). After all, the First and Second Parts of *Faust* differ more in ideas and language, and yet both are by the same author. It must no doubt be admitted that the whole method of expression and circle of ideas make the assumption of another poet appear the more obvious ; but there is no necessity to widen the cleft between them unduly, as Duhm, especially, has done. The possibility remains that only the prologue and epilogue are to be regarded as foreign bodies which the author found already in existence (40. 6 — 41. 34 might be *paraleipomena* from his own hand).

Not only the probability of this kind of gradual origin of the Book, and of the introduction of a different solution of the problem, but also the probability that the very statement of the problem has been altered, demand the closest consideration. Certainty is here not to be attained. And the same applies to the question of the author's date.

The first point to be noted is that poetic preoccupation with the suffering of the righteous goes back to very early times. We meet with it in Egypt and Babylon as early as the second millennium B.C.; in Egypt especially in the " Dialogue of the Man who is Weary of Life with his Soul," in Babylon in the poetic formulae of exorcism (cf. esp. KAT³, p. 385 ff.). It is certain therefore that the author in the poems in which he makes his hero complain and revolt against his fate, is often following an older practically conventional scheme (cf. *e.g.* chapter 31 with the second Surpu tablet in Zimmern, *Beiträge* I., p. 3 ff.). And this also supplies the explanation of the remarkable resemblances not merely with many of the psalms cited above, Lamentations 3, etc., but also between chapter 3 and Jer. 20. 14-18, and especially between 13. 17-28; 9. 15, 19 and Isaiah 50. 4-9. Similarly, the figure of Job as a typical righteous man had long been known in pre-Exilic times, cf. Ezek. 14. 14, 20, and different periods had added different traits to the portrait (cf. for Job as a prince 29. 9, 12, 14, 17, 25; 31. 36). Even apart from the popular story embodied in the prologue and epilogue, our Book has certainly a long history behind it.

That the earliest *terminus a quo* for the author is the year 722 is now generally accepted, on the ground of 12. 14-25 and 15. 19. The professional fashion in which the friends handle the doctrine of retribution makes it probable, however, that we must bring him down to the period Jeremiah-Ezekiel, cf. Jer.

31. 29 f.; Ezek. 18. 1 ff.; Deut. 24. 16. But on the other
hand there is no justification for saying that Job must be
placed after Ezek. 18, because it is there maintained that there
is no such thing as innocent suffering, and Ezekiel could not
have written thus if he had been acquainted with Job. There
is just as much and as little point in saying that the author of
Job could not have written this if he had been acquainted with
Ezekiel. It is time that an end was made of this pettifogging
criticism. Is it then not possible that one might have written
in Babylon so, and the other in Jerusalem, Teman or Egypt
have written otherwise? It would be just as true to say that
in post-Exilic times the poet would be forced to come to terms
with Isaiah 53. As we have seen above, the fact is, the original
Book of Job does not set out to solve the problem of retribution.
But it is clear enough that Ezek. 14. 14, 20 implies a knowledge
of Job 3—31.

The so-called literary borrowings prove nothing whatever.
Jeremiah 20. 14-18 and Isaiah 50. 4 ff. are branches from the
same tree. That Job 42. 17 is drawn from P (Gen. 35. 29;
25. 8) is surely a bold assertion. Still more curious is the view
that Job 15. 7 is a plagiarism from Prov. 8. 25, for that the
mountains are the most everlasting thing upon earth is a
familiar commonplace of Old Testament imagery, and the
" first man " of 15. 7 is in no way an allusion to the Wisdom
of Prov. 8. 25, but a quite independent reference to the
ancient oriental conception of the first man as the embodi-
ment of all wisdom (cf. Isa. 49. 2; 51. 16; Enoch 48. 3;
Dan. 7. 13).

Neither does the circle of ideas enable us to come to any
certain conclusion. It is true that Mal. 3. 13 ff. similarly
presupposes a time when doubts were felt regarding the Divine
retributive justice; but does not the same apply to Jer. 12. 1;
15. 18, etc.? That the author rejected for himself the hope
of a return from the realm of the dead, but was nevertheless
acquainted with it, cf. 7. 9 f.; 10. 21; 14. 7-22; 16. 22—the
famous passage in 19. 25 f. refers in my opinion to an experience in the hour of death, cf. NKZ, 1919, p. 232 ff.—is also
certain, but does not give us anything to take hold of, for the
Jews did not learn this belief first from the Persians; they
were familiar with it from early times through the Canaanites
and Egyptians (cf. Hos. 6. 1 ff.). And if it is said that Job 28
presupposes Prov. 1—9—in Proverbs confidence in the possibility
of possessing wisdom, in Job a resigned despair of doing so—
it is after all not uncommon to find an isolated sceptic renouncing

a good, while the optimistic multitude are still turning their hopes towards it.

The most we can do therefore is to place the author between Jeremiah and Malachi, between 600 and 450 B.C., recognizing that we are here in presence of a writer whose culture and whose wider than national purview render inappropriate the usual standards by which a date is fixed. He probably wrote elsewhere than in Jerusalem, indeed in some other country than Palestine. He is obviously familiar with the desert. It has been suggested that the description of the pariahs and cave-dwellers in 24. 4 ff. ; 30. 1 ff. takes us perhaps into the country east of Jordan. But on the other hand we may ask whether he might not have been a member of the Jewish colony in Egypt, which we now know to have been not inconsiderable as early as the sixth or fifth centuries B.C., and in which it is clear that literary interests and international culture were well represented. But on no grounds is the author to be brought down into the period after Ezra, for in that case he could hardly have failed to put into the mouth of the three friends, as representatives of the official piety of Jerusalem, some kind of reference to a will of God which had been clearly laid down in the Law.

The immense significance of this Book for the spiritual history of mankind is fortunately almost entirely independent of the question as to its date of origin. It would not lose its value even if it should be proved that whole generations had worked upon it. The problem of suffering has certainly *not* been solved by the poet. But all that is deepest and most impressive in what has been thought and

said on the basis of the Old Covenant concerning
the sufferings of the righteous is to be found here,
and the quite different lights which are cast upon
it from the different standpoints of the various
portions only increase the value of the Book.
What we cannot help seeing is that this Book is
written with the heart's blood, it has been won from
life by a struggle. A real solution of the problem
could not be offered until a new point of view had
been attained : " I hold therefore that the sufferings
of this present time are not worthy to be compared
with the glory which shall be revealed in us."

§ 4. *The Song of Solomon*

Rothstein, *Das Hohe Lied*, 1893 ; Budde, *Was ist das Hohe Lied?*
Preuss. Jahrbb., 1894, p. 92 ff. ; Haupt, *Biblische Liebeslieder*, 1907.

The " Song of Songs " depicts in glowing
oriental colours the love of Solomon and Shulamith. The synagogue, and, accordingly, the early
Christian Church, interpreted it allegorically of the
relation between God, or Christ, and the community
or Church. But for this interpretation there is not
a vestige of support in the text, any more than in
the case of Psalm 45. The song purports to exalt
the natural human love of bride and bridegroom,
but this too is for the Israelites a " fire of Yah " and
therefore something entirely religious, cf. 8. 6, 7
with Gen. 2. 24. Nevertheless the justification of
the inclusion of the Book in the Canon was debated
by the Jews themselves as late as the Synod of
Jamnia (A.D. 90–100).

There has been much controversy as to the species of
poetry to which the Song is to be referred. And the long
prevalent view that it is a dramatic operetta has still many

supporters. But it cannot be carried through without arbitrariness and artificiality. We owe the clue to the right understanding of it to Wetzstein, whose work was carried further by Budde. In Syria, down to present times, a marriage is, during seven days, celebrated with dances and songs, in which the bridal pair sit enthroned as King and Queen, while ancient stereotyped marriage-songs are sung about them ; the present collection of songs warrants us in concluding that the same custom was observed in Israel, and in seeing in it a cycle of these old popular marriage-songs.

The hypothesis which has lately been brought forward, but not yet fully worked out by Erbt (*Hebräer*, p. 196 ff.), that we have here Festal Hymns on the relations of the Sun-god (*Dods*, *Shelems*) and the Moon (*Shelamith*) may at the same time have a grain of truth in it, for these marriage customs no doubt go back to the long pre-Israelite cult of Adonis. For 5. 5-8 ; 3. 1 ff. (especially the " night-watchers ") there could hardly be a better explanation ; Bertholet has found a sporadic fragment of an Adonis Mystery-play in 4. 8 (cf. the Baudissin " Festschrift," pp. 47-53, and, in connection therewith, Jer. 22. 20, 22). But in Israel love and marriage became essentially something new, 8. 6 f. ; and the Song in the form that we possess it is simply nothing else than *a Collection of Israelitish Marriage-Songs*.

While that would admit of some of the songs being very early, the present redaction must be relatively late. The language points to the fourth or fifth century B.C. (In 3. 9 there is a Greek word, in 4. 13 a Persian word, the relative is always שׁ, etc.) Of the date of the original composition of one of the songs we get a hint from 6. 4, where Thirza appears alongside of Jerusalem as one of the principal cities (*i.e.* about 900) ; 5. 8 shows that the collection was made at Jerusalem.

Solomon is named as the author in the superscription merely because he is several times mentioned, 1. 5 ; 3. 6 ff. (doubtless also 6. 8), but 8. 11 implies that he was not the author of the Songs. The bride is called Shulamith (= female inhabitant

of Shunem) in 6. 13, doubtless in allusion to 1 K.
1. 3, 15 ; 2. 17, 21 f. ; it belongs to the playing of
the rôle of King Solomon in the marriage cere-
monies. As it was known from 1 K. 4. 32 that he
had composed songs, this was entitled his " most
beautiful song " (song of songs). We have to
thank the superscription for the preservation of this
writing, which is extremely valuable as a document
of the history of civilization as well as of the history
of religion.

§ 5. *The Book of Ruth*

Bertholet, *Stellung der Israeliten und Juden zu den Fremden*,
p. 145 f. ; Gunkel, *Ruth* in the Deutsche Rundschau, 1905, pp. 50-69 ;
Köhler, *Ruth*, Schweizerische Theol. Zeitschrift, 1920, pp. 3-14.

This Book narrates in the form of a romantic
story an episode from the latter part of the period
of the Judges, namely, how Ruth, the Moabitess,
became through her piety the wife of Boaz and the
ancestress of David ; or, perhaps, in view of 4. 16,
it is more correct to say, how Naomi, through the
Divine providence, obtained an heir (cf. Köhler).
Along with this it shows too the right of the Gentile
nations to share in Israel's blessings (cf. Jonah).
The basis of it must of course have been generally
known to be historical, cf. 1 Sam. 22. 3, for a free
invention on such a subject would have aroused the
sharpest possible opposition and would not have
proved what the author wanted to prove.

As regards its date, it could only have originated at a time
when the House of David still occupied the highest position
in the popular regard. After the fall of Zerubbabel, the story
would not have proved the author's point. A similar consideration completely disposes of the view that the Book was
a protest of those who in the time of Ezra and Nehemiah

Q

were unwilling to put away their foreign wives (so Bertholet). For the Moabitish strain in the ancestry of the fallen House would supply their opponents with an additional argument— quite apart from the fact that the action of Boaz was not entirely a voluntary one. On the other hand, the reference in 4. 7 to the usage prescribed in Deut. 25. 9 as belonging to " former times " points at earliest to the Exilic period.

The most probable date for the Book is therefore in the first years after the Return, when the problems connected with the adhesion of Gentiles to the Jewish community, and mixed marriages with them, were especially pressing (cf. Zech. 2. 11 f.; 6. 15; Isa. 56-66), and Deut. 23. 3 f. seemed to draw the line very sharply. To this period also the linguistic characteristics are most appropriate, while they also indicate that the narrative had already been current in the popular mouth (cf. König, *Einleitung*, p. 286 f.). 4. 18-22 is probably a later addition.

§ 6. *Lamentations*

Fries, *Parallele zwischen Thren. 4 und 5 und der Makkabäerzeit*, ZAW, 1893, p. 110 ff.; Löhr, ZAW, 1894, p. 51 ff.; 1904, p. 1 ff.

The Book of Lamentations consists of five poems, of which the first four are alphabetical and written in the Ḳinah metre. Their subject is in general—in chapter 3 there is also a reference to personal suffering—the destruction of Jerusalem in 586 B.C. As early as the LXX and in the Targums they are attributed to Jeremiah; indeed this tradition is already implied in 2 Chron. 35. 25, cf. Lam. 4. 20, which is mistakenly referred to Josiah.

This traditional view is, however, untenable and is now generally given up. It is excluded by 4. 20 itself, which refers to Jehoiakin or Zedekiah, about whom Jeremiah took an essentially different view; also by 2. 9 " her prophets also receive no revelation from Yahweh," and 3. 3, 53*b* ; 5. 7 ; and by the language. Finally, the poems cannot possibly be all by one author (in 1, ע comes before פ, in 2—4 the order is reversed, etc.).

Chapters 2 and 4 are probably from the beginning of the Exile (close affinity with Ezek. 27, etc.), by a writer who was of the entourage of the king, chapter 1 by one who was more or less contemporary with Deutero - Isaiah, in Babylon. The author of chapter 5 obviously lived in Jerusalem, but before the rebuilding of the Temple in the year 520, cf. v. 18, and must therefore have been either one of those who remained behind in the land (about 550) or one of the returning exiles (between 537 and 520). The latest of the poems, chapter 3, which attaches itself to chapter 2, is inferior in poetic value to the rest. It is an individual lament, and belongs to the category of the poetry of suffering, like the lamentations in Job, Isa. 50. 4-9, and many of the Psalms. It cannot be dated with certainty, but there is no reason to place it later than the fifth century B.C. It is possible that this poem is written in the character of Jeremiah, and that its author was also the compiler of this collection of "laments."

§ 7. *Ecclesiastes*

Bickell, *Der Prediger über den Wert des Daseins*, 1884 ; Pfleiderer, *Die Philosophie des Heraklit von Ephesus*, etc., 1886 ; Haupt, *Koheleth oder Weltschmerz in der Bibel*, 1905 ; Volz in SchAT, 1911.

In this Book, which is named in the LXX Ἐκκλησιαστής, the speaker is one who calls himself *Koheleth*, i.e. *contionator*, and identifies himself with a great and splendid monarch in Jerusalem, obviously intended for Solomon, who indeed is

directly designated as the " son of David " in 1. 1.
That this however is only a poetic assumption of
the character on the part of a later writer is obvious
from 1. 12, where he says, " I was king over
Jerusalem." Moreover, the consistently Aramaizing language, the Hellenisms and the familiarity
with the ideas of Greek philosophy are unmistakable evidences that the Book cannot have been
written before 300 B.C.

The writing presupposes a time of complete anarchy in the
land, cf. 4. 13-16; 10. 16-20; which points to the period of the
later Ptolemies and Seleucidae. Probably Friedländer (*ut sup.*,
151 ff.) is right in his view that 9. 13-18 alludes to the siege of
Syracuse by the Romans in 212 and its nine-year-long defence
by the aid of Archimedes (cf. the narrative in Polybius). In
that case the Book must have been written round about 200 B.C.
The author may perhaps have been a Teacher in Alexandria.

The fundamental idea of the Book, which recurs
in the most diverse forms, is that all earthly and
human things are vanity. The author is therefore
a sceptic, but he is not on that account a thorough-
going pessimist, for he believes in a living God,
3. 17 f.; 5. 1 f.; 9. 1; 11. 5. But he wrestles
with grave doubts. In this world he sees, like Job,
no evidence of retributive justice, and an after-life
is for him quite uncertain, 3. 20 f. But when all
is said and done he does find in this world some
permanent goods, viz., in the first place, wisdom,
7. 11 ff., and, yet more important, since even wisdom
cannot solve the ultimate enigmas, a rejoicing,
based upon the fear of God, in man's ordinary
lot. And thus, finally, in 11. 9 — 12. 7 he sets up
a positive ethic.

The author obviously takes up an attitude towards the
popular religion which is much freer even than that of Job,

and there is a whole world between him and Jesus Sirach
(Ecclesiasticus). It is indeed certain that, as he himself tells
us, 1. 13, 17, and as we can see for ourselves, foreign " wisdoms,"
Epicurean, Stoic and Heraclitic philosophy, confusedly inter-
mingled, had all influenced him (cf. esp. the wholly un-Jewish
idea of an eternal uniform flux of phenomena, and the exaltation of joy, 2. 24*a*; 3. 1-8, 22; 8. 15; 9. 3, 7; 10. 19; 11. 9*a*).
But at the same time he is not a philosopher ; the personality
of God, and the fact of a future judgement are for him fixed
points, although he is not able to reach them by pure thought
and his utterances in regard to them are self-contradictory,
cf. 2. 24*b*; 3. 10 f., 15, 18; 5. 1; 5. 2 ff.; 6. 2; 7. 13, 26, 29;
8. 15, 17; 9. 7; 11. 9; 12. 1, 7, though perhaps some of these
contradictions are to be ascribed to later pious corrections.

It is quite impossible to follow Siegfried in finding in the
Book a number of different hands (no less than 8 !), or Haupt
in his attempt to remove the contradictions by assuming a
series of different strata due to redactions. If *Koheleth* had
really been a *philosopher*, he would not merely have been
edited, but abolished. And to suppose a disorder in the text
due to displacement of pages of the MS., as Bickell has done,
does not really help matters. The confusion has its seat in
the author's own mind ; but for all that he was a thorough
connoisseur and incorruptible critic of practical life.

Verses 9-14 of chapter 12 are a later addition, and
no doubt some of the orthodox glosses which break
the connection in earlier passages are from the same
hand; cf. 3. 15 ; 7. 18; 9. 7? Ecclesiasticus (soon
after 200 B.C.) had, however, the whole Book before
him (cf. Nöldeke in ZAW, 1900, p. 90 ff.).

In spite of all the influences which he had received
from the recent influx of international culture,
Ḳoheleth remained at heart a believing Jew. In
the age-long struggle between faith and knowledge
the Book is a significant signpost, by which the Old
Testament points beyond itself to the necessity of
a faith of a new order. Ḳoheleth had indeed faith,
but love and hope were lacking to him. Contrast
Heb. 11. 1.

§ 8. *Esther*

De Lagarde, *Purim*, Göttingische Gelehrte Anzeigen 1890, p. 403 ; Zimmern, ZAW, 1891, pp. 157-69 ; Schwally, *Leben nach dem Tode*, pp. 42-45 ; Willrich, *Judaica*, 1990 ; Erbt, *Die Purimsage in d. Bibel*, 1900 ; Haupt, *Purim*, Beiträge z. Assyriologie, 1906 ; Jampel, *Das Buch Esther auf seiner Geschichtlichkeit kritisch untersucht*, 1907 ; Gunkel, *Esther*, 1916.

The Book recounts the frustration of a plot by Haman at the court of Xerxes against the life of all the Jews within the Empire, through the agency of the Jew Mordecai and his adopted daughter Esther, who is made Queen instead of Vashti ; and describes the deliverance of the Jews and their fearful vengeance upon their enemies. The main purpose of the Book is to show how the Feast of Purim, *i.e.* the Feast of Lots, arose, 9. 15-19.

The form of the statement in 1. 1 is itself sufficient to show that the Book cannot have been written until long after the time of Xerxes, and the language of the Book supplies further evidence that it cannot have been written before 300 B.C. Gunkel's former dating of it between Artaxerxes I. and Artaxerxes II. rests on an insecure foundation, viz., the absence of mention of the Apadana, the most important building in the palace of Susa. This would be equally well explained by dating the Book from the third century. The first trace of the Feast of Purim is found in 2 Macc. 15. 36 ; Sirach (Ecclus.) evidently knew nothing of it since he does not mention Mordecai in 44-49. But the Book must be based on some kind of historical foundation, for there must have been some reason for the introduction of this new, originally non-Jewish festival, and this is no doubt to be looked for in some occasion of persecution and deliverance of

the Babylonio-Persian Jews in the Persian period.
There is not a vestige of foundation for the hypo-
thesis that it is a reflection of the persecutions of the
Jews by Antiochus.

This historical basis has, however, not merely been made
to carry an imaginary superstructure but has probably also
been brought into connection with the ancient oriental myth
of the Battle of the Gods (Mordecai = Marduk, Esther = Ishtar,
the Agagite = Gog = Kingu ? ; with a secondary stratum
Haman = the Elamite God Uman, and Vashti = Mashti, so that
the defeated party bear the names of the Elamite divinities ;
which would go back to the period of the political opposition
between Assyria and Elam). And the Feast itself has non-
Jewish roots ; it corresponds in part to the Babylonian New
Year or Puchru festival, the festival of the assembling of the
gods, at which they assigned lots, in part to the Babylonian
Ishtar-Sakaean festival, cf. KAT³, pp. 515-20. Gunkel, with
arguments that deserve consideration, has lately disputed the
whole hypothesis of the mythological background, and sees
in the narrative only a historical romance. A decision cannot
be reached until we know with more certainty what the Feast
of Purim was before it was taken over by the Jews.

According to the results arrived at above, the
purpose of the Book is to recount how the Jews
in Babylon came to give a new interpretation to
this dual feast, and to take part in it, and, moreover, as a purely secular festival. In view of this
secular character of the feast, the Divine name is
entirely avoided in the Book, although the author
was obviously a believing Jew, cf. 4. 14 ; 8. 17.
We cannot therefore be surprised that the Feast
was only introduced in Palestine some decades after
the Maccabaean rising (not yet mentioned in
1 Macc. 7. 49), and that there was strong opposition
to the inclusion of the Book in the Canon (cf.
Megilla, 1. 7 in the Palestine Talmud).
The exclusive fanatical spirit which animates

the Book, though no doubt to a certain extent
excused by the equally fanatical persecution of the
Jews, shows the direction which was being taken
by the natural development of the Jewish mind;
and how wide was the departure by this time
from the path pointed out by a Deutero-Isaiah, a
Jonah and others of the prophets. Verses 20-32 of
chapter 9 are a later addition.

§ 9. *Daniel*

Meinhold, *Beiträge zur Erklärung des Buches D.*, 1888; Kamphausen, *Das Buch D. und die neueste Geschichtsforschung*, 1892;
v. Gall, *Die Einheitlichkeit des Buches D.*, 1895; Strack, article
"Daniel," in PRE³ (Real-Encyklopädie für protestantische Theologie
und Kirche); Jahn, *Das Buch D. nach LXX hergestellt*, 1904;
Böhmer, *Reich Gottes und Menschensohn im Buche D.*, 1906;
Hölscher, *Die Entstehung des Buches D.*, ThStKr, 1919, pp. 113-138.

The Book of Daniel consists of two parts: (*a*)
1-6, narrative of the experiences of Daniel and his
companions under Nebuchadnezzar, Belshazzar and
Darius the Mede in Babylon; (*b*) 7-12, four visions
of Daniel, in which he sees in various forms the
world-empires which are to follow one another from
the end of the Babylonian Exile onwards, the
persecutions which they are to inflict upon the
Jews, and the final establishment of the eternal
Kingdom of God.

That the Book does not date from the Babylonian Exile but from the Maccabaean period, is
proved to demonstration by the following among
other arguments. (1) The position of the Book in
the Canon and the absence of any mention of it in
Ecclus. 44-49. (2) Its language: 2. 4*b*—7. 28 are
written in West-Aramaic; 1; 8—12 in late Hebrew,
with Persian and Greek loan-words in both parts.

(3) The author has only a very inaccurate acquaintance with the history of the Babylonian Exile. There was no deportation in the third year of Jehoiakim (1. 1), and there was no son of Nebuchadnezzar named Belshazzar (which was the name of the son of Nabunaid), nor a Darius the Mede (which can at best be a pseudonym for Cambyses). (4) The Ptolemaic-Seleucid period, and the cruelties inflicted upon the Jews by Antiochus Epiphanes are described so specifically in chapters 7, 9 and 11 that these must be history and not prophecy. We can indeed fix the date of composition almost to the very month. It is most probable, in view of 8. 14, that the author had been present at the dedication of the Temple by Judas Maccabaeus (cf. 1 Macc. 4. 42-58) in the year 165 B.C. But it appears from 11. 40-45 that he does not yet know of the death of Antiochus Epiphanes in the winter of 164, so that the Book may be dated with the utmost probability about the end of 165 or beginning of 164. If, however, 8. 14 is taken to be a prophecy of the future, 8 and 9 must be dated a little earlier, and on the other hand 10 — 12 must be supposed to be written some months later.

While this problem may be considered to be in the main solved, there are still two others which await a satisfactory solution. The first is the extraordinary *change of language*, 1. 1—2. 4*a* in Hebrew, 2. 4*b*—7. 28 in Aramaic, 8-12 in Hebrew again ; the second, how far *older material* has been used as a basis. Of the first, a quite unsatisfactory explanation is generally given, viz., that the author wrote the whole Book in Aramaic, but later the beginning and end were translated into Hebrew in order to qualify it for admission to the Canon. Those concerned might, one would think, have let themselves off with something less than the whole of 8-12. And the second problem is far from having been studied, up to the present, with adequate thoroughness (only tentative beginnings by Strack and Meinhold).

Probably there is a connection between the two problems, perhaps in the form that the author in 1-7 was working on the basis of an *earlier Aramaic Daniel-Apocalypse* (cf. 7. 28a !), translated the introduction to this, 1—2. 4a, into the language which he himself wrote, and so transformed the visions of 2 and 7 that they might serve for the time of Antiochus also (*e.g.* 2. 41b-43 ; 7. 8, 20-22, 24 f.). In spite of much affinity there is, nevertheless, a different atmosphere in 8-12 from that of 1-7 ; the stormy days of Antiochus were scarcely the proper time for a leisurely dwelling upon the life story of Daniel such as we find here. In 8-12 there suddenly appear the angels Gabriel (8. 16 ; 9. 21), Michael (10. 13, 21 ; 12. 1) and so forth, of whom we have previously heard nothing whatever, and it is not until we reach these chapters that we meet with the detailed descriptions of the time of Antiochus. There is at present no possibility of dating more exactly this earlier Daniel-Apocalypse, or perhaps we should say biography, though the Greek loan-words in 3. 7 make the third century probable. König, Driver, Behrmann and others assume an old tradition (not, however, previously fixed in writing) as the basis of 1-7, but the exhaustive comparison between the language and ideas of 1-7 and 8-12 which has been recently made by Hölscher affords convincing proof of the correctness of our hypothesis.

Ezek. 14. 14 ; 28. 3, show that for the Jews of the Exile Daniel was a peculiarly wise and righteous man of bygone times. Just as the traits of the fallen king are transferred to Job, 29. 9, 12, 14, 17, so here there are transferred to Daniel the experiences of a pious Jewish seer of the Exile, and he thus gradually became one whom God honoured, like Enoch, by permitting him to share His own knowledge of the deepest mysteries of the future. Much of what is found in the Book which bears his name (the framework of the seventy years, the representation of two world-empires in images of various metals, or in the form of various beasts of prey, cf. Isa. 42. 2 ; Zech. 1. 18 ; Ps. 22. 23 ; the Son of Man who is hidden with God, Micah 5. 2 ; Isa. 49. 2 ; the King of the North, cf. Joel 2. 20, Ezek. 38 f., etc.) is very ancient apocalyptic material, to which the earlier prophets, as a rule, only make passing allusions, but with which they are quite well acquainted (cf. the express reference to older books in Dan. 9. 2). But nowhere else in the Old Testament is the Divine plan of the whole history of the world so clearly, comprehensively and definitely traced—the history of the nations, which *must* ultimately find its consummation in the Kingdom of the Son of Man, the Holy One ; that is, in the Kingdom of God.

§ 10. *Ezra, Nehemiah, 1 and 2 Chronicles*

Schrader, *Die Dauer des 2ᵗᵉⁿ Tempelbaues*, ThStKr, 1867, p. 460 ff. ; Smend, *Die Listen der Bücher Ezra und Neh.*, 1881 ; Kosters, *Die Wiederherstellung Israels* (German translation by Basedow), 1895 ; Hoonacker, *Nouvelles études sur la restauration juive après l'exil*, 1896 ; E. Meyer, *Die Entstehung des Judentums*, 1896 ; Geissler, *Die literarischen Beziehungen der Esramemoiren*, 1899 ; Nikel, *Die Wiederherstellung des jüdischen Gemeinwesens nach dem babylonischen Exil*, 1900 ; Sellin, *Studien zur Entstehungsgeschichte der jüdischen Gemeinde*, II. 1901 ; Fischer, *Die chronologischen Fragen in den Büchern Esra-Nehemiah*, 1903 ; Sachau, *Drei aramäische Papyrusurkunden aus Elephantine*, 1907 ; Jampel, *Die Wiederherstellung Israels unter den Achämeniden*, 1904 ; Rothstein, *Juden und Samaritaner*, 1908 ; Budde, *Bemerkungen zum Midrasch d. Bücher d. Könige*, ZAW, 1892, p. 37 ff. ; Keil, *Apologetischer Versuch über die Chron.*, 1833 ; Movers, *Kritische Untersuchungen über d. bibl. Chronik*, 1834 ; Graf, *Die geschichtlichen Bücher*, 1866, pp. 114 - 247 ; Wellhausen, *Prolegomena*⁴, pp. 169-228 ; Winckler, *A.T. Untersuchungen*, pp. 157-167 ; Klostermann, article " Chronik " in PRE³ ; Mosiman, *Eine Zusammenstellung und Vergleichung der Paralleltexte der Chronik und der älteren Bücher des A.T.*, 1907 ; Kittel, *Zur Frage der Entstehung des Judentums*, 1918.

That these four Books originally formed one great historical work is proved by the following circumstances. (*a*) The Book of Ezra in its present form cannot be by Ezra himself. The author sometimes makes Ezra speak in person, 8. 1 f., sometimes gives narrative matter about him in the third person, 10. 1 ff., and must have lived after the Persian period, *i.e.* at earliest about 300, as is shown especially by the expression King of the Persians, 1. 1 ; 4. 5, 24 ; 6. 14, etc. ; whereas contemporary sources, 4. 6 f., 23 ; 7. 11, say simply " the king." (*b*) It is equally impossible for the

Book of Nehemiah to be by Nehemiah, since the
list of the High Priests, 12. 11, 22, goes down to
Jaddua, who lived about 300, whereas Nehemiah
can scarcely have lived later than 400 B.C. (*c*) In
whole sections of these books we find exactly the
same language and the same set of characteristic
ideas as in the Book of Chronicles, cf. Ezra 3 ;
6. 16-22 ; Neh. 12. 1-30, etc. (*d*) Ezra 1. 1-3 coincides almost word for word with 2 Chron. 36. 22 f.

The purpose of the entire work was to give a
history of the holy community of God upon earth
from Adam to the restoration of the Jewish State
under Ezra and Nehemiah. In fulfilment of this
purpose the introduction, 1 Chron. 1-9, contains
genealogies from Adam to David, chapters 10-29
contain a detailed history of the latter, while
2 Chr. 1-36 contains the history of the royal
Tribe of Judah (cf. 1 Chr. 5. 2) from Solomon
to the deliverance from the Babylonian captivity,
Ezra 1-6, the reconstitution of the nation by Zerubbabel and Joshua, 7-10 the reforming work of Ezra,
Neh. 1-6 the building of the wall by Nehemiah,
7-13 his efforts at inner reformation, down to the
separation of the Samaritans and the establishment
of the purely Jewish State.

The whole work is dominated by levitical
and priestly ideals, and animated by the spirit of
the Priestly Writing. The author is primarily
interested in the history of the cultus ; even more
than the Deuteronomist he makes it his aim to
impart religious and moral lessons. This is the
source of his fondness for genealogies, the evidences
of the Divine election, for the cultual and liturgical
ordinances of the Kings, the omission of the whole

history of the Ten Tribes, which for him was a
profane history—an introduction, so to speak, to
the history of the Samaritans—his interest in all
statistical material—which for him is an illustration
of the Divine power and glory—along with his great
freedom in the handling of it—his demonstrations
of a constant Divine retributive justice in history.
The value of Chronicles as a historical source
is consequently very unequal. Over considerable
portions we can check it by the much earlier
Books of Samuel and Kings on which the work is
based, and find it sometimes expanding them for
didactic purposes, sometimes greatly abbreviating
them, as, for example, in the omission of everything
which would mar the ideal picture of David ; cf.
e.g. 1 Chr. 17. 13 with 2 S. 7. 14, etc.   On the
other hand, much of the additional matter which
it gives, which was long simply rejected off-hand
as unhistorical, has now, in virtue of our better
knowledge of the ancient east, again come within
the realm of historical possibility (cf. 2 Chr. 33.
10-13*a*, which stands in connection with the quite
unsuspicious verse 14, with Winckler's comments,
ut sup., and KAT³, p. 274 ff.).

How far the Chronicler had at his disposal other sources
for the pre-Exilic period in addition to the Books of Kings and
Samuel, is doubtful. He names a whole series of such books,
historical and prophetic, 2 Chr. 16. 11 ; 25, 26, etc. ; 2 Chr.
9. 29 ; 12. 15, etc. But probably the whole of these citations
refer to *one* great earlier work, that " Midrash of the Book of
the Kings " which is named in 24. 27, various sections of it
being named from the prophets who appear in them, cf. 2 Chr.
13. 22 ; 20. 34 ; 32. 32. The possibility that this Midrash,
from which the Chronicler took what he wanted for his purpose,
(cf. 2 Chr. 16. 11) may have contained, in addition to its edifying
matter, good historical information supplementary to that

given in Samuel and Kings, is of course evident, and how far
it did so must be examined in each particular case.   It appears
indeed almost certain that the Midrash was based not only
on our Books of Kings but also on the main source of these,
the now lost " Book of the History of the Kings," and that it
took from this the quite unsuspicious and in part excellent
information about the measures and experiences of some of
the kings which is not contained in our Books of Kings, cf.
2 Chr. 11. 5-12 ; 13. 19 ; 17. 7-9 (the *Sarim*, " princes," come
first ! Contrast 19. 4-11) ; 17. 14-18 ; 28. 12-15, etc. Cf.
ZEAT, p. 92 ff. In addition to this Midrash the Chronicler
had also at his disposal a large mass of pre-Exilic lists, both
genealogical and relating to the guilds, the latter of which he in
some cases mistakenly supposed to be also genealogical (cf.
Kittel on 1 Chr. 4. 15-23 ; and Sellin, NKZ, 1906, p. 753 ff.).

For the post-Exilic history the author drew on
valuable *sources* which were in direct contact with
the facts.   These, apart from the Books of Haggai
and Zechariah, which he uses merely to expand
his narrative in regard to the laying of the
foundation stone of the Temple (first in 537 and
a second in 520; but he mistakenly identified
Sheshbazzar with Zerubbabel), are mainly the
following : in Ezra 2 and Neh. 7 the lists of those
who returned between 537 and 520 and were recorded
in Jerusalem as citizens of the new State; in
Ezra 4. 7 — 6. 14 a fragment of an Aramaic source
which was either an earlier narrative of the rebuilding of Jerusalem (written by Nehemiah, or at
least in his time, cf. 2 Macc. 2. 13), or a self-
justificatory memorial to Susa by Tobias the
opponent of Nehemiah (cf. Tab'el 4. 7, and " the
eye of their God," 5. 5), and certainly contains some
important documents from the reigns of Cambyses
and Darius I., counterparts of the recently discovered papyri of Elephantine ; in 7. 12 — 9. 15 the
memoirs of Ezra, who here speaks in the first

person and reproduces in 7. 12-26 the *Firman* in
Aramaic which King Artaxerxes gave him to take
with him ; finally, in Neh. 1-7 ; 12. 31-40 ; 13,
the memoirs of Nehemiah.

The Aramaic documents, upon which doubt was thrown
for a time, especially by Kosters, who denies altogether the return
of the Jews from Babylon in the period 537–520, but also by
Wellhausen, Stade and others, are now again, especially since
the very able examination by Ed. Meyer, generally considered
to be authentic.   It is only necessary to compare them with
Ezra 1. 2-4 in order to recognize the difference between genuine
and apocryphal historical documents.   And Kittel has lately
come to the conclusion, on the basis of new evidence, that the
dating of the list of the returned Exiles (Neh. 7) as being from
the time of Cyrus, is confirmed.

We are justified in concluding from 1 Chr.
3. 19-24, where the genealogy of Zerubbabel is
carried down through nine generations, and from
Nehemiah 12. 11, 22, where the list of the High
Priests is carried down to Jaddua—*i.e.* to the time
of Alexander the Great—that the Chronicler lived
somewhere about 300 B.C.   It is possible that he
was one of the Levitical Temple-singers, in whom
he displays a special interest.

The first Book to be separated from the whole work and
received into the Canon, was, as its position shows, the Book
of Ezra.   It was not, however, received in the form in which
we now have it, but in an earlier form, with a different order,
which is preserved in the so-called " 3rd Ezra " of the LXX.
Next followed the Book of Nehemiah.   The Chronicles were
probably not received into the Canon until the last century B.C.

APPENDIX I

THE OLD TESTAMENT APOCRYPHA

AMONG the Introductions named in our introductory § 2 which deal with the Apocrypha and Pseudepigrapha are those of Koenig, Strack, Budde and Steuernagel. The best conspectus of the special literature will be found in Schürer's *Geschichte des jüdischen Volkes im Zeitalter Jesu Christi*, vol. iii. ³1898, ⁴1909. See also the relevant articles in Herzog's *Realencyklopädie*³. A work which is especially well adapted to give a student his first introduction to the subject is Kautzsch, *Die Apokryphen und Pseudepigraphen des A.T. übersetzt und herausgegeben*, 1900.

While Origen, no doubt influenced by the Jewish *genas*, "to hide," classed as apocryphal all those writings of which—in contrast with the Canonical writings—the use in public worship was undesirable, Jerome on the other hand applied the designation to all the Books not belonging to the Hebrew Canon, and the expression was soon transferred to those writings in particular which appear in the LXX, but are not in the Hebrew Canon. Of these the LXX contains twelve or fourteen.

1. HISTORICAL WRITINGS

(a) *The First Book of the Maccabees*

This Book narrates the history of the Jews from the oppression by Antiochus Epiphanes, 175, down to the death of the High Priest Simon in 135 B.C. The three leaders of the Jewish rising against this oppression were Judas Maccabaeus, Jonathan and Simon. The Book was originally written in Hebrew, after the death of John Hyrcanus in 105, but before the intervention of the Romans in Palestine in 63 B.C., some time, therefore, about 100 B.C., and is in the main quite trustworthy; 8. 22 ff.; 12. 6 ff., 20 f. were perhaps added subsequently but also before 63; on the other hand, the documents of the appendix, 14. 16—16. 24, date from the period after 47 B.C., for the letter given in 15. 16 ff. is identical with the decree of the Senate, which, according to Josephus, *Antiquities*, xiv. 8. 5, was made in that year.

(b) The Second Book of the Maccabees

This bears the same relation to the First Book that Chronicles bears to the Books of Kings, *i.e.* it aims at giving the history a religiously edifying form, offering, as it says of itself, wine mixed with water (cf. the narrative of the martyrdom of Eleazar, of the mother with seven sons, etc.). Its historical matter it professes to have drawn from the history of Jason of Cyrene, 2. 23. It follows the course of the Maccabaean rising only up to the victory over Nicanor in 161. It is not used by Josephus, but it is no doubt used by the author of the Epistle to the Hebrews, 11. 35. It appears to have been written shortly before A.D. 70, and since it was from the first in Greek was no doubt written, in spite of its Pharasaic standpoint, by a Jew of the Diaspora.

(c) The Third Book of the Maccabees

This describes how Ptolemy IV., Philopator (about 200 B.C.), who was at first hostile to the Jews became friendly towards them. It was presumably written in the time of the Emperor Caligula, that is to say about A.D. 40.

(d) The Third Book of Ezra *

The Canonical Ezra is counted as 1 Ezra and Nehemiah as 2 Ezra. 3 Ezra is an extract from the earliest form of the Chronicler's work. It begins with the reforms of Josiah and breaks off in the middle of the reforms of Ezra. It is, therefore, a precursor of the Canonical Book of Ezra, and was probably not separated off in its present form until the time of Rabbi Akiba (about A.D. 120). Its most outstanding peculiarity is

---

* The " 1 Esdras " of the A.V. Apocrypha.

the section 3. 1—5. 6, the story of the minstrel-contest of the pages before Darius, in which Zerubbabel wins the prize with his eulogy of woman and truth. Josephus uses it freely, but not as canonical.

(e) The Book of Judith

Celebrates the vengeance which Judith took upon Holophernes, Nebuchadnezzar's general, at the siege of Bethulia, *i.e.* Jerusalem. If the narrative has a historical basis, this must be sought in the siege of Jerusalem by Bagoses, the general of the Persian King, Artaxerxes Ochus. The Book was written during the Maccabaean rising or shortly afterwards, and must have been written in Hebrew or Aramaic, as several errors of translation show.

(f) The Book of Tobit

This deals in an edifying fashion with the blinding of Tobit in Nineveh, the journey of his son Tobias under the protection of the angel Raphael to Ecbatana, his return thence and the healing of his father. The Book was probably written about 100 B.C.; there are, however, no definite historical allusions by which to determine its date more exactly. The law of marriage with the next of kin, which was abolished about the time of the birth of Jesus, was still valid; the writer does not appear, from 14. 5, to have been acquainted with the splendours of the Herodian temple, so that it must certainly have been written before 25 B.C. It has even been proposed, in view of 14. 4-6, to date it from the pre-Maccabaean period. Its place of origin was perhaps Egypt. Its acquaintance with the story of the " Grateful Dead Man " and the Aḥiḳar legend (cf. 1. 18 f.; 11. 17; 14. 10) are significant. The form of the text varies very much in Greek, Latin and Aramaic.

(g) Additions to the Book of Esther

A dream of Mordecai and its interpretation, an edict of Haman and an edict of Mordecai. The time of origin is quite uncertain; Josephus was acquainted with these additions, cf. *Ant.* xi. 6.

2. Didactic Works

(a) The Wisdom of Jesus the Son of Sirach
(Vulg. and A.V. Ecclesiasticus)

According to the prologue, this Book was translated from Hebrew into Greek about 130 B.C. in Egypt by a descendant of the author. He speaks of the latter as πάππος μου. If this means here, as it usually does, the grandfather, the latter must have written about 200 B.C. This would be quite consistent with the account of the High Priest Simon, 50. 1-4, cf. Josephus, *Antiquities*, xii. 3. 3. Others, with less probability, refer the description to Simon the Just, about 290 B.C., and understand πάππος in the general sense of ancestor. The *terminus ad quem* is certainly the year 168. The contents of this collection of aphorisms has a close resemblance to Proverbs, except that here the influence of the Law and the Priesthood is more noticeable. Since 1896 large fragments of the Hebrew Sirach, which had been lost since the eleventh century, have been brought to light in Cairo, amounting to some three-fifths of the text, the principal being 39. 15—49. 11 (by Lewis and Gibson, Schechter, Margoliouth).

(b) The Wisdom of Solomon

As the title indicates, the author conceals himself under the pseudonym of King Solomon. But it is clearly evident from the circle of ideas that he was an Alexandrian Jewish philosopher of the last century B.C. Platonic or Stoic philosophy appears in the doctrine of the pre-existence of the soul, 8. 20, and its imprisonment in the body, 9. 15. This writing marks the transition from the Old Testament *Ḥokhmah* to the philosophy of Philo. Wisdom is already thought of as a Hypostasis standing between God and the world (cf. 10-12), as the Logos does later in Philo.

(c) The so-called Fourth Book of the Maccabees, or, Concerning the Self-mastery of Reason

This proceeds from the same school as (b). Here it is especially Stoic influences which are prominent. The martyrdom of Eleazar and the seven brethren (cf. 2 Macc. 6 ; 7) is turned to the uses of edification, and it is shown by this example that faith and rational thought must rule the natural feelings and that when they do so true happiness results. The writing is probably to be dated before A.D. 70.

(d) The Prayer of Manasses

This is supplementary to 2 Chron. 33. 11-13. It serves to give a still more edifying form to the story of the conversion of King Manasseh in Babylon, in connection with which a whole cycle of legends gradually grew up, cf. Tobit 14. 10, etc. It has been conjecturally assigned to the Maccabaean period.

3. IMITATIONS OF THE PROPHETS

(a) The Book of Baruch

The hero of this Book is the well-known disciple of Jeremiah. 1. 1—3. 8 tells of the deep impression made by a book written by him upon the captives in Babylon. The Book is then sent to Jerusalem, with money for sacrifices, and a request to pray for Nebuchadnezzar and Belshazzar. 3. 9—5. 9 contain the actual Book of Baruch which is mentioned in 1. 3, consisting of both calls to repentance and words of consolation (so, rightly, Koenig). The date of the Book is not certain. As, in consequence of the broad-minded universalistic spirit, the Maccabaean period is out of the question, views regarding the date vary between 200 B.C. and A.D. 70. In the latter case the two kings named might be thought of as standing for Vespasian and Titus. Hilgenfeld and Schürer assign the two parts to different dates.

(b) The Letter of Jeremiah

This is an apocryphal imitation of Jeremiah 29, although in the LXX it follows Lamentations. It contains a polemic against the foolish worship of idols. Consequently its date is probably between 200 and 175 B.C. It is pre-supposed in 2 Macc. 2. 2.

(c) Additions to the Book of Daniel

The Prayer of Azarias, the Song of the Three Children in the fiery furnace, the Deliverance of Susanna by Daniel, Bel and the Dragon. These all must have originated about the end of the second century B.C., whether first written in Hebrew is disputed; in the case of the first two, however, this is probable, since there stand between them three narrative verses which would very appropriately fill the gap in the Canonical Daniel between 3. 19-23 and verse 24. They must, therefore, have been removed from there, along with the prayer and the song of praise, when the Book of Daniel was received into the Canon; and this implies that the prayer and song had been interpolated there before the Greek translation was made (cf. Rothstein in Kautzsch's *Die Apokryphen des A.T.*).

APPENDIX II

THE MOST IMPORTANT OLD TESTAMENT
PSEUDEPIGRAPHA

THE name characterizes these writings as professing to be by authors from whom they are not in reality derived. For the most part they are apocalyptic writings which had already been rejected by the Synagogue of the first century A.D. in Palestine. The LXX also did not admit them. Augustine and Jerome opposed them energetically. In consequence they disappeared—with the exception of 4th Ezra (2 Esdr.), which held its place in church use down to the sixteenth century—only continuing to be held in honour in some of the more remote churches, like that of the Abyssinians. It is only in quite recent times that their importance for the history of religion has been recognized.

1. *The Letter of Aristeas*

This letter, written in the language of the κοινή, which is our source for the legend of the origin of the LXX (vv. 301-311), professes to be written by a heathen official of Ptolemy II., Philadelphus, who questions Eleazar the High Priest and the translators of the Old Testament regarding the Jewish Law (121-171). It was, however, quite certainly written by a Jew in Egypt, under the Ptolemies, and before 63 B.C. He drew much of his material from Hecataeus of Abdera.

247

2. *The Book of Jubilees or Little Genesis*

The names are explained by the contents, the author dividing his history into " jubilees " which consist of seven seven-year periods. He casts Gen. 1—Ex. 12 into a legendary form, which is supposed to be received by Moses on Sinai from the " Angel of the Countenance." The Book seems to have been put into its present shape by a Pharisee of the last century B.C. (Belief in Angels ; pre-existence of the Law ; high value placed upon animal sacrifice). It has been preserved to us only in an Ethiopic translation, and, in part, in a Latin translation. It will be a task for future critics to determine whether the basis of the Book does not go back to the pre-Maccabaean period, to which Bohn has already proposed to refer its composition.

3. *The Book of Enoch*

This was originally written in Hebrew or Aramaic, but has come down to us only in an Ethiopic, and in part in a Greek, translation. (The so-called Slavonic Enoch is a translation of a later Greek offshoot from it.) The larger part of it was discovered as recently as 1887 in the course of excavations in Egypt. It is a composite work, the various parts being of very different dates. The main portion consists of chapters 1-36 ; 72-105, a history of the theocracy in visions, beheld by the Enoch who was translated to the Divine presence. It also contains an account of the Fall of the Angels, some astronomical material, stories of dreams and hortatory discourses. The author of the Epistle of Jude quotes it in verse 14. From the fact that in chapter 90 the line of governors appears to be carried down to John Hyrcanus (died 105 ; according to others, however, the " great horn " of verse 9 = Judas Maccabaeus) it may be conjectured with some approach to certainty that the Book was written under Hyrcanus ; though it is possible that 92-105, in which the historical background is a period of severe persecution of the Pharisees, were written a little later, under Alexander Jannaeus. But the whole book also includes pre-Maccabaean material, cf. esp. the so-called 7 or 10 weeks' Apocalypse 92 ; 93. 1-14 ; 91. 12-17.

A specially difficult critical problem is offered by the Similitudes, chapters 37-71. While a number of critics take the view that these also pre-suppose the period of the conflict between the Pharisaic party and the last Hasmonaean princes (*c*. 70 B.C.)—or at least, since chapter 56 pre-supposes the

Parthian invasion of Palestine (40–38 B.C.), date from the
reign of Herod I—others take them to be of Christian origin,
and yet others assume that at least the so-called " Son of
Man" passages and the "Chosen One" passage, 40. 5, are due
to Christian interpolation. This controversy is still unsettled,
but the first-named view has on the whole the greater probability
in its favour, since we hear nothing of the crucifixion and
resurrection; and if it is correct, it is of the very greatest importance for the history of the Messianic Hope, because we find
here not only, as in Daniel, the title Son of Man for the Deliverer,
46. 4 f. ; 51. 3 ; 52. 4 ; 61. 8 ; 62. 2, etc., but also the explicit
doctrine of his pre-existence, 48. 3 ; 62. 6 f. ; 70. 1 ff., which
in Daniel is only to be read between the lines.   But even apart
from this, the Book of Enoch has claims of the highest interest
as a typical specimen of Jewish Apocalyptic, as an evidence
of the Pharisaic expectation of the Kingdom of God, and as
a proof-passage for the contamination of Jewish belief with
Perso-Babylonian elements in the last pre-Christian period.

4. *The Assumption of Moses*

This Book contains an address of Moses to Joshua in which
he foretells the future course of history ; it is obviously not
now complete, and has only been preserved in Latin. The
author of the Epistle of Jude must, in verse 9, have been drawing
on the now lost conclusion. The work seems to have been
written shortly after the death of Herod I., cf. 6. 6, 8 f. The
text which has come down to us is translated from the Greek,
but whether this in turn goes back to an Aramaic original
is uncertain.

5. *The Vision of Isaiah*

This writing, which has been preserved in an Ethiopic
translation, consists (1) of the martyrdom of Isaiah, 2-5, telling
how the prophet was sawn asunder in the reign of Manasseh
(remarkable parallels with the Iranian legend of Dschemschid).
This is of Jewish origin. It was known to the author of the
Epistle to the Hebrews, 11. 37. (2) the Vision of Isaiah,
6-11 ; the two parts have been connected by a Christian
redactor by means of chapter 1 and 11. 42 ff.

6. *The Apocalypse of Baruch*

This narrates the revelations received by Baruch before
and after the destruction of Jerusalem by the Babylonians.

This is obviously a veiled allusion to the taking of the city by the Romans. As Papias, *c.* A.D. 160, was familiar with, and influenced by this Apocalypse, it must have been written between A.D. 70 and 160. If, as is probable, it was written before 4th Ezra, *i.e.* before 96, that, taken in conjunction with the accurate knowledge which it shows of the circumstances of the destruction, would fix its date between still narrower limits. It has been preserved in Syrian, Greek (with Christian interpolations) and Old Slavonic translations, but it was originally written in Hebrew.

7. *The Fourth Book of Ezra* (*2nd Esdras*).

This is also a Jewish Apocalypse, consisting of seven visions. It was written in the reign of the Emperor Nerva, 96–98, cf. 11. 35 ; 12. 2, 28. Whether originally in Greek or Hebrew is a matter of controversy. It has come down to us in Latin, Syriac and Ethiopic versions. A feature of special importance is the evidence which it gives of the general belief, outside the bounds of the Christian community, in the reality of " pneumatic " experiences (" speaking with tongues," etc.), and another thing which it shows is that in the Jewish community there was still, even subsequently to A.D. 70, a lively expectation of the coming of a Messiah designated as Son of God, the " Son of Man," cf. 7. 28 ; 13. 3 ff. ; 14. 9, etc.

8. *The Testaments of the Twelve Patriarchs*

This also was, according to the now prevailing view, written by a Jew, shortly after the destruction of Jerusalem by Titus, though containing later Christian additions. It has been preserved in a Latin and an Armenian translation. In the latter some of the Christian additions are absent. But even in the main Jewish document different sources can be distinguished, and it is a matter for future investigation whether one of these does not go back to pre-Maccabaean times (*e.g.* Levi 14-18 ?). Each of the twelve sons of Jacob appears and relates his life-story, and connects with it exhortations for posterity. The most remarkable are those of Levi and Judah.

9. *The Sibylline Oracles*

Under this title there have been brought together very various prophetic writings, in all fourteen Books. They are

in part of Jewish origin (Book 3-5, some of the material of
1 ; 2 ; 11 ; 14), in part Christian. The date of the various
Jewish elements is also very various. The oldest, which is
III. 97-807, in which the time of Ptolemy VII., Physcon, is
represented as the Times of the End, must have been written
about 140 B.C. ; and in addition to this several groups of verses
date from the last century B.C.   The main bulk of the collection
originated in the first and second centuries A.D.   The oracles
are written in Greek hexameters.

10. *The Psalms of Solomon*

These, eighteen in number, were obviously originally composed in Hebrew, but they have come down to us only in Greek.
The earliest of them pre-supposes the deposition of the Hasmonaean dynasty and the taking of Jerusalem by Pompey,
the latest (Ps. 2) makes a clear allusion to the death of the latter.
They must, therefore, have been written between 63 and 40 B.C.
They form a very valuable source for our knowledge of the
religious attitude of the Pharisees, especially their Messianic
expectations.

11. *The Odes of Solomon*

These, forty-two in number, were edited in 1909 by Harris on
the basis of a Syriac MS. Five of them were already known
from the Coptic *Pistis Sophia*. The keen discussions of the
last few years as to whether they are a product of Jewish gnosis
of the first century A.D. worked over by a somewhat later
Christian reviser, or whether they are directly Christian, or
Jewish-Christian, compositions of the second century, have not
so far led to any generally, or even predominantly, accepted
results.

In addition to these more important Pseudepigrapha, there are also Books of Adam, a Testament of Abraham, of Job, of Moses, etc.

C. THE HISTORY OF THE COLLECTION AND CANONIZATION OF THE OLD TESTAMENT BOOKS

Strack, article " Kanon " in HRE³, 9 ; Wildeboer, *Die Entstehung des Kanons des A.T.* (translated by Risch), 1891 ; Buhl, *Kanon und Text des A.T.*, 1891 ; Duhm, *Die Entstehung des A.T.*, 1897 ; Budde, *Der Kanon des A.T.*, 1900 ; Hölscher, *Kanonisch und Apokryph*, 1905 ; Koenig, *Kanon und Apokryphen*, 1917 ; Haenel, *Der Schriftbegriff Jesu*, 1919.

IN the sixteenth, seventeenth and eighteenth centuries it was the prevailing opinion (especially since Elias Levita † 1549) that Ezra, or the Great Synagogue founded by him, created the Canon, a view which, indeed, goes back to 2 Esdr. 14. 44, and is also found in Irenaeus (*Adversus Haereses*, iii. 21. 2) and Tertullian (*De cultu feminarum*, i. 3). This view has now generally been rightly given up, for the Old Testament certainly contains writings which are later than the time of Ezra (Chronicles, Daniel, Ecclesiastes, etc.), and the " Great Synagogue," although it is already referred to in the Talmud (*Baba Bathra*, 14*a*), never had any real existence, but is, as Kuenen in particular has proved, only a reflection of the assembly of the people in Neh. 8-10. The fact is that we have not here to do with a single act, taking place once for all, but with a historical *process* of long duration. The Canon in the form in which it has come down to us, itself indicates by its division into three or four different collections, that it arose by successive stages.

Finally, we have to distinguish between the collection of the writings and their canonization, although, as regards the first two parts of the Canon, these were in practice exactly coincident.

The concept of the Canon (the word, originally Semitic, then adopted in Greek = plumb-line, hence standard, is first used with reference to the Scriptures by the Church Fathers of the fourth century), in its full extent and used with full consciousness, first meets us in Josephus (*Contra Apionem*, I. 8), about A.D. 100. He speaks here of twenty-two sacred Books (he therefore counts Ruth as belonging to Judges, Lamentations to Jeremiah, otherwise it would mean that Ecclesiastes and the Song of Solomon were not counted.

The characteristic marks of sacred scripture which he here gives are that the various Books (*a*) are derived from the period between Moses and Artaxerxes, *i.e.* from prophets, and are therefore inspired (" but while from Artaxerxes to the present time many books have been written, they are not of the same authority with the former books, because there has not been an exact succession of the prophets "); (*b*) that in contradistinction to all profane literature they have a sacred character; (*c*) their number is limited; (*d*) their wording cannot be tampered with.

There we have already the conception of the Canon all complete; even the Talmud adds nothing further to this, except that it, like 4 Ezra (2 Esdr.),* everywhere reckons the number of the Books as the sacred number twenty-four (as to their

---

* The oriental versions in 2 Esdr. 14. 44-46 make the number 94, less 70 which are to be kept secret.—Translator.

order cf. *Baba Bathra*, 14*b*, where, moreover, the
authors are named, and Ezekiel and the Twelve
Prophets, Daniel and Esther, are said to have been
" written " by the men of the Great Synagogue).
The Talmud describes the Books as " defiling the
hands," *i.e.* from their sacred character making
washing necessary after handling them, being, so to
speak, *tabu* (cf. Mishna, *Jadaim* iii. S ; *Seder Olam*:
" From the time of Alexander onwards it was only
the wise who worked, before that the Holy Spirit ").

While it is quite certain that Josephus did not
independently create his conception of the Canon
as a new thing, but received it from tradition, we
cannot fix the time of its formation, for the precise
reason that it grew up gradually. It can be
confidently asserted, however, that the conception of
the Canon in its full extent did not yet exist in the
second century B.C. For not only did Jesus Sirach
(Ecclus.) himself (immediately after 200 B.C.) bring
his teaching directly into line with that of the
prophets, without appearing conscious of any
qualitative distinction as between a norm and that
for which it serves as norm, cf. 24. 33 ; 47. 20 ;
50. 29, but even his grandson (about 130 B.C.)
sees in the writing of his grandfather a direct
continuation of the Law and the Prophets and
remaining Books. " Jesus Sirach," he says,
" having much given himself to the reading of
the law and the prophets and the other books of
our fathers . . . was drawn on also himself to write
somewhat pertaining to instruction and wisdom."

While this compels us to conclude that the whole
conception of the Canon, as found in Josephus,
only took definite form in the last century B.C., or

first century A.D., among the Palestinian Pharisees, it had nevertheless a long history behind it. It was only the *negative* attributes of exclusive inspiration, inviolability of the text and absolute separation from all profane writings which were previously lacking ; in a *positive* and practical sense a Canon, *i.e.* a Divinely given norm for the estimation of the world, of history and of life in general, had been in existence long before ; indeed, since ever there was a religion of Israel at all.

It is often said nowadays that the canonization began with the solemn institution of Deuteronomy in 622 B.C. But, after all, Deuteronomy as then made public, underwent repeated further expansions, and its introduction was only a further step on the same road which was entered upon at Sinai, as is evidenced by the Decalogue, the Book of the Covenant, the Law given at Shechem, etc. As early as Amos 2. 4 and Hos. 8. 12 we find the normative function of the Divine law fully recognized. And what other significance than that of canonization has the laying up of the *Laws* in the ark of the Covenant, Deut. 10. 1 ff., or beside it, 31. 26, or before Yahweh, 1 Sam. 10. 25, or before the sacred stone in Shechem, Jos. 24. 26 ff., or the permanent record of them upon the stone there, Deut. 27. 8 ? It is true that the express laying of a curse upon any one who " addeth thereto or taketh therefrom " is found for the first time in Deut. 4. 2 ; 12. 32 ; but that belongs to the formulae of primitive legislation, which may in the case of some of the older laws have been accidentally dropped in the course of the various redactions. According to the Blessing of Moses, the Levites received then the charge to " guard God's word and preserve his Covenant," Deut. 33. 9. Indeed, in Oriental antiquity in general a religion without a fixed inviolable Divine law is inconceivable. Hammurabi calls down the curse of all the gods upon any one, who, in his divinely sanctioned laws, " alters anything, deletes anything, changes the wording," and so forth. Is not that a Canon ? It is just because Law is surrounded with this awe-inspiring atmosphere that the introduction of a new legal code is always associated with the sharpest birth-pangs and disturbances. Indeed such a thing was only possible so long as there remained sufficient spiritual energy to enable men to brave the curse, to create a new thing in the consciousness that they themselves possessed the Spirit of God, that they were not leaving the old paths, but were merely giving to the intentions of the original law-giver—and so to the intentions of God Himself—a more appropriate expression. This power made itself manifest in Judah for the last time in the days of Ezra, in the year 444 B.C., and so ended the age-long process of the canonization of the Law. A glance at the writings of the Chronicler suffices to show how, by about 300 B.C., an authority is attributed to the Torah which is nothing less than Divine. If, even after this, alterations were made in the letter and even in peripheral ordinances (cf. Ex. 35-40), these were of such a character that the people scarcely noticed them—mere scholars' work having nothing to do with the inner and essential life, cf. ZEAT, p. 95 f.

The case is similar in regard to the collection of the prophets, the so-called earlier as well as the later—here, too, there is a long historical process. It is indeed a characteristic of the development of a sacred literature in Israel in contrast with that of other nations of the ancient East that this literature was never limited to a Divine Law *alone*, but included also a sacred *history*, and its interpretation by the discourses of Divinely commissioned *Prophets*. The collection of the former, the historical Books proceeded indeed almost *pari passu* with that of the Torah, for the latter never existed in isolation but was from the first most closely connected with the history of the founding of the nation, and it continued to be preserved in a framework of historical writings. How important a rôle was played by the sacred history for Amos and, still more, for Hosea, not to speak of Deut. 32, etc. ! It may be confidently asserted that every historical " source " of priestly authorship— and that includes the Yahwist as well as the Elohist—was held to be sacred and normative, as indeed is shown by the fact that the narratives were read at public worship and on feast days (cf. Jos. 24. 1 ff. ; 1 Sam. 12. 7 ff. ; Deut. 31. 9 ff.). So the compilation, under Hezekiah, of the ancient laws was associated with a compilation of the ancient narratives of the sacred history, in which God had manifested his power, righteousness and mercy. The admission of Deuteronomy to its place of authority was closely followed by the great Deuteronomic historical work which extends from Genesis 2 to 2 Kings 25, and the canonization of the Torah was also a canonization of the history which prepared the way for the Law, as well as of its continuation down to the death of the law-giver. This was

certainly followed, only a few years later, by that of the Books
from Joshua to Kings ; Ezra and Nehemiah, in their discourses
and prayers, have before their minds the same well-established
conception of the history. Thus practically the whole of the
historical matter had taken shape from the time of the Great
Deuteronomic work of the Babylonian exile, and only the Book
of Joshua was subjected to further revision and expansion on
the basis of the Priestly Writing. On the other hand, this
collection, as thus sanctioned, was as yet no hard and fast
norm, in the sense of excluding all other historical writing as
profane or forbidden, as indeed the work of the Chronicler,
about 300 B.C., with its numerous deviations from the earlier
Books, itself suffices to show. But the position in the Canon
which was later on assigned to this work shows that, although
it was certainly more in harmony with the taste and tendencies
of the period, it was never accorded the same degree of respect
as was given to the earlier Books, these having once for all
in the era of the re-establishment of the nation as a religious
entity, been made the foundation of its existence.

Israel had never been able to think of its relationship to
God apart from men of God, seers, prophets and the like, by
whom the immediate living spiritual communion between God
and His people was maintained. And from the possession of
such teachers and leaders resulted a consciousness of universal
knowledge of the will of God ; a secret will of God, elsewhere a
sine qua non of ancient oriental religions, and in them the special
domain of the priesthood, is here, and here only, unknown.
Even the earliest of the " literary " prophets thankfully acknowledge that God has always quickened men to be interpreters of
His will, Amos 2. 11 ; 3. 7 ; Hos. 12. 13 ; Micah 6. 4 ; Jer. 7,
25, etc. But during the Exile the sense of dependence upon such
predecessors became stronger, as we see in Ezekiel and Deutero-
Isaiah ; and Zechariah, especially, appeals to them at every step,
1. 4 ; 7. 4 ff. ; until finally, those who came forward as spokesmen
for God no longer came forward in their own names and their
own personalities, but wrote anonymously or under ancient
names. The more men became conscious that the Divine
Spirit no longer worked upon living personalities directly and
without intermediary (cf. Ps. 74. 9, from the late Persian
period), the stronger was their dependence on the Scriptures
which they owed to the former Men of the Spirit. The norm,
the standard of life given by the prophets to the nation, remained
from this time forward firmly established, Ezra 9. 11 ; Neh.
9. 26, 30. And, accordingly, the prophetic Canon must, as a

S

matter of fact, have been formed in or immediately after the Ezra - Nehemiah period, the last Book admitted (Malachi) dating just before that. In Ecclus. 49. 10 the collection of the prophets appears as a long-established fact, and Isa. 34. 16, Dan. 9. 2, also allude to it. But here, again, the formation of the collection did not exclude the possibility that the individual writings might receive interpolations by anonymous hands. The collection was not looked upon as different in an absolute sense from all other religious literature, but as superior to it ; as sacred, yet not in the *noli me tangere* sense.

It was considerably later before the collection of the remaining sacred writings, the hagiographa, into a whole, was taken in hand, the nucleus being the Psalms and the Proverbs—there had indeed been collections of psalms and proverbs even in the pre-Exilic period. The first clear trace of a collection of these written products of the religious life of the community is found in the Prologue of Ecclus., about 130 B.C., where besides the prophets there are named " the others that have followed in their steps," and, a little further on, " the law, the prophecies and the other writings." Next, a passage from the Psalter (Ps. 79. 2, 3—probably written in the fourth century B.C.) is definitely cited about 100 B.C. as " scripture " (1 Macc. 7. 16, 17 literally, " according to the words which he wrote "). From the statement in 2 Macc. 2. 13 f., though it, of course, itself only dates from the first century A.D., it must be taken as a well-established earlier tradition that on the one hand Nehemiah had collected the historical books, the prophets, *a* psalter (literally " Books of David "), and the correspondence with the Persian Kings (Ezra 4-6, etc.), and, on the other, that Judas Maccabaeus set on foot a collection (additional to the above) of writings of the men of earlier times, which came to be conterminous with the so-called *Kethubim*. In any case, this statement is so remarkable in its silence regarding the Torah and Ezra that it cannot simply be dismissed as worthless. And, as a matter of fact, the prologue of Ecclus. is confirmatory evidence that already, before 130, such a collection had not only been formed, but had even been translated into Greek. It is, of course, also evidence that this collection of Judas, as we have seen was the case with the earlier ones, did not exclude additions.

In *Alexandria*, we must bear in mind, the conception of a closed Canon was unknown. Here there were taken up into the collection of sacred writings all those which served the purposes of edification. Here, indeed, inspiration was not thought of as temporally limited ; every wise and virtuous man was held to be inspired—though that did not prevent the Torah's being given a position above all other books, and regarded as a book possessing Divine authority and constituting a norm for the religious life (cf. Philo). In view of these considerations we are forced to the conclusion that it was not in Alexandria but in Palestine, in the last century B.C., in Pharisaic circles, that the final step was taken by which the conception of the Scriptures as the sacred foundation and norm of the whole life of the religious community—which had obtained as regards its first two parts since the time of Ezra and Nehemiah, and as regards the third since the Maccabaean period—passed into the conception of a whole which was distinguished from all other religious literature in virtue of having been composed by inspired men, a whole to which nothing could be added and from which nothing could be taken away.

This conception was undoubtedly current among the Jewish People in the time of Jesus and His Apostles. " The Scripture " or " the Scriptures " are for them something established and unquestionable, sacred, inspired, normative, cf. Lk. 24. 27, 44 ; Jn. 5. 39 ; Rom. 3. 4 ; 9-11 ; 1 Cor. 9. 9 ; 15. 3 ; Gal. 3. 22 ; 4. 30 ; 2 Tim. 3. 16, etc. That the Chronicles at that time stood in the last place may be seen from Lk. 11. 51 (cf. 2 Chr. 24. 20 ff.). Apart from the Epistle of Jude (vv. 9 and 14), there is not a single passage where an extra-Canonical work is cited as authoritative " Scripture."

There are, no doubt, various allusions to writings, some of which must have been known to and read by the New Testament writers, but all the passages cited in proof of this are quite uncertain (1 Cor. 2. 9; Eph. 5. 14; Lk. 11. 49; Jn. 7. 38; Ja. 4. 5 f.; Mt. 27. 9; Heb. 11. 35 f.).

But even if it did really happen two or three times, these exceptions would only prove the rule, since, as the New Testament writers absolutely always use the Alexandrian translation, this regular ignoring of the extra-Canonical parts of it must have had some very strong reason. If in Gamaliel's days there was still controversy as to whether Ezekiel and Proverbs should be " hidden," that only refers to the question whether they were to be used in public worship or no ; it makes it all the more certain that the Canon was already in existence. And if we still hear in the time of Josephus of opposition to certain works of the Canon (only, however, the Song of Solomon, Ecclesiastes and Esther), about which there was a debate at the Synod of Jamnia (between A.D. 90 and 100), the result of this debate shows that these Books must have been long before received as Canonical ; it was simply that their contents created difficulties for the theory of Canonicity.

On the other hand, we must once more emphasize the fact that Jesus and His Apostles nowhere and never (not even 2 Tim. 3. 16 ; 2 Peter 1. 20 f. is post-Apostolic) bring forward a particular *theory* of the inspiration of the Scriptures in contrast with other religious literature, precisely because " Scripture " to them was not a lifeless writing, but the voice of the Living God. Since it was for them a source of life, from which streams of life flowed out to them (Jn. 5. 39), they had no need to engage in toilsome speculations as to how it arose. Accordingly, they are entirely free from any slavery to the letter, but often quote with complete freedom, cf. 1 Cor. 1. 19 ; Eph. 4. 8, etc. The designation, " the Law and the Prophets," Mt. 5. 17 ; Lk. 16. 16, or " the Law, the Prophets and the Psalms," Lk. 24. 44, shows that *in practice* they even made distinctions of degree within the Scriptures (moreover, the Song of Solomon and Esther are not cited, Ecclesiastes, if at all, only in Jn. 3. 8). And, indeed, Talmudic Judaism retained in no small measure the consciousness of such a distinction, as is shown by its comparing the threefold division of Scripture to the threefold division of the Temple—Fore-Court, Holy Place, Holy of Holies (cf. *Meg.*, 26*b*, 27*a* ; *Dikduke*, § 3).

As regards the motive which led, in the first century B.C., to the marking-off of these twenty-four Books as sacrosanct to the exclusion of all others, we have no means of definitely ascertaining it ; we can only conjecture. According to Josephus, the determining point of view was that prophetic inspiration extended from Moses to Ezra and Nehemiah ; and this is evidently so far true, for it supplies the best explanation of the exclusion, *e.g.*, of Ecclesiasticus, while the Song of Songs and Ecclesiastes, which circulated under the name of Solomon, Daniel, which ostensibly belonged to the period of the Exile, and Esther, dating from the time of Xerxes, were received into the Canon.

But the really difficult question is why precisely inclusion within this period was made the criterion.

According to Hölscher, it was specially designed to
oppose the rank growth of *Apocalyptic* literature,
which adopted especially the pre-Mosaic names
(Adam, Enoch, the Patriarchs, etc. ; for their
multitude cf. 2 Esdras 14. 46, where the author
speaks of seventy secret writings). But, as against
this view, Schürer had already rightly urged (Theol.
Literaturzeitung, 1906) that there was no antithesis
between the Pharisaic Legalism and Apocalyptic,
and, moreover, that Abraham, for example, ranked
as a prophet. We cannot therefore limit the motive
in this way ; we might just as well assume a special
intention to oppose the *philosophic* literature which
was pouring in from Alexandria ; or others, of
which we know nothing at all, cf. Ecclesiastes 12. 12.
When all is said, we must seek the deepest motive
in the consciousness of spiritual poverty which
characterized that period in Palestine. It was felt
that the Maccabees had entered upon a path which
led farther and farther from the Divine will and
more and more in the direction of worldliness, and
those who desired to lead the People back into the
way of the Fathers, at the beginning of the first
century B.C. (? under Alexandra, 75–67), conscious,
as we have said, of their own spiritual poverty,
learnt to rely exclusively upon the will of God as
revealed to the Fathers. But where was this
revealed will to be found ? Already for centuries
past the answer had been : in *the Law and the
Prophets*. And the historical limits for these were
known, Moses and Ezra-Nehemiah, the latter of
whom had already formed a collection ; and so,
among the writings which had later become attached
to these, only those which fell between the aforesaid

limits could be held to have a valid claim. (When the Talmud takes, not Artaxerxes but Alexander as the lower limit, it has in mind the "Great Synagogue," but the Talmud reckons between the rebuilding of the Temple and the Fall of the Persian Empire, only thirty-four years, cf. *Seder Olam*, p. 91). We have thus a direct bridge between passages like 1 Macc. 4. 46; 9. 27; 14. 41, in which, about 100 B.C., we find the melancholy recognition that the *prophetic* spirit has been entirely extinguished, and that passage of Josephus, according to which guidance and salvation are to be found only in that which has been revealed by God through the prophets.

It is no doubt true that this selection and isolation of the Books of the Canon opened the way to the later irreligious *worship of the letter* both in Church and Synagogue, and that only by deliberately shutting the eyes to the light of truth can it be maintained that, without exception, the Books admitted by the Pharisees were superior from the ethico-religious point of view, more fully inspired by the Spirit of God, than those which they excluded (compare Ecclesiastes with Ecclesiasticus, Esther with Tobit, the Song of Solomon with the Psalms of Solomon, etc.), but it is no less true that the Divine directive providence must, in a special sense, have watched over the process of canonization. It was, indeed, only by this means that the wealth and fullness of the Divine revelation which had been vouchsafed to ancient Israel, the Divine purpose of salvation as manifested under the Old Covenant, was preserved from being stifled by the rank growth of a religious literature of inferior order. And while this collection is, in the first place, rendered sacred to the Christian by the attitude which the Lord and His Apostles assumed towards it—and towards it alone—as the *sacred archives of the preparatory stage of the Divine revelation*, all unprejudiced criticism confirms the view that *these Books alone give us a true representation of the spiritual life which, under the Old Covenant, was called into being by the Divine revelation and special guidance, and they alone preserve to us the prophecies, contained in prophetic words*

and actions, of which Jesus Christ is the fulfilment and con-
summation.   From this central significance the extra-Canonical
writings are in a greater or less degree removed (cf. Buhl,
ut sup., p. 72).   That conclusion will be disputed only by those
who strain out gnats and swallow camels.

In the post-Apostolic Church, in which most of
the teachers, since they knew no Hebrew, used the
LXX, the distinction between the Canonical and
the other sacred writings was for a time almost in
abeyance.   But so soon as the Church—in the days
of Origen—faced with the opposition on the one
hand of the sects, and on the other of the Synagogue,
which had now generally accepted the Palestinian
Canon, felt the need of deepening the foundation
and developing the form of its teaching, it gradually
became conscious of the higher value of the Canonical
Books as compared with all other Jewish religious
literature.   And while in the Greek Church the
Apocryphal Books took more and more the position
in contrast with Canonical, of edifying literature of
which the public reading as such was permitted, in
the Latin Church, Jerome following in the footsteps
of Julius Africanus, contended vigorously for the
exclusive validity of the " hebraica veritas."

The varying position assigned to the Hebrew Canon in
contradistinction to the Apocrypha in the various Christian
Confessions, the varying views of the sense in which Scripture
was to be regarded as the Word of God, the various conceptions
of inspiration, and finally, the various estimates of its significance
for the Church of the present day, lie beyond the limits of Old
Testament Introduction and belong to the history of Scripture
as a whole, or, in certain aspects, to Dogmatics.   For an introduction to these questions see, among other works, H. Schultz,
Das A.T. und die evangelische Gemeinde, 1893 ; Kautzsch, *Die
bleibende Bedeutung des Alten Testaments*, 1902 ; Öttli, *Die
Autorität des A.T. für den Christen* (Bibl. Zeit- und Streitfragen,
II. 2) ; Seeberg, *Offenbarung und Inspiration* (*ibid.* IV. 7-8).

CHRONOLOGICAL CONSPECTUS OF THE DEVELOPMENT OF THE OLD TESTAMENT LITERATURE

Pre-Mosaic Era.—Gen. 14, originally a Canaanite record of a deed of arms of Abraham the Hebrew ; 9. 25-27, Noachic prophecies (possibly of the latter part of the period of the Judges) ; 4. 23 f., the Song of Lamech.

Mosaic Era (about 1300 B.C.).—Exodus 15. 21, Song of Miriam at Red Sea ; 17. 16, Saying about Amalek ; 20. 1-17, the Sinai Decalogue ; Num. 6. 24 - 26, the Aaronic Benediction ; 10. 35, Invocation at the moving of the Ark ; 21. 14 f., List of the stations of the Ark (cf. 33. 1 ff., basis) ; 21. 17 f., Song of the Well ; 21. 27-29, Taunt-song against Sihon ; Ex. 20. 23—23. 19, Book of the Covenant of the Plains of Moab (cf. ref. to permanent record in Shechem).

Period of the Judges (1250–1050 B.C.).—Judges 5, Song of Deborah ; Ex. 15. 1-18, expanded Song of Triumph at Red Sea ; Gen. 49, Blessings of Jacob (with the exception of vv. 8-12) ; Deut. 33, Blessing of Moses ; Ex. 34. 10-27, the wrongly so-called Yahwistic Decalogue; Deut. 27. 15-26, the Shechem Decalogue ; Oracles upon the Patriarchs ; Adoption and recasting of Canaanitish-Babylonian myths ; Oral elaboration of the stories of the Patriarchs and of the Hero-stories of the Pentateuch, Joshua and Judges.

The Davidic Period (about 1000 B.C.).—2 Sam. 1. 19-27, David's Song of the Bow ; 3. 33 f., Lament for Abner ; Ps. 18, cf. 2 Sam. 22 ; 2 Sam. 23. 1-7, the so-called Last Words of David ; Gen. 49. 8-12, the oracle on Judah in the Blessing of Jacob ; Num. 24. 3-9, 15-24, the prophecies of Balaam ; probable compilation of the " Book of the Valiant " and the " Book of the Wars of Yahweh " ; Beginning of the reduction to writing of the Yahwistic Source.

Solomonic Period (about 950).—Completion of the Yahwist (from Gen. 2 to 1 Kings 2) ; Solomon's words at the Dedication of the Temple, 1 K. 8. 12, 13 (LXX) ; Annals, which can still be traced in 1 K. 4-7 ; 9 ; 10 ; Beginning of the composition of the proverbs collected in Prov. 10-22.

900–800 B.C.—The Elohist (first " edition," Gen. 15 to Joshua 24, in Shechem or Bethel ; the last, from Gen. 15 to 2 K. 3, in Mizpeh ?) ; Obadiah 1-10, the Ephraimite stories of the prophets in 1 K. 17—2 K. 13 ; Deut. 32, the Song of Moses (?).

Period of Jeroboam II. (about 750).—Isaiah 15 f., Prophecy about Moab. The Prophet Amos (about 760). The Prophet Hosea (750–25).

Period of the Fall of the Northern Kingdom (735–722).—Isa. 2. 5—10. 4 ; 11. 1-10 ; 14. 24-27 ; 17. 1-11 ; 28. 1-6 ; Micah 1.

Period of Hezekiah (722–699).—Isa. 1. 2—2. 4 ; 10. 5-34 ; 14. 29-32 ; (15 ; 16) ; 17. 12-14 ; 18 ; 19. 1-15 ; 20 ; 22 ; 23. 1-14 (?) ; 28. 7—33. 24. Micah 2-5, North Israelitish Annals brought to Jerusalem (?). The biography of Solomon in 1 K. 3-11. Yahwistic and Elohistic Sources worked up together (?). The nucleus of Prov. 25-29. The " royal " Psalms, also hymns of praise, psalms of penitence and of " the poor," in Ps. 2-41 ; 51-72. The main part of Deuteronomy.

Period of Manasseh (698–643). — Micah 6. 1—7. 7 (?). Nucleus of the Law of Holiness reduced to writing, Lev. 17-26 (not in Jerusalem), also other parts of the later Priestly Writing (perhaps in Mizpeh). A biography of Isaiah (cf. Isa. 7 ; 20 ; 36-39) ; Isa. 19. 16-25 (?).

Period of Josiah (640–608).—Zephaniah. Discovery, in 622, of Deuteronomy, and, soon after, expansion of it by the insertion of the " You " sections, hortatory passages and the historical introduction, 1. 1—4. 4 ; E worked up together with it (?). The Prophet Nahum.

Period of the last Jewish Kings (608–586).—The writing of the first roll of Jeremiah, 604 B.C. ; subsequent expansions of this. First redaction of the Books of Kings by the so-called Deuteronomist. Psalms of suffering and lamentation in the first two books of the Ps. Prov. 22. 17—24. 34.

Period of the Babylonian Exile (586–536).—Completion of the Writing of Jeremiah by Baruch in Egypt. The Prophet Ezekiel in Babylon (Call, 592, last words, 570); Lamentations 2 and 4; On the basis of a working-up together of JE with D, the great historical work Gen. 2 to 2 K. 25. About 550 the anonymous prophecies against Babylon, Isa. 13; 14; 21; Lamentations 1; from 545 onwards the first of the Cyrus prophecies of Deutero-Isaiah; 539–8, the Writing of Deutero-Isaiah (Isa. 40-55).

Period of the Return (537–520).—Isa. 56-66 (?); Lam. 5; Neh. 7; Ps. 137; Jer. 50; 51.

Period of the rebuilding of the Temple (520–516).—Haggai; Zech. 1-8; Ruth.

About 500.—The Priestly Writing, in Babylon. The Book of Job (in Egypt ?).

About 470.—Lam. 3; Malachi; Obadiah.

Ezra - Nehemiah Period (458 *to about* 420).—The Priestly Writing worked up with JED and the Pentateuch promulgated. Ezra's Memoirs; Nehemiah's Memoirs; the Aramaic Source dealing with the Restoration in Ezra 4-6. Jonah.

About 400.—Collection and redaction—in the main corresponding to what has come down to us—of the " Earlier " and " Later " Prophets. Joel.

In the Fourth Century B.C.—Isa. 24-27 (?), 34; 35 (?). The main body of Psalms 42-49; 73-150. Proverbs 1-9. Song of Solomon.

About 330.—Habakkuk.

About 300.—The work of the Chronicler (including Ezra and Nehemiah). Esther (?).

About 200.—Zech. 9-14. Ecclesiastes (in Alexandria ?).

Maccabaean Period (*after* 168).—Daniel, 165. Very soon after 164, collection of the remaining sacred writings added to the Torah and the Prophets.

About 75 B.C.—Final canonization of Old Testament in its present extent, in Jerusalem.

INDEX

Abiathar, perhaps the writer of J, 114

Abraham, shown by Gen. 14 to be a historical personage, 50

Ahijah of Shiloh, spiritual father of the Elohist, 70

Aḥikar, story of, referred to, 243

Akiba, Rabbi, 18, 242

Amos, his origin, 166; his Book, 167 f.; not the creator of ethical monotheism, 168; Egyptian parallels to his representation of the future, 170

Apocalypses, Isa. ch. 24-27, 137 f.; ch. 34, 35, 138 f.; Joel, 163 f.; Obadiah, 172; Zech. ch. 14, 191; Daniel, 232; Baruch, 249

Apocalyptic, Ezekiel not the father of, 154; Deutero-Isaiah first representative of, 146; opposition to, on the part of those who formed the Canon, 262

Aristeas, Letter of, 247

Assumption of Moses, 249

Babylonio-Assyrian literature, 5 f., 177, 181, 199, 220

Balaam, Oracles of, 36 f.

Baruch, redactor of Book of Jeremiah, 149 f.; Book of Baruch, 245; Apocalypse of B., 249 f.

Book of the Covenant, 42 ff.

" Book of Jasher," 8, 9

" Book of the Wars of Yahweh," 8, 9

Canon of O.T., 252-64; Josephus' conception of, 253; gradual development of this, 255 ff.; Canon in Alexandria, 258 f.; attitude of Jesus and Apostles towards, 259 f.; motives for its fixation, 261 f.

Chronicles, Books of, 235 ff.; sources of, 237 f.

Daniel, Book of, 232; earlier basis of, 233; additions to, 245 f.

David, as collector of psalms, 9; as composer of psalms, 202 f.

Deborah, Song of, 101

Decalogue, 40 ff.; so-called Yahwistic D., 45 f.

Deutero-Isaiah, 140 ff.

Deuteronomist, in Pentateuch, 92; in Joshua, 98 f.; in Judges, 102; in the Books of Samuel, 116 f.; in the Books of Kings, 121 f.; connected historical work, 124 ff.

Deuteronomy, 73 ff.; combination of, with E and J, 91 ff.

Dikduke Haťamim, 19, 261

Doxologies, in Amos, 169; at close of the divisions of the Psalter, 196

Ecclesiastes, 227 f.

Ecclesiasticus. *See* Jesus Sirach

Egyptian literature, 5, 133, 170, 207, 220

Elephantine papyri, 133

Elohistic Source, 61 ff.; place of origin, 63; further developments of, 64 f.; connection with Yahwistic Source, 68 f.; continuation in Joshua, 98 f.; in Judges, 103 f.; in Samuel, 114 f.

Enoch, Book of, 248

Ephod, 41, 87, 105, 162, 203

Eschatology, in Isaiah's promise of salvation, 132; in Isa. 32 and 33, 134; in Deutero-Isaiah, 142; Hosea, 161 f.; Joel, 164 f.; Amos, 168 f.; Micah, ch. 4 and 5, 176 f.; Nahum, 181; Zephaniah, 186;